CW01095174

# Intertextual and Interdisciplinary Approaches to Cormac McCarthy

# Routledge Studies in Contemporary Literature

# Intertextual and Interdisciplinary Approaches to Cormac McCarthy

Borders and Crossings

**Edited by Nicholas Monk**
**with a Foreword by Rick Wallach**

Routledge
Taylor & Francis Group
NEW YORK   LONDON

First published 2012
by Routledge
711 Third Avenue, New York, NY 10017

Simultaneously published in the UK
by Routledge
2 Park Square, Milton Park, Abingdon, Oxon OX14 4RN

*Routledge is an imprint of the Taylor & Francis Group,
an informa business*

Typeset in Sabon by IBT Global.
Printed and bound in the United States of America on acid-free paper by
IBT Global.

*Library of Congress Cataloging-in-Publication Data*
    Intertextual and interdisciplinary approaches to Cormac McCarthy :
borders and crossings / edited by Nicholas Monk ; with a foreword by
Rick Wallach.
        p. cm. — (Routledge studies in contemporary literature ; 6)
    Includes bibliographical references and index.
    1. McCarthy, Cormac, 1933—Criticism and interpretation. 2. Intertextuality.
I. Monk, Nicholas.
    PS3563.C337Z73 2011
    813'.54—dc22
    2011011237

ISBN13: 978-0-415-89549-1 (hbk)
ISBN13: 978-0-203-80380-6 (ebk)

This book is dedicated to Edwin T. (Chip) Arnold

# Contents

# Figures

# Foreword

## NEW HORIZONS IN MCCARTHY SCHOLARSHIP

My colleague Nick Monk has had the difficult but gratifying task of constructing this landmark volume from amongst the many excellent presentations to the Fourth International Conference on Cormac McCarthy in Coventry, England, in June of 2009.[1] How different his choices have proven to be compared to when Wade Hall and I sorted the papers from the first conference on McCarthy's work at Bellarmine College in Louisville in 1993. Back then, the field was wide open. Few had read, much less written about, this underappreciated author's work so that just about any approach to it was novel. We were still looking for the most basic variety of interrogations in those days for what would become *Sacred Violence: A Reader's Companion to Cormac McCarthy*. Formalist, deconstructive, mythographic, feminist, psychological, historical, and biographical readings were all still mostly wanting. Biography was surely the most difficult approach. McCarthy's career-long reticence about himself had been compromised in print only once, in an interview he had given to the *New York Times*.[2] Although his revelations about venom components of the Mojave rattlesnake were fascinating (a longtime armchair herpetologist, I own a baby rattlesnake myself, a local pygmy rattler named Friendo after a comment made by Anton Chigurh in *No Country for Old Men*), they were so merely in passing to any literary critic without my particular idiosyncrasies. From the point of view of working critics of McCarthy, though, his remark "The ugly fact is that books are made of other books" was the mother of all of his few analytical observations in print. It was as if the master had emerged from silence only to license us to fan out through the intertextual to hunt down his . . . and with the passage of nineteen years I still cringe a little when I write this . . . *literary influences*.

"The intertextual" was a sort of proto-cyberspace poststructuralists (like me) invented to drive home the point that *all* texts extended nodelike out of some metatext that transcended temporal and linguistic barriers, made a hash of genre theory, and, spearheaded by a group of continental theorists—usual suspects who for our purposes might as well remain

nameless, and their enthusiastic ivy league factotums here in America—
even killed the author graveyard dead while this same archetypal literary
fabricator went right on dreaming dreams of *faux* individuation. And I
dare say the idea of the intertextual—and all of the problems, paradoxes,
and excesses which are its companions—well served its purpose for many
decades, and will go on being a useful generator of ideas and relations
between texts into the future. That was then. It would be more accurate to
speak of "intermediality" than mere intertextuality now.

 We met in Coventry in June of 2009 following the most productive
period of McCarthy's career and surely the most dramatic expansion of his
profile and readership. It had long been his pattern to publish a novel every
four to six years, but then the two-year interval from 2005 to 2006 saw
the release of *No Country for Old Men* and *The Road*, and the play *The
Sunset Limited*. The film of *No Country* was released in 2007 and won the
Academy Award for best picture in 2008; *The Road* went into cinematic
production that same year; and *Sunset Limited* was being staged by numerous theatrical companies nation- and worldwide. Also during this time, to
the mixed shock and horror of his longest-term readers on one hand and
to the delight of his more recent converts, in July of 2008 McCarthy broke
once more with his traditional taciturnity to appear in a series of televised
interviews with Oprah Winfrey and was featured in several more interviews in periodicals.[3] For the first time, really, the Cormackian scholars at
Warwick were talking at least as much if not more about film, television,
theatre and general stagecraft in relation to McCarthy's *ouvre* as they were
about other texts. "Influence" was giving way to "interrelatedness". The
discussion had shifted away from the old model of "the intertextual" to
something more like science fiction master William Gibson's concept of
"the matrix," where ideas and images themselves, not merely "discourses"
in the textual sense, found interrelation in a postverbal environment. If you
were there and you didn't notice the sea change in the dialogue, you just
weren't paying attention.

 It seemed fitting, then, that the 2009 Warwick conference, sponsored in
part by the Cormac McCarthy Society, should be cosponsored by, and meet
at, the CAPITAL Center, the University of Warwick's superb multimedia
and theatrical facility.[4] I think it's fair to say that for the first time, the theatre auditorium became more than just a seating facility where participants
read or sat and listened. Ideas of performativity saturated the entire conference, and they dominate this collection as well, and the essays selected
for this volume are solidly indicative of how far beyond textual interro-
gation per se critical appreciation of Cormac McCarthy's work has gone.
Most of these pieces, as Nick Monk's introduction demonstrates, reach
past McCarthy's own works, and thence beyond their presumed textual
antecedents, to intersect with issues of performance, re-presentation, and
medium-as-message. This is quite an evolution from the days when critics struggled to come to terms with a McCarthy whose work, stylistically

especially, seemed to cut so sharply against the grain and fashion of contemporary literature. Instead, the phase of scholarship represented here is all about siting McCarthy not just in the context of American letters, but in terms of American, and beyond that Western, and even beyond that, human, culture as a whole.

Rick Wallach
Miami, Florida
February 16, 2011

## NOTES

1. Prior conferences outside the US, at roughly three-year intervals, included Berlin, Reims, and Manchester.
2. Woodward, Richard B. "Cormac McCarthy's Venomous Fiction." *New York Times Magazine* 19 Apr. 1992: 28–31.
3. For a regularly updated list of these interviews, articles, and studies, check the online bibliography at the Cormac McCarthy Society's website at <www.cormacmccarthy.com> (accessed 10 January 2010).
4. CAPITAL, standing for "Creativity and Performance in Teaching and Learning," was one of the Higher Education Funding Council of England (HEFCE's) Centres of Excellence in Teaching and Learning (CETLs), and a collaboration between the University of Warwick, the Royal Shakespeare Company, and other theatrical organizations. The 70 CETLs were created in universities by HEFCE in 2005 with a grant of over £300 million. CAPITAL was initially established to use theatre performance skills and experience to enhance student learning. The early focus was the application of performance in the theatrical sense (the use of acting and other stage skills for teaching and learning, the engineering of production, writing for performance, theatre as a research medium, and the rehearsal process).

# Acknowledgments

The editor would like to thank Carol Chillington Rutter, Susan Brock, Helen Neal, and Ian O'Donoghue (CAPITAL Centre, University of Warwick); Elizabeth Levine and Diana Castaldini (Routledge); Helen M. Dennis, and Thomas Docherty (Department of English, University of Warwick); The Cormac McCarthy Society; Laura Monk, Margaret J. Monk, Peter Monk, Marianne DeKoven, and John McClure.

# Introduction

## Nicholas Monk

O boy!—a contact sheet with twenty shots of McCarthy in his Bearden scriptorium, with more books stacked up on the table behind McCarthy and me going blind as a monk trying to make them out—John McPhee's *Giving Good Weight*, an old John Player Motor Sport Yearbook, Ernst Cassirer's *Substance and Function and Einstein's Theory of Relativity*, Banesh Hoffmann's *The Strange Story of the Quantum*, Harold Blumenthal's *Sacco and Vanzetti*, Hans Reichenbach's *The Philosophy of Space & Time*, Carolyn Kolb's *New Orleans*, Gregory Bateson's *Mind and Nature*, Peter Forbath's *The River Congo*, Freeman Dyson's *Disturbing the Universe*, a book on Kant, John Locke's *Essay Concerning Human Understanding* in two volumes, F. Max Muller's translation of *The Upanishads, also* in two volumes, John R. Cooke's *The Border and the Buffalo*, Weston La Barre's *The Human Animal*, George F. Ruxton's *Adventures in Mexico and the Rocky Mountains*, T.E. Lawrence's *Seven Pillars of Wisdom*, the novel *Silence* by Shusako Endo.

Peter Josyph's keynote presentation at the twenty-fifth anniversary conference for *Blood Meridian* in San Marcos, Texas—a fragment of which is reproduced above—concerned his mission to track down the photographer who produced the shots for the cover of the first edition of *Blood Meridian or the Evening Redness in the West.* Josyph's delight at not only finding the photographer concerned but also getting sight of the uncropped originals was, and is, manifest. All of us who listened to the address were electrified by this glimpse into the influences upon a writer whose intellectual hinterland we still know relatively little about.[1]

Further glimpses into McCarthy's reading were available to those of us fortunate enough to have access to the newly expanded McCarthy collection in the Alkek library.[2] A number of the contributors to this volume have used the archive to support and inform their work, and in my own research I was intrigued by a variety of unpublished passages, notes, and corrections. My sense, as I dipped into the materials, was of a meticulous, precise, but, most of all, widely read writer. Just one example is the draft of *Whales and Men*—McCarthy's unpublished film script—in which there are quotations from Thomas Beston's *Outermost House*; a complete rendering of Ezra Pound's beautiful translation of an eighth-century Chinese poem, "The River Merchant's Wife"; and three lines of poetry from Padraic

Colum, one of the leading lights of Ireland's Celtic revival in the early twentieth century. There are also fragments from Dylan Thomas, and mentions of Cervantes, Handel, Melville, Dobie Gray's "Drift Away," and Mozart.[2] Perhaps most tellingly, however, for those of us looking for McCarthy's influences, there is a handwritten note in the margin of page 95 of the draft that reads as follows: "WITT: A philosophical problem has the form: 'I don't know my way about'". There is a strong case for interpreting WITT as Wittgenstein, and in the passage just below the marginal note McCarthy has the character, John, say,

> [T]he whales have made mutes of us. There is nothing to say . . . We all have these assumptions about logic and language and intelligence and there is no ground for them. What argument could you advance for the principles of logic that did not presuppose them? We occupy a small band of visible light, a small band of audible sound, a small band of shared existence. We are imprisoned by what we know. (96)

It would take time of course, and a keener philosophical mind than mine, to begin to unpick the links between Wittgenstein's thinking and McCarthy's, but it seems to me that the text itself legitimizes the speculation the note invites, and in doing so authorizes us to pursue our compulsion to further probe and analyze work that has been, and continues to be, richly productive for critics and scholars.

It seems timely, therefore, that a collection of essays on McCarthy should adopt as its focus the intertextual and interdisciplinary nature of his work.[3] As all the essays in this volume remind us, literary works cannot exist free of the accretions of cultural influence that develop as the novel forms in that culture, and in the mind of its author:

> [T]he frontiers of a book are never clear-cut: beyond the title, the first lines and the last full stop, beyond its internal configuration and its autonomous form, it is caught up in a system of references to other books, other texts, other sentences: it is a node within a network . . . The book is not simply the object that one holds in one's hands . . . Its unity is variable and relative. (Foucault 23)

This is not so different from the view of T. S. Eliot in "Tradition and the Individual Talent" that "no poet, no artist of any art, has his complete meaning alone. His significance, his appreciation is the appreciation of his relation to the dead poets and artists" (38). Nor, indeed, from that of Samuel Johnson who noted that Shakespeare had, indirectly, absorbed the literary influences of his time and that these provided "a stock of knowledge sufficient for a mind so capable of appropriating and improving it" (143).

So while it is true that a significant proportion of McCarthy scholarship refers in a fragmentary or tangential fashion to his literary influences—and it is rarely possible as one reads the critics to imagine that McCarthy sprang fully formed as a novelist into the world in the Western deserts or the Southern mountains—a more detailed analysis of some these influences might be regarded as overdue.[4] Through my own contribution, therefore, and those of David Williams, Megan McGilchrist, Jan Nordby Gretlund, Euan Gallivan, John Ferer, and Michael Madsen, we seek to draw back the curtain on some of McCarthy's literary interlocutors, as well as revealing and analyzing some of the fiction's key contemporary intertexts, showing a complex and possibly underestimated body of influence. Williams' contribution looks at classical philosophy in relation to *Blood Meridian*, McGilchrist compares Gawain and John Grady Cole, and Gretlund's piece reviews McCarthy's literary forbears in the South. Moving into the twentieth century, Ferer's article juxtaposes Jean Toomer's neglected poem "Blue Meridian" with *Blood Meridian*; Gallivan's take on Beckett and McCarthy seeks to explore the work of two authors who are both fascinated by "nihilism"; and my own essay compares aspects of McCarthy's work with contemporary Native American literature.[5]

In addition, while not losing sight of its central importance, we look beyond the novel both to other genres in McCarthy's *oeuvre*, and to the way these genres have influenced McCarthy's writing. Dianne Luce's piece, for example, that acknowledges *The Road* as a species of "anti-pastoral," but uses the aesthetics of landscape painting to identify a kind of Burkean sublime in the painterly style of the fiction, falls into the category. As does Ciarán Dowd's analysis of the mixed genres of novel and drama in *The Sunset Limited*; while John Cant's comparison of *No Country for Old Men* in each book and film reveals much about both. We also want to show in this collection that, beyond the range and richness of traditional scholarship, literary analysis itself can sometimes be innovative in its form. The production of the *Sunset Limited* was precisely this kind of work, as were Peter Josyph's paintings and his accompanying presentation. At this level, art and performance become alternative ways to "read": it can be argued, for example, that performance close-reads any kind of fiction, poetry, or drama (or theory come to that) in a way that cannot help but develop an array of meaning as complex and generative as that offered by the standard form of the paper presentation.

Josyph's paintings produce something akin to this in their crystallization of the response of one artist to the work of another. At its simplest Josyph's collection of paintings, "Cormac McCarthy's House," created over a ten-year period, might be viewed as an *homage* to a writer that fascinates Josyph, yet Josyph's work is literary criticism at its most insightful, and to hear or read him on McCarthy is to be offered a rare glimpse into the glittering reflection of McCarthy's work in his own. To be exposed to the shifts in focus that result is to understand the works of both artists in a fresh way. The paintings express the notion I mention of "critical innovation" with absolute clarity, and can move the observer into an altogether more immersive experience of McCarthy's work. A genuinely immersive experience was also part of our intention when we invited Tom Cornford to direct a rehearsed reading of *The Sunset Limited* at the Warwick conference. Cornford's experience as a theatre director at the Globe in London and as Artist in Residence at the CAPITAL Centre revealed themselves in an extraordinary performance of the play that transcended its advertised status as a rehearsed reading. Josyph's detailed and engaging interview with Cornford offers a rare insight into both McCarthy as a playwright and the process of directing such a piece and supports my claim that this collection is performative of its interdisciplinary theme in the sense that it includes contributions from an artist, a theatre director, and a philosopher, as well as from literary critics.

Just as McCarthy's works are shot through with the influence of others, so are our own as critics. We find ourselves revisiting the thoughts of our predecessors, and tracking back—sometimes inadvertently—to themes in McCarthy that have pre-occupied critics endlessly over the decades since Vereen Bell began the process in earnest in 1983. The essays in this volume both return to old conversations and begin new ones—Ciarán Dowd's take, for example, on the spiritual/metaphysical is significantly different from my own and both, in turn, differ from Jan Nordby Gretlund's. The venerable bogeyman of nihilism appears in a number of essays, John Ferer's and Euan Gallivan's perhaps most notably, and is tackled in a number of different ways—some feel McCarthy may well have concluded *The Road* differently as a younger writer, others see no convincing redemption from bleakness, and still others continue to see hope enduring in the work. Evil receives a new take in Michael Madsen's essay; David Williams looks at violence, but through the lens of Classical philosophy; and romance is once more present in both my own contribution and that of Megan McGilchrist—alongside notions of chivalry and honour.[6] John Cant takes up the tension between novels and films, and between high and low culture; and the sublime and the pastoral surface in Dianne Luce's essay; while the landscapes of both the South and the Southwest continue to inform the criticism in subtle ways and at many levels. As editor, I am persuaded these essays stand as new and significant scholarship in their own right, but my hope is that they also function in conversation with one another as part of a performative intertextual enterprise.[7]

## NOTES

1. Peter Josyph. "Judging *Blood Meridian or the Evening Redness in the West* by its Cover." Twenty-fifth Anniversary Conference for *Blood Meridian*. The Alkek Library, Texas State University, San Marcos. 28 October 2010.
2. We are very grateful to Katy Salzmann and her staff at Western Texas State University San Marcos' Southwestern Writers Collection at the Wittliff Collections for their tolerance of our *en masse* descent upon their library.

3. I have avoided a narrow definition of "intertextuality" in this introduction and elsewhere, as I want the readings of McCarthy's work in this collection to be free of conformity to structuralist/poststructuralist—or indeed any other—formulas of interpretation. This is not to diminish the influence of critics like Kristeva, Barthes, and Foucault, nor to denigrate any of the essays in the collection that employ their thinking, but merely to express the hope that the catholic approach I have taken to the notion of intertextuality might influence the reader to consider creating her/his own definition. For the purposes of this volume, therefore, an intertextual or interdisciplinary approach describes, merely, the crossing of the border of one genre or text by another, and the trace, or traces, that crossing leaves.
4. All references are to the McCarthy Collection, Box 97, Folder 6: 25–94.
5. See Dianne Luce's painstaking and detailed bibliography on the Cormac McCarthy Society website for examples of work that looks at McCarthy's influences.
6. I should acknowledge that this work has been begun by James Lilley, and is highly developed in Jason Mitchell's article. Also Kenneth Lincoln's book is valuable in this area.
7. The collection is divided into three sections. The first deals with literary intertexts pre-1900 (three essays), the second deals with painting, film, and theatre (six essays, two in each genre), and the final section addresses intertexts post-1900 (three essays).

## WORKS CITED

Cormac McCarthy Papers, Southwestern Writers Collection, The Wittliff Collections, Texas State U, San Marcos.

Kermode, Frank, ed. *Selected prose of T. S. Eliot*. London: Faber and Faber, 1975.

Lilley, James D. "'The Indian with a Camera': Resistance and Representation in Silko and McCarthy." Proceedings of the Third Annual International Conference on the Emerging Literature of the Southwest Culture (privately distributed). El Paso: U of Texas at El Paso, 1997. 394–97.

Lincoln, Kenneth. *Cormac McCarthy: American Canticles*. New York: Palgrave Macmillan, 2009.

Luce, Dianne. *Cormac McCarthy: A Bibliography*. 2007. 17 Feb. 2011 <http://www.midlandstech.com/edu/ed/eng/biblio.htm>.

Mitchell, Jason P. "Louise Erdrich's *Love Medicine*, Cormac McCarthy's *Blood Meridian*, and the (De)Mythologizing of the American West." *Critique* 41.3 (Spring 2000): 290–304.

Woodhuysen, H. R., ed. *Samuel Johnson on Shakespeare*. London: Penguin, 1989.

# 1  *Blood Meridian* and Classical Greek Thought

## *David Williams*

In this essay I will argue that the central themes of *Blood Meridian or the Evening Redness in the West* can be seen more clearly when they are examined through the lens of classical Greek thought. That *Blood Meridian* owes a great deal to epic, philosophy, and tragedy is agreed upon, yet its roots in classical Greek thought remain largely unexamined. This is surprising given that epic, philosophy, and tragedy are all products of the Greek mind. It is not difficult to find scholars noting connections to epic (Lincoln), philosophy (Frye 4), and tragedy (Bloom 11), but I will argue that if we establish the precise connections that *Blood Meridian* shares with these areas of Greek thought we can more clearly elucidate its central themes and gain a more precise picture of the Judge. In the first section, on epic, I will argue that the sense in which *Blood Meridian* is an epic can be established by showing the connections that it shares with the *Iliad*. I will contend that *Blood Meridian* is not simply epic in terms of subject matter or scope, but that its central focus is the same as that of the *Iliad*; namely, it is concerned with the nature of *force*. In the second section, on philosophy, I will show that *Blood Meridian* engages precisely those issues that concerned the first Greek philosophers and will contend that an elucidation of these issues can be used to characterize the philosophical positions that support the Judge's moral and scientific pronouncements. My argument will be that the Judge quotes early Greek philosophers such as Thales and Anaximander because he shares their philosophical position. In the third section, on tragedy, I will argue that, with an understanding of how *Blood Meridian* is connected to the *Iliad* and its concerns with necessity, equality, and chance (first section), and how early Greek philosophers responded to those concerns (second section), we are in a position to read *Blood Meridian* as a work of Greek tragedy. I will contend that McCarthy's work is a true work of tragedy in the precise sense of pitting two irreconcilable metaphysical options against each other. I will conclude in the last section by suggesting a possible way of identifying a Homeric trajectory in McCarthy's work that begins in *Blood Meridian* and culminates in the Border Trilogy.

## BLOOD MERIDIAN AS EPIC

*Blood Meridian* is often characterized as standing in the tradition of epic or "prose-epic" (Bloom 10). I find this characterization accurate, but not very helpful. There are numerous works that are characterized as epic in the history of literature, and it would seem that if the characterization of epic is to add to our understanding of *Blood Meridian*, then some measure of specificity is required. I am going to argue that characterizing *Blood Meridian* as an epic can be more useful if it is compared with a specific epic, namely the *Iliad*. The most obvious connection between *Blood Meridian* and the *Iliad* is that both works take war as their subject matter and use historical events (or what would have been taken to be historical events in the case of Homer) to investigate the human condition and the nature of the cosmos. Homer uses the events of the Greek invasion of Troy to construct a narrative that investigates the human condition.[1] Similarly, McCarthy uses the historical realities of the Glanton gang's murderous expeditions in the borderlands of Texas and Mexico between 1849–50 as a way to investigate the human condition through an examination of its past.

The most striking feature linking *Blood Meridian* and the *Iliad* is, however, what I am going to call the problem of *force*. I intend to use Simone Weil's interpretation of the *Iliad* from her seminal "*Iliad*, Poem of Might" (*L' Iliade ou le Poème de la Force*) as a way of understanding the central issues of the *Iliad* and then argue that a concern for these same issues is shared by *Blood Meridian*. My claim is that applying Weil's reading of the *Iliad* to *Blood Meridian* brings about two clear interpretative results: first, a better understanding of the central philosophical issues engaged by *Blood Meridian* and, second, a clearer picture of the Judge. Weil's argument is that "*force*" (translated as "might" below) is the central character in the *Iliad* and that Homer is engaged in a search to understand this principle. I will argue that *force* can be analyzed in terms of equality, necessity, and chance, and I will show how *Blood Meridian* employs these concepts, thereby placing it more clearly in the tradition of a particular epic—in this case the *Iliad*. Weil characterizes the *Iliad* as follows:

> The true hero, the real subject, the core of the *Iliad* is might. That which is wielded by men rules over them, and before it man's flesh cringes. The human soul never ceases to be modified by its encounter with might swept on, blinded by that which it believes itself able to handle, bowed beneath the power of that which it suffers. Those who dreamt that might, thanks to progress, belonged henceforth to the past, have been able to see its living witness in this poem: those who know how to recognize it throughout the ages, there at the heart of every human testament, find here its most beautiful, most pure of mirrors. (24)

*Force* in the *Iliad* is not simply that which is employed by human actors but a principle of "geometric strictness" (Weil 35) that transcends personal intentions and actions. It is an ontologically real measure or ratio that can be defined as that which makes a person subjected to it into an object.

One could read the *Iliad* and *Blood Meridian* as putting forth a kind of nihilistic relativism: life as an endless and futile struggle to wield violent control over others lest we become victims, and that the ends of violence are entirely self-centered. I want to argue that this reading is mistaken. Violence, as portrayed by McCarthy and Homer, is a constant that seems to operate with the kind of necessity that points to the possibility of intelligibility. The *Iliad* is distinguished from Near Eastern epics such as *The Epic of Gilgamesh* because the Greek epic is a search for regularity, law, purpose, and order. Neither the gods nor the universe itself is chaotic and entirely unpredictable. That there are constants in human behavior such as the attraction to violence, and the absolute equity according to which the *force* of violence respects neither the just or the unjust, does not resign one to the inscrutable whims of fate or the actions of unintelligible gods, rather it leads one to a search for order and the possibility of regularity in the functioning of the universe. Weil's fundamental insight that the *Iliad* is about *force* can be useful in understanding *Blood Meridian* as work of epic. In order to substantiate this claim I will argue that Weil's notion of *force* can be understood in terms of three distinct notions: necessity, equality, and chance. Analyzing *force* as a concept containing the aforementioned three aspects will provide a way of connecting *Blood Meridian* with the *Iliad*, and will offer a means for discussing the philosophical issues found in *Blood Meridian* that are concerns of the next section.

In what sense can the sort of violence portrayed in both the *Iliad* and *Blood Meridian* be linked with necessity? I think that there are two distinct ways in which the connection can be established. First, it is the case that human beings are both attracted and repelled by violence. Second, violence functions in a way similar to a physical force like gravity. Consider the following passage from *Iliad*, book 16. Patroclus has taken the field against the Trojans in Achilles' armor and is presenting a formidable challenge on behalf of the Argives. In this scene Patroclus has just killed Pronous and now turns to engage a Trojan charioteer:

> And next he went for Thestor the son of Enops
> cowering, crouched in his fine polished chariot,
> crazed with fear, and the reins flew from his grip—
> Patroclus rising beside him stabbed his right jawbone,
> ramming the spearhead square between his teeth so hard
> he hooked him by that spearhead over the chariot-rail,
> hoisted, dragged the Trojan out as an angler perched
> on a jutting rock ledge drags some fish from the sea,
> some noble catch, with line and glittering bronze hook.

So with the spear Patroclus gaffed him off his car,
his mouth gaping round the glittering point
and flipped him down facefirst,
dead as he fell, his life breath blown away. (425–46)

The simile of the fisherman is used by Homer to convey the perspective of both victor and the vanquished and forces us to reflect on the attraction and repulsion we feel relative to both wielding as well as undergoing violence: "The lines combine two contrary emotions: man's instinctive revulsion from bloodshed and his susceptibility to the excitements of violence. And they are typical of the poem as a whole" (Knox 29). The ability to portray violence from the dual perspective of dominator and dominated is central to the *Iliad*'s understanding of the human condition and reveals our fascination with controlling the *force* of violence. We are both repelled and attracted by the kind of violence portrayed in *Blood Meridian*. Critics have not failed to note this tension when approaching McCarthy's violent Western (Bloom 5).

Weil compares the attraction of violence and domination in all forms to a *force* like gravity (Weil, *Gravity and Grace*): we are irresistibly drawn to it as a constant, and the regularity of our attraction to it marks it as something that is out of our control. The violent *force* exercised by Patroclus over Thestor will very quickly be turned against him and result in his own violent death at the hands of Hector. We are drawn to this drama of *force* because there seems to be a kind of necessity, akin to physical laws involved. Control and retribution seem to operate with the kind of necessity that governs physical laws such as gravity. The universe, then, confronts us with the equity of *force*. It is the necessity inherent in acts of violence and their attempt at control that the Judge identifies when he declares that human beings are born for games and that even a child will recognize the lack of nobility in work, but identify its presence in games (249). This is because risk and the mastery of it are like *force*s of attraction. We are creatures that crave control, but ultimately that control will elude even those most practiced and skilled, and this, according to the Judge, is what makes war the ultimate game and the super science that contains all trades (249).

The idea that violence is bound up with a kind of necessity that functions in a law-like fashion gives rise to a notion of equality: if everyone is attracted and repelled by violence and if violence operates in a law-like fashion like gravity, then is it not the case that the universe displays a kind of basic equity? The light of the sun, like gravity, is impartial. Even those most skilled at violence (Achilles, Patroclus, Hector) are subject to it. The characters in the *Iliad* are not divided into any sort of hierarchical sorting of weak and strong, victor and vanquished, suppliant and master; rather everyone, including Achilles, is compelled to bow before *force*. The genius of the *Iliad* on Weil's reading is not the discovery of a truism, such as "live by the sword, die by the sword" rather; it is the discovery of *force* as a metaphysical principle of necessitated equality (see McCarthy 248 for a discussion between the Judge and the gang on this particular notion). The *Iliad* and its portrayal of the equity of *force* brings about the idea "of a destiny beneath which the aggressors and their victims are equally innocent, the victors and the vanquished brothers in the same misfortune" (Weil 39).

This idea that the universe presents us with a chilling impartiality is clearly at work in *Blood Meridian*. That the universe appears to us as ultimately impartial, as evidenced by the impartiality of *force*, to the fate of any particular thing is one of the central problems of *Blood Meridian*. What is the meaning of existence relative to nature? In attempting to make sense of the world we are confronted with what McCarthy calls a "strange equality." I take the following to state the basic problem of equity in *Blood Meridian*:

> The horses trudged sullenly the alien ground and the round earth rolled beneath them silently milling the greater void wherein they were contained. In the neuter austerity of that terrain all phenomena were bequeathed a strange equality and no one thing nor spider nor stone nor blade of grass could put forth claim to precedence. The very clarity of these articles belied their familiarity, for the eye predicates the whole on some feature or part and here was nothing more luminous than another and nothing more enshadowed and in the optical democracy of such landscapes all preference is made whimsical and a man and a rock become endowed with unguessed kinships. (247)

The universe confronts us with a blind equality: no particular thing holds sway over any other, and no apparent teleological pattern is forthcoming. It presents us with an "optical democracy." While a Nietzschean, or Heideggerian, or Darwinian reading is possible here, I think that it is the Homeric one that will shed the most light and help us to place *Blood Meridian* in the tradition of the ancient epic.

The notion of equality in McCarthy's phrase "strange equality" needs to be distinguished from its contemporary political usage and the latter's association with rights. I am asserting that the "strange equality" put forth by McCarthy is like the equity of *force* found in the *Iliad*; it does not necessarily provide the basis for political rights, but presents the problem of why any particular thing should hold sway over any other particular thing. This notion of equity is present in *Blood Meridian* in the following examples. First, there is a strict equality that controls and directs the affairs of the Glanton gang. I am not referring to a notion of political equality whereby rights are granted and democratic structures are enforced via a social contract, but the sort of equality that exists by *force*. Glanton's gang is clearly no democracy, but the equality among its members is strictly maintained by Glanton (whose leadership is based on his ability to use *force*). Despite Glanton's extreme racism the black Jackson is treated equally according to the rules of equity that apply to *force*: "There were two fires in this camp and no rules real or tacit as to who should use them" (106). The white Jackson seeing the black Jackson seated at what he takes to be the wrong fire (his own) warns him away with drunken oath and gesture. The narrator intones ominously that "beyond men's Judgments all covenants were brittle" (106). When the white Jackson draws a gun and threatens to kill the black Jackson unless he moves to the other fire, the black Jackson looks to Glanton for a judgment: "He looked to where Glanton sat. Glanton watched him. He put his pipe in his mouth and rose and took up the apishamore and folded it over his arm" (106). Moments later the black Jackson decapitates the white Jackson and the men move away without speaking.

There is neither condemnation nor retribution by any member of the gang, and they leave the white Jackson sitting unburied, upright and headless. "They had not gone forth one hour upon that plain before they were ridden upon by the Apaches" (107). There is the recognition here that *force* is a principle that moves with an inexorability that is beyond human control: the black Jackson decapitates the white Jackson while the gang looks on, but in rapid succession they all will be "ridden upon" by the Apaches and black Jackson will soon die at the ferry (273). Patroclus gaffs Thestor from his chariot with great martial skill, but will quickly suffer a gruesome death at the hands of Hector. Homer's portrayal of the equitability of bloodshed is echoed clearly in *Blood Meridian*: "Among their barbarous hosts they had met with neither favor nor discrimination but had suffered and died impartially" (227). If it is the case that the universe displays necessity and equity, then what is the source of that necessity and equity? In the *Iliad* we see *force* operating according to a strict pattern of equality, and this raises the possibility that there is a kind of necessity or measure of regularity exhibited by the cosmos. However, the fact that this pattern is ultimately inscrutable raises the problem of chance.

That Homer is clearly dealing with issues pertaining to order within the universe, and their relationship to necessity and chance, can be seen in the following passage from book 16. Here Zeus watches Patroclus (almost immediately after Patroclus has gaffed Thestor from his chariot and killed him) close on the Trojan Sarpedon for battle. Zeus is considering plucking Sarpedon, his own son and much beloved, from the battle when Hera addresses him as follows:

> But Queen Hera, her eyes wide, protested strongly:
> "Dread majesty, son of Cronus—what are you saying?
> A man, a mere mortal, his doom sealed long ago?
> You'd set him free from all the pains of death?
> Do as you please, Zeus . . .
> but none of the deathless god will ever praise you.
> And I tell you this—take it to heart, I urge you–

if you send Sarpedon home, living still, beware!
Then surely some other god will want to sweep
his own son clear of the heavy fighting too.
Look down. Many who battle round King Priam's
mighty walls are sons of the deathless gods–
you will inspire lethal anger in them all. (427)

Here we have two distinct possibilities regarding the governance of the universe, but no clear position as to how things actually run. It could be the case that Zeus runs the world and can decide Sarpedon's fate, and if so then we can attribute a kind of teleological governance to the universe: there is a thinking intelligence that directs (or could direct) events. Or it could be the case that even Zeus must follow the dictates of fate ("a mere mortal, his doom sealed long ago?"). Homer is investigating the problem of the how the universe actually runs and whether it is governed by a teleological intentionality (e.g., the mind of Zeus) or whether it operates according to blind chance (the fates).

The tension described above also drives *Blood Meridian*. The Judge and the Glanton gang under his influence opt entirely for the "chance" side of the dilemma. The Judge's claim that "anything is possible" (245) is not born out of some kind of naïve hope or idealism; rather it is rooted in the rejection of any kind of teleological principle or intentionality governing the cosmos. The order that one sees in creation is the order that one has imposed by thinking it so, the mind being simply one fact among others (245). The Glanton gang is inextricably bound by the workings of chance because the affairs of the gang are ultimately governed by chance, and a violation of the results of chance is a violation of the equality and necessity that bind the gang together. If one has rejected that the affairs of the world are teleologically directed, then one has accepted the role of chance and has given it one's allegiance, which is why the Glanton gang is about the trade of war because it, according to the Judge, is god (249). The following example illustrates the role that chance plays in the operation of the gang and how, according to the Judge, their violation disrupts the essential fabric of the gang. In an encounter with General Elias' Sonoran cavalry three men are killed, and four of the seven wounded cannot ride. The wounded unable to ride will need to be killed (or presumably suffer a worse fate at the hands of the enemy), and lots are drawn to decide who must do the killing.

McCarthy describes how Glanton places arrows, some of which have red flannel strips attached, into a quiver: "When the kid selected among the shafts to draw one he saw the Judge watching him and he paused. He looked at Glanton. He let go the arrow he'd chosen and sorted out another and drew that one. It carried the red tassel (205). Despite having drawn the red tassel, the kid does not kill Shelby, one of the wounded men that he was charged with dispatching. This is a pivotal moment in the narrative as it marks the kid off as one not willing to obey the dictates of chance. As I will show later, it is this moment as perceived by the Judge that removes the kid from the fabric of the gang: if he is no longer willing to follow the principles of equality, chance, and necessity, he has violated the bonds that connect Glanton's gang. It is not the kid's misplaced clemency (Shelby most likely had to endure a worse death at the hands of the Sonoran cavalry than by the kid), but his failure to adhere to the rules of *force* that brings him into conflict with the Judge.

Such arguments help to elucidate the notion that *Blood Meridian* belongs to the tradition of ancient epic. These notions, however, do not appear as McCarthy's concerns in *Blood Meridian* alone, they can be found in his earlier work as well. In a passage from the conclusion of *The Orchard Keeper*, McCarthy's first novel published twenty years before *Blood Meridian*, Homeric themes of chance, necessity, and strange equality are sounded just as strongly as in *Blood Meridian*:

> Young Rattner finished his cigarette and went back out to the road. An aged Negro passed high on the seat of a wagon, dozing to the chop of the half-shod mule-hooves on the buckled asphalt. About him the tall wheels veered and dished in the erratic parabolas of spun coins unspinning as if not attached to the wagon at all but merely rolling there in that quadratic symmetry by pure chance. He crossed the road to give them leeway and they swung by slowly, laboriously, as if under the weight of some singular and unreasonable gravity. (244)

Here we find the necessity of mathematical notions ("parabolas" and "quadratic") conjoined with equality ("symmetry") and juxtaposed with chance ("spun coins" and "pure chance"). Taken together they combine as "the weight of some singular and unreasonable gravity," i.e., *force*.

## *BLOOD MERIDIAN* AS PHILOSOPHY: PRESOCRATIC THOUGHT AS A RESPONSE TO THE HOMERIC PROBLEM OF *FORCE*

My argument has been that we achieve a greater understanding of *Blood Meridian* as an epic when it is compared with a specific epic, namely, the *Iliad*. The central concern of the *Iliad* is the nature of *force*, and I have claimed that *force* can be understood in terms of equality, necessity, and chance. The claim, then, is that these notions are central to understanding *Blood Meridian*. I have also claimed that *Blood Meridian* engages philosophical issues. To understand the nature of *Blood Meridian*'s philosophical engagement I am going to examine how the tradition of Greek philosophy responded to the philosophical questions of equality, necessity, and chance raised by Homer. Homer sets in motion the search for order and regularity in the universe and raises questions regarding the nature of this order: is it mind driven (teleological) or driven by a purposeless necessity alone (chance)? In order to see more clearly the philosophical aspects of *Blood Meridian* it will be necessary to briefly examine how Greek philosophical thought picked up Homer's questions and developed them. It is my contention that a clearer understanding of the tradition of naturalistic materialism in Presocratic Greek philosophy will provide a more complete picture of the Judge as he represents this tradition and quotes thinkers such as Thales and Anaximander (the first Presocratic philosophers) with specific intent. I am going to argue that the tradition of Greek naturalistic philosophy can be used to understand more clearly the Judge's scientific and moral pronouncements.

The origins of Greek philosophical thought are often construed as discontinuous with Homeric epic (i.e., the scientific picture of the world supplants by literary or mythic portrayals), but a more cogent account portrays the development of Greek philosophical thought as continuing the line of inquiry articulated in works like the *Iliad*. The "Presocratic" philosophers (roughly 625–475 BCE) were the first to offer explanatory structures that we would today recognize as scientific. Figures such as Thales, Anaximander, Pythagoras, Xenophanes, and Democritus put forth explanations that were reductive, naturalistic, and analogical and contained a concept of causation sufficient to generate causal laws. One of the central difficulties in the history of ancient Greek philosophy is accounting for how this type of thought came to be articulated and developed. It is with recognition of the complexities involved that I would like to argue that Presocratic thought constitutes a continuation of the Homeric inquiry into the nature of *force*. The move of the Presocratics is to accept the Homeric assertion of a metaphysically real equality and try to account for it via a different form of explanation, i.e., those forms of explanation that we now call scientific, rather than those that construe the investigation in terms of story and chronology, as poets like Homer and Hesiod had done.

*Force* as identified by Homer became, in the hands of thinkers like Thales and Anaximander, a reductive and naturalistic principle of nonteleological necessity. Thales (the very first of the Presocratics), for example, maintained that everything is water. If the former holds, then the cosmos and everything in it is subject to a new kind of analysis because we can now distinguish the question, "What is a thing made of?" from the question, "How did this thing come to be?" (The Homeric account answered the former in terms of the latter, e.g., if one wishes to know why Achilles is so great, one would appeal to origins). If, however, one can analyze the world solely in reductive material terms, it is science and not religion or history that provides the best account of necessity. An example of this naturalistic pattern of explanation can be found in the Presocratic philosopher, Democritus. Democritus asserted that the world was composed of atoms (literally, "uncuttables") that moved in a void. The atomism of Democritus was not the result of empirical investigation as in the case of contemporary physics pertaining to atomic science, but a way of explaining how change and permanence could be reconciled:

the movement of atoms accounted for the different phenomena we perceive, but existence of ultimate building blocks that moved according to necessity provided the conceptual basis for the justification of knowledge claims. For example, the movement and configuration of atoms in the human body could explain the phenomena of love as a chemical state, but to ascribe any purposive or teleological function to love over and above atomic motion was to move beyond what could be rationally understood. Aristotle states that "Democritus leaves aside purpose, but refers all things which nature employs to necessity" (Curd 80). The analogue in contemporary science is the mechanism of natural selection: species are evolving in particular ways that are governed by physical laws of necessity, but there is no *telos* or purpose toward which those forms are evolving.

Democritus held that notions such as equality, necessity, and chance are evinced by the universe, but whereas Homer seems to leave open the possibility that the equity displayed by the universe points to a higher moral order or teleological governance, Democritus maintained that any appeal to purpose or governing principles beyond the material are beyond the reaches of reason. Democritus maintains that it is by "convention [or, custom], sweet; by convention, bitter; by convention, hot; by convention, cold; by convention, color; but in reality, atoms and void" (Curd 87). In other words, properties such as color and taste, and by extension moral properties such as goodness or beauty are mere conventions (like the rules of baseball, they can be changed); all that can be said to be real are atoms and their movements since these are, by necessity, unalterable. Homer's investigation of *force* leaves open the question of whether the universe is teleologically directed or not. Later philosophical thought, however, sought to settle this issue, and the debate between naturalism and teleology became one of the central issues, if not the central issue, in ancient Greek philosophical thought. Plato sums up this debate well in *Phaedo*. In *Phaedo* Socrates explains his first encounter with "Presocratic" philosophy; he mentions specifically Anaxagoras and notes that he was persuaded by the arguments of thinkers like Anaximander (a thinker upon which the Judge discourses in *Blood Meridian*). While sitting in prison waiting to be executed, Socrates relates to his interlocutors that in his youth he was an avid student of the "philosophy of nature": "It seemed to me a superlative thing—to know the explanation of everything, why it comes to be, why it perishes, why it *is*" (Plato 96a).

But Socrates explains that he became disenchanted with natural philosophy because it tried to explain things like the generation of animals and thought itself via material "mechanisms" such as a fermentation of the hot and the cold:

> It seemed to me very like a case in which someone says that Socrates does what he does by virtue of mind or intentionally, and then, trying to give explanations for all the things I do, says that I am sitting here

[in prison] because my body is composed of bones and sinews . . . So when the bones are raised up in their sockets, the sinews by relaxing and contracting, make me able to bend my limbs now, and that is the explanation of why I am bent into a sitting position here. (Plato 98c)

Explaining Socrates' refusal to leave prison by reference to his "bones and sinews" would constitute a mechanistic, or purely material, explanation. Let us call explanations of the sort that appeal only to bones and sinews M-type explanations. But, as Socrates goes on to state, he came to reject M-type explanations:

By the Dog, these bones and sinews would long ago have been in Megara or Boeotia, acting on their judgment of what was best, if I had not thought it righter and better to submit to whatever punishment the city imposes rather than run away. To call such things as bones and sinews explanations is too ridiculous. If you want to say that without having bones, sinews and whatever else of this kind I have I couldn't carry out what seems good to me, you would be right; but to say that I do what I do . . . because of these things, and not through my choice of what is best would be a very large piece of lazy thinking. (Plato 99b)

Socrates does not think that his present situation can be explained by reference to the mechanistic facts of his bones and sinews alone, for these do not explain what power it is that arranges bone and sinew "for the best." Complete explanation for Socrates involves reference to bone and sinew *as well as* purpose. Let us call explanations of the sort that appeal to "purpose," in addition to "bone and sinew," T-type explanations.

The passages given above from the *Phaedo* set out the broad parameters of the debate between the materialist who advocates explanations of type M and teleologists such as Socrates, Plato, and Aristotle who advocate explanations of type T. I will argue that understanding these arguments and the philosophical distinction between the two positions are requisite for understanding the dispute between the Judge and the kid in *Blood Meridian*. The Presocratic revolution regarding explanation not only led to the birth of nonteleological reductive Western science as we understand it today, it provoked attacks on conventional moral notions in the following way. Democritus maintained that everything contained in the universe was a result of the movements of atoms and postulated a material and nonteleological conception of the world wherein all sense perceptions and thoughts were ultimately reducible to the movement of atoms. Democritus held that "In reality we know nothing about anything, but for each person opinion is a matter of reshaping [of the soul atoms by the atoms entering from without]" (Curd 87). While Democritus seemed to resist the implications of his materialistic physics for morality, certain thinkers from a class of itinerant teachers called "sophists" embraced them gladly, developing positions on law and morality that appealed not to theology or convention, but to a reductive and nonteleological view of nature. If one claims ala Democritus that everything is a matter of atoms in motion, then not only do the conventional claims of morality have no hold on us, but they are mere projections created by the human mind.

Here is the argument up to this point: *Blood Meridian* and the *Iliad* are attempting to deal with the same problem. What is the problem of *force*? The *Iliad* raised the problem of a teleologically understood universe versus one that runs according to chance. Plato articulated the distinction between the types of explanatory structures that correlate to naturalistic materialism and teleology. I argue in the next section that the Judge accepts entirely that the universe is governed by chance and in so doing puts forth explanatory structures that are materialistic. I do not argue that the Judge's nemesis, the kid, knowingly argues for or articulates a teleological position, only that he opposes him and that this constitutes the tragic tension of *Blood Meridian*.

## *BLOOD MERIDIAN* AS TRAGEDY: JUDGE AND KID AND THE METAPHYSICS OF OPPOSITION

As stated at the outset, *Blood Meridian* is often characterized as a work of tragedy (Bloom 11). Again, as in the case of the labels "epic" and "philosophical," we need to clarify how the term in question is being applied if we are to make interpretive use of it. A general definition that seems to capture the essence of Greek tragedy holds that it "stresses not the orderly process of transition from one stage of life to another but the in-betweenness, the marginality, and the ambiguity in the juxtaposition of the two stages" (Segal 35). To choose a well-known example, we have in Sophocles' *Antigone* a number of tensions: the tension between the growing power of state institutions and the need to maintain their stability against the power of familial ties, and the tension between the unwritten divine law of tradition and the written conventions of a developing legal system brought about by the innovation of literacy. What Sophocles throws into relief for the audience is the tension between two opposing ideas and the subsequent difficulty of the middle ground. This dialectical way of fleshing out ideas is central to Greek thought. It is the *modus operandi* of Greek philosophy (Socrates, Plato), history (Herodotus and Thucydides) and literature (Homer, Aeschylus, Sophocles, Euripides). Greek tragedy searches out the borderlands between concepts, and aims its *elenchus* less at precise definitions (as does Socrates) than at the territory between the extremes. McCarthy's title, *Blood Meridian or the Evening Redness in the West*, indicates that the novel will be about boundaries and the ambiguity between stages. Whether those stages are understood geographically (the borderlands of Mexico and Texas), politically (the unsettled aftermath of previous military conflicts), or otherwise *Blood Meridian* is tragic in the general sense out-lined above.

I want to argue, though, that *Blood Meridian* is tragic precisely because it sets out two metaphysical extremes and places them at odds with each other. The tragic tension in *Blood Meridian* is between the kid and the Judge. I will suggest below that we can understand the Judge as a meta-physical extreme that uses the argumentation of naturalist Presocratic phi-losophy. I will argue that the role of the Judge can be interpreted using the Presocratic response to "strange equality" outlined above in the section on philosophy. The advantage of correlating the Judge with Presocratic thought is that two of the most important foci of his character, science and law, can be linked. The Judge is a scientist and his expertise runs the gamut from the application of scientific technology to philosopher of science. Here is what I take to be the essence of the Judge's position:

> The man who believes that the secrets of the world are forever hidden lives in mystery and fear. Superstition will drag him down. The rain will erode the deeds of his life. But that man who sets himself the task of sin-gling out the thread of order from the tapestry will by the decision alone have taken charge of the world and it is only by such taking charge that he will effect a way to dictate the terms of his own fate. (199)

In the passage above the Judge is defending his claim that a reduction-ist, nonteleological science will be "suzerain of the earth" (198), and his defense contains the same type of explanatory structure to which the Pre-socratics appealed, namely, that proper explanations involve a search for the single thread of the tapestry or a single causal principle by which the world runs. This thread, once discovered, will not be anything mysterious, but, *contra* religion and superstition, remove mystery: as the Judge claims, "The mystery is that there is no mystery" (252).

If nonteleological necessity governs the world, then there are no con-straints to what is possible (245), and history is not necessary (explains the Judge expunging history). McCarthy has the Judge quote the Presocratics Thales and Anaximander (239) because the Judge's response to the "strange equality" of the world is the same as theirs. Significantly, McCarthy groups Thales and Anaximander with Coke and Blackstone, the latter both legal theorists and natural law jurists. It is to the connection between science and law that we now turn. In addition to the Judge's scientific acumen, he is a purported expert in the law. As discussed above, the naturalistic science developed by Thales and Anaximander led to the naturalistic legal notions of historical sophists such as Thrasymachus, Gorgias, and Protagoras. I am claiming that the development of scientific forms of explanation were inextricably linked to law and ultimately to critiques of religion. Many of the sophists were well known for their antagonism toward traditional religion, and it is unsurprising that the first time we encounter the Judge he is stirring up trouble for traditional religious practices by accusing an itinerant preacher of congress with a goat (something he later admits to be a lie). The Judge could have been portrayed in any number of ways, why the conjunction of law and science?

The answer is because one's conception of law is based upon one's conception of the order (or lack thereof) of the universe. Echoing sophists such as Gorgias and Thrasymachus the Judge declares that

> Moral law is an invention of mankind for the disenfranchisement of the powerful in favor of the weak. Historical law subverts it at every turn. A moral view can never be proven right or wrong by any ultimate test. A man falling dead in a duel is not thought thereby to be proven in error as to his views. His involvement in such a trial gives evidence of a new and broader view. (250)

This "broader view" is the empire of chance and necessity, of strange equality. It is this "broader view" that allows the Judge to claim that war is the super science and "the ultimate game because war is at last a forcing of the unity of existence. War is god" (249). McCarthy aligns the darkest characters of the border fiction with the coin, the dance, and violence and all ultimately subscribe to a view of the universe that is wholly devoid of teleological direction. For the Judge it is chance and necessity all the way down; the Judge cannot be divided back to his origins (309) anymore than chance and necessity can be divided back to theirs.

The Judge personifies the trajectory of Presocratic thought as it develops a response to the fundamental insight of the *Iliad*: philosophy and science began with an examination of the Homeric notion of *force* operable in the cosmos, but characterize this *force* as nonteleological and reducible to naturalistic principles. The Judge does not, however, represent McCarthy's final word in *Blood Meridian*. I will argue that McCarthy's response is Homeric in the following sense: contra the Judge, there is something in the universe that resists and is not reducible to strange equality—and that is mercy. This metaphysical option is represented by the kid. In Simone Weil's view the *Iliad* does not simply portray a blind, but equitable, *force* by which the world runs, rather the *Iliad* argues that the only thing not entirely subject to the empire of *force* is human connection in the forms of mercy, friendship, and hospitality: "All that has no part in war, all that war destroys or threatens, the *Iliad* envelopes in poetry; this it never does for the facts of war" (50). Hospitality, mercy, friendship, and love are beyond the interlocking systems of necessity found in strange equality and the necessity that governs reductionist science. Weil puts it this way:

> Whoever does not know just how far necessity and a fickle fortune hold the human soul under dominion cannot treat as equals, nor love as himself, those whom chance has separated from him by an abyss. The

diversity of the limitations to which men are subject creates the illusion that there are different species among them which cannot communicate with one another. Only he who knows the empire of might and knows how not to respect it is capable of love and justice. (52–53)

The *Iliad*, then, sets up a metaphysical opposition between *force* and those forms of human interaction that transcend *force*. Weil refers to this metaphysical opposition as the tension between "gravity" and "grace" (*Gravity and Grace*).

Though a killer and a scalper like the rest of the Glanton gang it is the kid alone who threatens the Judge's reign of necessity by the extension of mercy to those around him. Our moral assessment of the kid does not matter. What matters is how the Judge perceives him: "There's a flawed place in the fabric of your heart. Do you think I could not know? You alone were mutinous. You alone reserved in your soul some corner of clemency for the heathen" (299). If the Judge is the personification of *force*, then the kid signifies the only thing not subject to the Judge's domain. The element that threatens the Judge's domain is, as identified by the Judge himself, clemency or mercy. I think that it is a testament to the literary skill of McCarthy that the metaphysical opposition to the Judge is found in a violent, illiterate murderer, whose ability to connect to other humans is quite limited. It is, however, this character, as stated by the Judge himself, that brings the greatest threat to the reign of *force*. The challenge to the Judge's reign is the extension of mercy. The kid is not a hero, and his challenge to the Judge is unintentional and unreflective, but there is no denying that he does extend aid to others, and this, according to the Judge, is how he broke faith with the gang. To cite those examples that the Judge will recall, he removes the arrow from Brown's leg when no one else is willing (162), when wounded men unable to ride in the flight from Elias must be killed, the kid, who has drawn the red flannelled arrow like Tate, relieves the latter of his duty as executioner, and ultimately allows Shelby (one of those slated for killing) to live (206–09), and the kid does not abandon the priest when he seems to be mortally wounded (295). The Judge cites each of these instances—Brown, Tate, Shelby, and the priest—in his final encounter with the kid (331).

The kid, then, has violated the rules of the dance according to the Judge. The dance for the Judge is like the movement of atoms for Democritus and is based entirely on necessity and chance. The Judge accepts the Democritean reality that there is no overarching teleological principle, and this means that intelligibility will be found not in teleological explanations, but in war, the ultimate expression of necessity and chance. "Only that man who has offered himself up entire to the blood of war . . . only that man can dance" (331). The kid has violated the dance by his extensions (however misguided) of mercy, and, again, in his case against the kid the Judge lists every man in succession to whom the kid has extended mercy: Brown, Shelby, Tate, and the priest (331). The kid's reply is one that is beyond his full comprehension but is a full repudiation of the Judge's worldview of the universe as a dance of necessity and chance: "Even a dumb animal can dance" (331). At its most basic, this remark recalls the fact that a bear was just dancing on the stage (prior to its being shot and killed), but at its most philosophical it is an argument that there is a distinction between a being that can think for itself—whose mind is not simply one fact among the "strange equality" of all facts and who is capable of even the slightest transcendence over those facts—and the true dancer as understood by the Judge. The former can, on occasion, break the cycle of necessity ultimately governed by chance through the extension of mercy, while the latter can never transcend *force*, but is bound to it. This is the tragic tension of *Blood Meridian*.

*Blood Meridian*, like the *Iliad*, then, puts forth a metaphysic of opposition. By pitting the Judge against the kid, McCarthy infuses *Blood Meridian* with the same response to *force* as the *Iliad*. The following passage, although used to describe a landscape, holds for the ontological arrangement of the Judge and the kid: "they lay opposed to each other across the earth, the sun whitehot and the moon a pale replica, as if they were the ends of a common bore beyond whose terminal burned worlds past all reckoning" (86). The kid, Blasarius, born of the Leonids, is fire, while the moon-like Judge constitutes a mere lunar reflection of fire. McCarthy's characterization of the Judge's luminosity as lunar and thus secondhand, gives ontological primacy to light of the kid, but not by much. The transcendence that the kid represents is hardly a match for the Judge who does not merely defy systems but is in fact system itself. The Judge is physical, scientific, rhetorical, military, emotional *force*. The Judge himself has identified the threat to his system, and it is mercy that rejects systematization, even when that mercy is found in individuals that are ignorant and violent.

## *BLOOD MERIDIAN* AND THE TRAJECTORY OF THE BORDER TRILOGY

The tragic tension of the *Iliad* is this: on the one hand there seems to be a *force* operable in the universe that is displays equity and necessity, but is ultimately governed by chance. War is the ultimate expression of *force,* and our feeble attempts to master *force* animate the majority of our actions. On the other hand, there are moments of human connection brought about by love and mercy that are not subject to *force*; in fact, merciful actions have the power to break the domination of *force* if only for the briefest interval. I have attempted to show that one could read the development of contemporary science as being built on the naturalistic patterns of explanation articulated by the Presocratics and that those patterns of explanation are built on the Homeric idea that there seems to be a kind of regularity in nature that operates according to chance and necessity. This seems to be the perspective of the Judge. Homer, however, does seem to hold out the possibility that through human connection via love and mercy we can transcend the bounds of necessity imposed upon us by *force*. McCarthy seems to at least recognize the very dim possibility of this option in the kid.

I do not intend to make an extended argument for the following claim, but will submit it as a way of attempting to round out the overall picture of *Blood Meridian* and its connection to the Greek epic tradition. *Blood Meridian*, like the *Iliad*, is about war and uses war and violence as a means of investigating the human condition and the nature of the cosmos. The intent of both works, arguably, is to specify the parameters of the problem, not necessarily to suggest a final answer. It is, though, possible to read Homer's other great epic, the *Odyssey*, as a response to the problems raised in the *Iliad*. The *Odyssey* is not about war, but about *nostos*, or homecoming, and the central issue is the establishment of good *xenia*,[2] or hospitality: a form of the very thing that could break alter the reign of *force* in the *Iliad*. *Blood Meridian* and the Border Trilogy seem to share a similar relationship: the former establishes the problem, and the latter delves into the question of how one can return, how one can make things right given the human condition and the metaphysical realities of *force* in the cosmos. The Border Trilogy never leaves behind the issues of *Blood Meridian*, but like the *Odyssey*, turns its attention to *xenia* and the conditions that allow for return and grace.

## NOTES

1. There exist tremendous difficulties pertaining to the authorship of the Homeric epics. I intend to sidestep the complexities involved and will simply refer to the author of the *Iliad* and the *Odyssey* as Homer.
2. This term is very difficult to render into English as it can mean guest, host, stranger, friend, and foreigner. It is often translated as *hospitality*. Significantly, it is one of the epitaphs for Zeus, *Zeus Xenios*.

## WORKS CITED

Bloom, Harold. Introduction. *Blood Meridian or the Evening Redness in the West.* By Cormac McCarthy. New York: The Modern Library, 2001.

Curd, Patricia, ed. *A Presocratics Reader.* Trans. Richard McKirahan. Indianapolis: Hackett, 1995.

Frye, Steven. *Understanding Cormac McCarthy.* Columbia: U of South Carolina P, 2009.

Homer. *The Iliad.* Trans. Robert Fagles. New York: Penguin, 1991.

Knox, Bernard. Introduction. *The Iliad.* By Homer. Trans. Robert Fagles. New York: Penguin, 1991.

Lincoln, Kenneth. *Cormac McCarthy: American Canticles.* New York: Palgrave Macmillan, 2009. 30.

McCarthy, Cormac. *Blood Meridian or the Evening Redness in the West.* 1985. New York: The Modern Library, 2001.

———. *The Orchard Keeper*. 1965. New York: Vintage, 1993.

Plato. *Phaedo*. Trans. H. Tredennick. *The Collected Dialogues of Plato*. Ed. Edith Hamilton and Huntington Cairns. Princeton: Princeton UP, 1961.

Segal, Charles. "Greek Tragedy and Society: A Structuralist Perspective." *Interpreting Greek Tragedy: Myth, Poetry, Text*. Ithaca: Cornell UP, 1986.

Weil, Simone. "*The Iliad*, Poem of Might." *Intimations of Christianity Among The Ancient Greeks*. London: Routledge, 1998. 24–55.

———. *Gravity and Grace*. London: Routledge, 2002.

# 2   The Ties that Bind

## Intertextual Links between *All the Pretty Horses* and *Sir Gawain and the Green Knight*

*Megan Riley McGilchrist*

*All the Pretty Horses* bears the signs of various influences. In John Grady Cole we may catch sight of the long shadow of the Virginian; get a glimpse of Natty Bumppo; hear more than an echo of the voice of Huck Finn. And one mustn't forget Holden Caulfield, skirting dissolutely around the edges of the text. Like Holden, John Grady's spiritual alienation comes into focus with a death. But John Grady is a complex character, one who does more than share psychic space with any number of possible protagonists. In this essay I will argue that the character of John Grady Cole in *All the Pretty Horses* has much to do with the figure of the medieval knight, and specifically that paragon of the genre, Sir Gawain, as he is depicted in the eponymous fourteenth-century poem, *Sir Gawain and the Green Knight*. The knight errant is a character whose motivations exist largely in the realm of the idealistic and illusory, formed in feudal patriarchy. John Grady's similarity to this traditional character in chivalric quest literature is obvious, and has been discussed by Charles Bailey in a paper first presented at the 1998 colloquy of the Cormac McCarthy Society in El Paso, Texas. Briefly, Bailey suggests that the *All the Pretty Horses* is based upon medieval chivalric romances. He sees John Grady in terms of the questing knight errant; Alejandra as the unobtainable lady; the *cuchillero* in Saltillo as the traditional evil adversary. However, I would like to argue that not only does John Grady embody many of the attributes of the medieval knight errant, he also resembles a very specific one: Sir Gawain. Intertextual studies are problematic if one is seeking to prove an intentional link between texts, and clearly, there is no way of knowing whether McCarthy had *Sir Gawain and the Green Knight* in mind when writing *All the Pretty Horses*. But congruencies exist between the texts, which suggest that both works are dealing with themes which are paradigmatic, and indeed may reflect similar historical milieus. It is the issue of parallel structures suggesting archetypal themes with which I am most concerned.

*Sir Gawain and the Green Knight* is an example of the fourteenth-century alliterative revival which consciously looked back to the Anglo-Saxon period. The similarities with an earlier tradition do not end with the verse style. Gawain himself is a transitional figure, somewhere between the stoical, long-suffering, fearless Anglo-Saxon hero and the "meek in love and stern in battle" (Lewis 195) late Medieval knight whose courtesy, gentleness, and devotion was a development beyond the earlier figure. Similarly, McCarthy's young cowboys are rooted in the mythology of a vanished past, characters who live by a code articulated in a world which no longer exists, if indeed it ever did. Their similarity to Gawain lies in the fact that they truly believe they are invoking the ideals of a quasi-chivalric tradition. But they, unlike Gawain, are transitional to nothing. John Grady's adventures do not lead him to knowledge or redemption, or show the way to a new kind of Western man, but rather reveal the vacancy of placelessness and lack of identity. This suggests a postmodern reworking of the chivalric motif expressed in *Sir Gawain and the Green Knight*.

The poem requires the reader to understand it on a number of different levels. Initially appearing to be a tale of Christmas magic and monsters, it soon becomes clear that there is much more to it than that. Equally, while *All the Pretty Horses* may look like a Western, even the most casual reader soon becomes aware that there is much more going on in the novel than a simple tale of Western adventure:

> To a certain degree nearly every narrative of any sophistication enter-tains us or holds our attention by first setting up and then subverting or denying certain expectations on our part. There are narratives, how-ever, that indulge in this practice to a suspicious extent. As a result, we are constantly made aware of our presuppositions. We are forced to question our own perception. (Ganim 376)

Ganim argues that *Sir Gawain and the Green Knight* is such a narrative, proceeding through the medium of disorientation to take the reader on a journey from order to disorder and back again. He continues:

> The delicate balance of the poem always threatens itself but always returns safely from excursions into disorder, into the seemingly incon-sequential, into details so minute that to follow the poet's eye is to lose oneself in the trees, to be lost in a forest to which, until we finish the poem, we have no map. (383)

This maplessness, the excursions into disorder, the minutiae of detail, along with many other elements present in both works, are all aspects of *Sir Gawain* which we may also see exemplified in *All the Pretty Horses*.

Early in both works, their authors historicize events which are to follow. *Sir Gawain* opens with an invocation of antiquity, emphasizing its retro-spective gaze:

> Sithen the sege and the assaut was sesed at Troye,
> The borgh brittened and brent to brondes and askes,

The tulk that the trammes of tresoun ther wroght
Was tried for his tricherie, the trewest on erthe.
                    (Cowley 51, 1–4)

By speaking of Troy before even beginning his story, the poet places the action within a historical/mythical milieu. The mention of treason and trickery in the poem's opening also gives us a clue as to what we may expect to follow in the story, as does the implicit reference to Helen, the very archetype of the faithless woman. The poet gives us some further background:

Hit was Ennias the athel, and his highe kynde,
That sithen depreced provinces, and patrounes bicome
Welneghe of al the wele in the west iles.
Fro riche Romulus to Rome ricchis hym swythe,
With gret bobbaunce that burghe he biges upon fyrst,
And nevenes hit his aune nome, as hit now hat;
Tirius to Tuskan and teldes bigynnes,
Langaberde in Lumbardie lyftes up homes,
And fer over the French flod Felix Brutus
On mony bonkkes ful brode Bretayn he settes wyth wynne.
                    (51, 5–15)

This passage gives us Camelot's lineage, descending from Aeneas who left the ruined city of Troy and went to Rome, and his grandson Felix Brutus who crossed the "French flod"—the English Channel—and founded Britain. The poet thus places his mythic story within a historical framework with which his audience would have been familiar.

By invoking the glorious ancients the poet also suggests a similar significance for his knights, equating them with the heroes of antiquity. The poet was writing with the benefit of hindsight, in an era which must have seemed much less appealing than Arthur's. The fourteenth century saw the worst outbreaks of the Black Death in Europe, the Hundred Years' War with France, the Peasant's Revolt, and the beginnings of the end of traditional mounted warfare as gunpowder became more common. Therefore, the stories of King Arthur and the Round Table were, by the end of the fourteenth century, already archaic. The chivalric tradition was fast fading. As the disintegration of a feudal society progressed and was replaced by a preindustrial world, the third estate—peasants, labourers, and artisans—gradually gained greater privileges and standing. Therefore by the time the poet was writing *Sir Gawain and the Green Knight*, the tradition he was invoking was already gone, and the figure of the medieval knight was largely symbolic. In *All the Pretty Horses* we see a similar framing of events. First there is an invocation of the ancient past of the Comanches, their "transitory and violent lives" (McCarthy 5), which flags a connection with John Grady Cole and his mother's uncles, the seven "wild Grady boys" who all died young. This is followed by the history of the family ranch, which places John Grady in historical time and place. Additionally, the setting in time, post-World War II, reminds the reader from the very outset that we are in an altered world, forever distanced from the assumed innocence of an earlier age.

At this point a brief summary of Sir *Gawain and the Green Knight* may be useful. In the poem, King Arthur's court is visited at Christmastime by a giant green knight who challenges the assembled company to join him in an exchange of blows in which one knight will strike the Green Knight, but in one year's time that knight will have to allow the Green Knight to do the same. None of Arthur's knights volunteer for this challenge until Gawain, the king's nephew, does so to prevent the king from offering himself. Gawain beheads the Green Knight who, revealing his supernatural origins, does not fall, but picks up his own head and departs, reminding Gawain from his bodiless mouth that he will have to seek him out at his Green Chapel in one year. One year later Gawain duly sets out from Camelot to fulfill his part of the bargain. After hard traveling he arrives at the castle of Sir Bertilak, just in time for Christmas. Bertilak is a large, garrulous, red-haired knight who welcomes Gawain and treats him as an honored guest. Gawain spends Christmas at Bertilak's castle in company with many knights and ladies, not least of whom is the host's beautiful wife, whom the poet compares to Guinevere, describing her as even more beautiful than Arthur's queen. Also present in the court is an aged crone who clearly has a position of honor in the court, but whose identity is not revealed until the end of the story. When Gawain says that he must leave after Christmas, Bertilak persuades him to stay until the New Year when he will be guided to the Green Chapel which is nearby. Bertilak then goes hunting for three days, insisting that Gawain stay home and sleep. They make a pact that each will give the other whatever he has gained during the day.

Bertilak hunts, bringing home a large number of deer the first day, a wild boar the second, and finally a fox, a shameful trophy for the knight, a "foule fox felle" (124, line 1944) on the third day of the hunt. At the castle, Gawain stays in bed each day until he is awakened by Bertilak's wife who tries, ever more persuasively, to seduce him, but without success. On the third and final day she persuades Gawain to accept a magic green girdle which she unwinds from her own waist, telling him it will keep him safe. She also admonishes him not to tell her husband of the gift. On the morning of New Year's Day, Gawain departs for the Green Chapel. Before long, he encounters the supernatural Green Knight, as promised. Gawain prepares to receive his blows and at first flinches, drawing the derision of the Green Knight. The second time the Knight deliberately misses him. The third and final stroke draws blood but does not seriously harm Gawain, who leaps up, ready to do battle. But instead of fighting, the Green Knight reveals all the mysteries of the story to Gawain. He tells him that the nick he received was for accepting the girdle and not speaking, and that the Lady's seduction was his plan, for the Green Knight is Bertilak. The entire plot was created by the sorceress Morgan le Fay, the aged crone, who wanted to spoil Guinevere's Christmas. In the end Gawain returns to Camelot, shamed, wearing the green girdle as a mark of his disgrace. The court all adopts green girdles to honor Gawain. The reader is finally admonished, "Hony soyt qui mal pence" (146, line 2531). Its literal translation from Old French is "Shame be to him who thinks evil of it," and it is the motto of the chivalric Order of the Garter.

Although he has similarities to both the Anglo-Saxon and later Anglo-French tradition, Gawain is a considerably less complex figure than some other medieval knights. It is important to note that although the Gawain Poet was contemporary with Chaucer, he was not writing in a cultural centre. *Sir Gawain* was written in the Midlands, an area which was to a degree untouched by the fashions of literary London. The poem also reveals the effect of the earlier Anglo-Saxon tradition. Certainly the use of the alliterative style points to this. The French influence which transformed the fierce Anglo-Saxon warrior of *Beowulf* into the courtly lover of the late fourteenth century had smoothed out some of the rough edges of the warrior in Gawain, but his own conflicts were still comparatively simple. The tension that plagued so many medieval knights, that of a division of loyalties between one's lord and lady is shown in silhouette in the episode of Lady Bertilak's attempted seduction of him, but the figure of the knight suppliant, as seen in Palamon and Arcite in Chaucer's *Knight's Tale,* or the full-blown love affairs of Tristan, Troilus, or Launcelot, are not yet part of the depiction of the knight in the poem. Gawain, unlike Malory's knights, is ever chaste, despite the reputation which precedes him to the castle of Sir Bertilak of being a great lover. Indeed the company at Bertilak's feast expect to "lerne of luf-talkying" (85, line 927) from their guest.

As Gamin has noted, the style and content of *Sir Gawain and the Green Knight* "contributes to a process of disorientation" (376), forcing the reader to examine her perception and the presuppositions upon which that perception is based. Clearly *Sir Gawain* is disorienting. From the arrival of the giant green man at a peculiarly childish Arthurian court, and his subsequent headless departure, to the final revelation that the charming red-haired Bertilak was the Green Knight, the plot is full of strange revelations and surprises. Morgan le Fay's motives are never clear, and Gawain's own disgrace seems largely self-inflicted. And of course the question remains as to why Gawain felt compelled to join the Green Knight in his bizarre game of blows in the first place. In fact it is clear that Gawain did not need to behead the Green Knight at all; all that was asked for was an exchange of blows. Victoria Weiss has persuasively argued that,

> His failure to see an alternative to his action is striking, especially since indications that he might emerge from this situation honorably and unharmed are offered to him prior to chopping off the Green Knight's

head . . . there is a suggestion . . . that Gawain is free to choose how he will wield the ax, and a hint that there may be more to the acceptance of the challenge than simply demonstrating one's strength. (364)

This argument suggests that the testing of Gawain began long before the Lady entered his chamber, calling into question the very premises upon which Arthur's court is founded. Seeing Gawain in this way suggests that the purportedly civilized behavior which the tradition of courtly love with its chivalric component brought to Britain was in fact nothing of the kind, and that the Green Knight paradoxically represents a more peaceful world, arriving with his holly branch and the offer of a Christmas game.

The poem may also be read as a cultural *Bildungsroman*, pitting a youthful Gawain against not only the Green Knight, but also the older world which he represents: ancient, natural, Celtic, magical. The Green Knight's arrival in Camelot is really not so different from Grendel's arrival at Hrothgar several centuries before. He does not "hate the sound of harps," as Grendel does, but the Green Knight's desire to upset the festivities does perhaps point to a similar ancient malice directed against the new order. In another layer of complexity Gawain pits the newly acquired chivalric value of courtesy against a determined onslaught of female sexual predation which, had it succeeded, would surely have resulted in his death at the hands of the Green Knight, suggesting an anti-female subtext to the work. This is a point to which I will return, but at this point it is worth pointing out that female power is also a central issue for John Grady Cole.

With its boy protagonist, John Grady Cole, *All the Pretty Horses* is, on one level, a *Bildungsroman*; so is *Sir Gawain and the Green Knight*. Gawain leaves Arthur's youthful court on a journey into the wild which will test his knightly honor, chivalry, and faith, but arguably he begins his journey having already erred by his too hasty assumption that the initial blow he should give was a beheading blow. John Grady Cole leaves Texas in search of a new world in the old world of Mexico, and a new identity for himself, but he too is operating by flawed reasoning. He believes that it is his right as an American to simply take what he likes once he is in foreign territory. Gawain too is entering into an older world: the world of the Green Man, Celtic, magical, pre-Christian, even prehuman. His journey sets him against giants, monsters, forest creatures, nature itself. Both young men find something less straightforward than they expected:

What John Grady Cole also finds when his old world fails him, is that the "new" world he finds is in fact far older and more complex than the world he fled, and is dominated by class and elite interests which mirror the economic interests which dominate his abandoned western landscape, and have made his family ranch unviable. He has substituted the Hispanic south for the West in his catalogue of desired space . . . In the valley of the Hacienda de Nuestra Señora de la Purísima

Concepción are "fishes not known elsewhere on earth," (9) suggesting an isolated, ancient world, more ancient than even John Grady's nostalgia allows for: an unknown Eden beyond his reckoning. At the hacienda, he encounters a social system, and a code, exemplified by the Dueña Alfonsa, far more archaic and systematized than any he has known in Texas. (McGilchrist 162)

So too does Gawain encounter a world which is "other," peopled by strange and confusing characters, and full of old dangers and new temptations.

Both knight and cowboy represent cultural archetypes. John Grady Cole is a cowboy's cowboy: brave, stoical, taciturn, and an expert horseman. Gawain is the best of all medieval knights, his perfection represented by the pentangle on his shield, which the poet tells us had a specific meaning:

Fyrst he was funden fautles in his fyve wyttes,
And efte fayled neuer the freke in his fyve fyngres,
And alle his afyaunce upon folde was in the fyve woundes
That Cryst kaght on the croys, as the crede telles;
And quere-so-ever thys mon in melly was stad,
His thro thoght was in that, thurgh alle other thynges,
That alle his forsnes he feng at the fyve joyes
That the hende heven-quene had of hir chylde;
At this cause the knyght comlyche hade
In the inore half of his schelde hir ymage depaynted,
That quen he blusched therto his belde never payred.
(75, lines 640–50)

Here the poet tells us that Gawain is faultless in his wits; his five fingers were never at fault. His faith was founded in the five wounds of Christ, his fortitude in the five joys of Christ's mother, whose image he had painted on the inside of his shield to give him strength. John Grady has no such spiritual models, but we know he feels himself to be a cowboy of the old school, and that he is guided by that platonic conception of himself. We see it in his actions—his self-conscious posturing in the theatre in San Antonio when he goes to see his mother in a play; his tacit acceptance of his role of silent desperado when he and Rawlins ride away from their homes en route to a new life in an old world they believe is theirs for the taking.

The terrible irony is that John Grady's self-image is in large part derived from a mythology which had become, by 1949, largely cinematic. However, in this too, he and Gawain have equivalence. By the fourteenth century feudalism was on its way out in Britain, and the virtues of knighthood, originally those qualities of a good warrior, had become transmuted into qualities of nationhood, and as such were the stuff of romantic tales. Jennifer Moskowitz has written that:

[T]he knight's portrayal underwent a change concurrent with the soci-
etal move toward industrialism and nationalism. In literature, he came
to embody the desired attributes of the nation itself. Geoffrey of Mon-
mouth's The History of the Kings of Britain (c 1135), includes King
Arthur and emphasizes the warrior-knight ideal. Geoffrey's narrative
already demonstrates a clear agenda—that of national pride, Christianity, and a strong judicial system. (Moskowitz 3)

Equally, John Grady Cole is reenacting a dead past. The mythic figure of
the brave cowboy, as we know, was largely invented, his literary identity
constructed for similar reasons as the identity of the literary figure of the
medieval knight:

[I]f we look closely at [D.H.] Lawrence's identification of the cowboy
as "the essential American soul," we find that the qualities ascribed to
the cowboy are identical to those of the English knight. Thus, the two
are related; in fact, the cowboy can be seen as the American incarna-
tion of the knight . . . [T]he cowboy would serve a similar purpose for
America as the knight had served for England. More than simply folk-
lore comes through the literature, however. The knight as a representa-
tive figure of nationalism and capitalism carries over to the cowboy, for
he occupies a position remarkably similar to the knight, and his movement from historical figure to literary and cultural figure is similar as
well. Indeed, as with the medieval knight, the historical cowboy bears
little resemblance to the literary one. (Moskowitz 3)

This suggests that as "essential souls" of their respective countries the cowboy and the knight are the repositories of national identity. That both Sir
Gawain and John Grady Cole have this role in eras when national identity
was perceived to be changing is significant, and supports my view that these
texts may be looked at in terms of their paradigmatic qualities. Having
established the larger correspondence, I would now like to look at details
of more specific similarities between both works.

Both Gawain and John Grady Cole set out on horseback on journeys
with no clear destination, John Grady to a mapless Mexico, Gawain to
the mysterious "Grene Chapel" whose location is entirely unknown. John
Grady is looking for something to which he feels he is entitled, enacting
a latter-day model of Manifest Destiny, choosing for his "virgin land,"
Mexico, a space in which he believes the ordinary rules of life do not apply.
In fact he finds a world in which there are many more rules than he might
have imagined. His problem is that he does not know what those rules are.
Similarly, in his travels Gawain is entering into a world in which the parameters of reality slip; people are not who they seem to be; things are not what
they appear to be. The rules of chivalry do not offer solutions to the conun-
drums Gawain faces. For both Gawain and John Grady, familiar referents

are lost. On their journeys, John Grady and Gawain encounter trouble of various kinds, involving people, animals, and bad weather. (Gawain additionally meets wodwos—wild men of the woods. Perhaps a parallel might be the wax-makers in *All the Pretty Horses*). Both travel through beautifully described strange and alien landscapes which finally lead to apparent havens. And both Gawain and John Grady find their havens to be illusory, hiding a preexisting danger which waits for each of them.

I suggest that both John Grady and Gawain also fight battles of a sort with landscape and the natural world. The landscape reflects their solitude and peril. John Grady is constantly at war with hostile landscapes, both before reaching the Hacienda, and after his departure. It is on his return journey to Texas that the world becomes especially forbidding. The sun rarely shines on his travels, and landscapes are barren, volcanic, forbidding. Rain, like tears, is constantly dripping from the brim of John Grady's cowboy hat. There is little food for either men or horses in the empty terrain through which he travels. All these things reflect the state of John Grady's heart. Similarly Gawain's quest takes him out of the world of Camelot into a harsh and strange wilderness in which he suffers from cold and loneliness, fear and self-doubt, accompanied only by his faithful horse, Gryngolet. However, Gawain's most significant conflicts with nature occur before his battle with the Green Knight, arguably himself a representation of the natural world.

The parallels continue and become more striking. Both Gawain and John Grady encounter beautiful and seductive young women whose attentions cause them major problems. Both women, arguably, represent something other than themselves, which is that which their admirer *truly* desires. Alejandra represents land, the possession of which would give John Grady back the identity he lost when his mother told him he could not keep the family ranch. Not only does Alejandra represent the land he so desires, she is the land in the sense that she is the heiress of the hacienda. The metaphor of land as female is unambiguous in this case. (A point of intratextual parallelism here is that John Grady's father, another landless cowboy, only came into possession of land when he married John Grady's mother, also an heiress to a large family ranch). Alejandra, in her willful pursuit of John Grady, is expressing a disdain for the powers which surround her but which eventually separate the two young lovers. However, she colludes, albeit unhappily, in this separation and acknowledges her position in the nexus of father-aunt-society.

As Alejandra represents land, and thus identity, the Lady in *Sir Gawain* represents life, salvation from the awful fate awaiting Gawain at the Green Chapel. In the poem, the lady's attempted seduction of Gawain is done at the behest of her husband, who is himself acting on the instructions of Morgan le Fay. This places the Lady near the bottom of a power structure which is controlled by an older female, but it places Gawain even lower. All characters in *Sir Gawain* are acting roles which are determined by the will of Morgan le Fay. In this case the Lady's gift of the "grene girdel" represents Gawain's desire for life, as she, the Lady, *represents* life in all her ardent and beguiling seductiveness. And yet this too is a mask. How she would have behaved had Gawain given in to her blandishments is something we will never know. Narratively, in the case of the poem, it is impossible.

In both of the young men's perceived havens there is an elderly woman who appears to hold the reins of power. The Dueña Alfonsa's relationship with Alejandra, while protective, is also parasitic. The Dueña lives through Alejandra, seeing in her the life she herself lost through revolution and the disfigurement of her hand in a hunting accident. For all her wisdom and experience, the Dueña is embittered, and she herself is unable to move beyond the social structure in which she has been placed. She is a powerful female, and yet she is powerless in her own life.

Morgan le Fay herself is seen but silent in *Sir Gawain*, and we are told that it is through her that the Green Knight holds his powers: "Thurgh myght of Morgne la Faye, that in my hous lenges" (143, line 2446). She is Arthur's half-sister (and in some stories the mother of his son, Mordred) and acquired her skill at sorcery from Merlin, with whom she had a love affair. Her role in the affair of the beheading game and its consequences is central. She sent Bertilak to Camelot in the guise of the Green Knight to ascertain whether the tales of the knightly prowess of the court were true. She also had a more sinister aim: to frighten Guinevere to death. This second goal is never adequately accounted for, nor is it questioned by any of the players in her game. Her power clearly has its limitations, as does her wisdom; we are never told of any fear felt by Guinevere. Arthur lightly tells her not to worry, "Dere dame, to-day demay yow never / Wel bycommes such craft upon Chritmasse" (69, lines 470–71), and that is the end of it.

A further parallel between the works exists in the fact that both hosts eventually betray their guests in one way or another. The Hacendado turns John Grady and Rawlins over to the Federales without hearing their side of the story of Blevins and the horse. Of course he has in the meantime learned that John Grady has been having an affair with his teenage daughter, so perhaps his behavior is understandable. Bertilak, testing Gawain's fidelity by means of his wife, doubly betrays him. In trying to entrap Gawain he is also trying to kill him, for if Gawain had succumbed to the Lady, clearly, he could not have revealed it to Bertilak and would therefore not only have forfeited the exchange of winnings game, but also put himself in mortal danger.

The games in *Sir Gawain*—exchange of blows and exchange of winnings—have dark subtexts. When Gawain interprets the exchange of blows as an invitation to behead the Green Knight, it is arguably a castration metaphor. The Green Knight's survival of his own beheading thus posits a kind of vitality in the ancient world which far surpasses that of the new order. In the exchange-of-winnings game the descriptions of the hunting and slaughter of the animals offers a parallel to the "hunting" of Gawain by the Lady. We can only assume that had she triumphed Gawain's slaughter would have been as grisly as that of the beasts. These games, if they are games at all, are of the most serious kind. Life and death hang upon them, and yet they must be played with the same good humor as games of the usual sort. In *All the Pretty Horses* John Grady and the Dueña play chess, the most medieval of games. Although it is ostensibly an amusement, the deadly seriousness of its implications is clear to both the Dueña and John Grady. When she loses a game the Dueña states, "That was foolish of me, she said. The queen's knight. That was a blunder. You play very well" (133). When she finally wins, the Dueña "used an opening he'd not seen before." In a clear fore-shadowing of coming events, the passage continues, "In the end he lost his queen and conceded" (134).

John Grady, the queen's knight, does indeed lose all. Later, John Grady and the Hacendado, Alejandra's father, face each other as adversaries over a billiard table in the unused but still consecrated chapel of the hacienda, a medieval setting in decoration and atmosphere:

> He pulled a tasseled chain and lit an ornate tin chandelier suspended from the ceiling. Beneath it an antique table of some dark wood with lions carved into the legs. . .At the far end of the room was a very old carved and painted wooden altar above which hung a lifesize carved and painted wooden Christ. (McCarthy, 143)

The Hacendado even says to John Grady, "Beware gentle knight. There is no greater monster than reason" (McCarthy, 146). Bringing Cervantes into the situation naturally brings Arthur, and Arthur brings Gawain. Watched by Jesus, John Grady and the Hacendado play against one another, just as Gawain and the Green Knight meet in the Knight's "grene chapel" to fulfill the terms of *their* game. That McCarthy was at least glancing toward *Sir Gawain and the Green Knight* in this passage seems likely.

Another point of intertextual collision is in the very youthfulness, indeed immaturity of both cowboy and knight. We know that John Grady has grandiose notions of entitlement; he is the living manifestation of the doctrine of Manifest Destiny, albeit in an attractive and nonviolent young man. He rejects his mother, who attempts to rein in his extravagant fantasies, departing without a word of farewell, to find what he believes he is owed. This is coupled with a self-identification with the nostalgic image of the cowboy of the past. Although Gawain does not have a particular sense of entitlement, he too identifies with the imagery of an idealized form. The pentangle painted on his shield symbolizes this perfection. Geraldine Heng has argued that Gawain's pentangle

> Stands . . . for an aspiration, a psychic yearning that takes up and re-enacts an archaic preoedipal moment of fantasmic plenitude—the moment of presubjectal infancy, where loss and uncertainty, division, are still absent—since it leads back inexorably, umbilically, via the

route of an uncut knot, the pentangle, to the (divine) mother whose image appears on the other side. (504)

This yearning for "fantasmic plenitude" in the case of John Grady Cole might be said to be the yearning for the land, coded as female, before the incursion of modernity, which he articulates in his desire to be "one of the old waddies" and before the reality of his powerlessness in the face of the financial impracticality of keeping the family ranch forced his mother to sell it. The paradox with which John Grady simply cannot live, and for which reason he simply vanishes, is that his mother, whom he regards as the one who ought to be providing him with his desires, is the very person who takes away what he most wants.

Similarly, Gawain, skilled in "luf-talkyng" (85, line 927, and used to being the servant of an idealized vision of womanhood, the Virgin, discovers that real women—using Bertilak's Lady as his proof—are faithless. This results in his antifemale diatribe in lines 2411–28 in which he sarcastically refers to the courtesy of Bertilak's wife and the ladies of the court before launching into a litany against duplicitous women through history, drawing us back to the beginning of the poem and the unspoken reference to Helen of Troy. Both Gawain and John Grady finally perceive themselves to be disgraced. Upon his return to Texas, John Grady confesses his disgrace to the judge who restores his horses to him. Gawain tells his disgrace to the court of Arthur, who laugh at him, mocking the serious Gawain, and wear green girdles as a mark of solidarity. Both John Grady's judge and Arthur's court believe the young men are being too hard on themselves, but the self-imposed disgrace does not leave either of them. They have broken their own rules, and neither will forgive himself for not being perfect. Their sense of disgrace also calls into question the principles of their respective societies, those principles they feel they have failed.

Perhaps the greatest similarity between the two works is the extraordinary passivity with which both characters respond to manifestations of feminine will or power. Gawain literally hides under his covers when Lady Bertilak first appears in his chamber:

And as in slomeryng he slode, sleyly he herde
A littel dyn at his dor, and derfly upon;
And he heve up his hed out of the clothes,
A corner of the cortyn he caght up a lyttel,
And waytes warly thiderwarde quat hit be myght.
Hit was the ladi, loflyest to beholde,
That drow the dor after hir ful dernly and stylle,
And bowed towarde the bed; and the burne schamed,
And layde hym doun lystyly, and let as he slepte.
(95, lines 1182–90)

Gawain first hides, and when hiding fails, he simply resists the Lady, verbally jousting, but being careful not to be in any way discourteous. This too is a kind of game, and one that Gawain plays well. Gawain's chivalric code prevents him from acting on the desire he clearly feels, and his resistance to the Lady's overtures is expected. Yet he finally does accept the lady's "girdel" made of "grene sylke." The color ought to have been a warning, but Gawain takes it when he is told it will save his life in his confrontation with the Green Knight. The green girdle is certainly a sexual signifier, showing that Gawain is now the Lady's possession, and when the Green Knight tells Gawain it is his, the magnitude of the mistake of passively accepting the "girdle," thus acknowledging the power of the Lady, and by association, the Green Knight/Bertilak, is made clear.

In reference to the veiled reality of female power in the poem, Geraldine Heng has noted that

> Repeatedly crisscrossing the narrative plane established by such characters as Gawain, Arthur, and Bertilak and by the worlds of the two courts are, after all, the reticulated angles and interstices of a feminine nexus, a spacing of women; and this other script, read for itself, recuperates the movements of another desire, in a feminine narrative folding into and between the masculine. (501)

By substituting John Grady, his father, and the Hacendado, for Gawain, Arthur, and Bertilak, and "two ranches" for "two courts," one may apply Heng's comment equally and with as good effect to *All the Pretty Horses*. This feminine narrative, "folding into and between the masculine," is in both works the unspoken text. Here we have works in which the archetypal knight/cowboy figure is invoked as a comment upon national aspiration, and yet in both works it is in the feminine that power truly resides.

John Grady's wordless departure to Mexico, never to see his parents alive again, is made in reproach to his mother who has told him a simple truth and has remained unmoved by his objections. Powerless, he appeals to other powerless males: his father, the lawyer Franklin, and Rawlins. Later, Alejandra is in complete control of their brief relationship. She begins it with a display of power—taking the stallion from John Grady and riding it away, leaving him to return barefoot in an obvious emasculation of him. This makes John Grady's previous rides upon the stallion seem like a child's naughtiness, and indeed Alejandra tells him, "You are in trouble," like a mother admonishing a naughty child (McCarthy, 131), further establishing her dominant role. Later, in the prison, it is only the Dueña Alfonsa's money which saves him from certain death. Finally Alejandra abandons him and returns to her enchanted life, the question of possible pregnancy never even being mentioned, which suggests that John Grady may in fact be even further disempowered. That two healthy teenagers could have unprotected sex for upwards of three months without becoming pregnant seems unlikely.

In *All the Pretty Horses,* John Grady's mother is mirrored by the Dueña Alfonsa; both take away from John Grady the thing he most desires. Both speak to him across the expanse of long wooden tables. Both represent the wounding feminine which he reacts against. I have written elsewhere that,

> At this point it is appropriate to point out that John Grady's reaction to the wounding feminine is to adopt a highly stylized, almost parodic version of what he regards as masculine, the idealized cowboy, in reaction to those aspects of the feminine which he cannot control (his mother selling the ranch, his girlfriend dropping him, Alejandra choosing father over lover). When events occur over which he has no control, John Grady becomes the horseman of history: a Texan Leatherstocking. The response to contrary events is flight to the wilderness, in which identity may be re-established by acts of heroic indifference to pain, death and danger. It is also significant that when he finally looks towards an actual female again, in *Cities of the Plain,* he chooses not a strong and willful aristocrat who has the means to defy his wishes, but a helpless, diseased, victimized child. (158)

John Grady disappears; he acquiesces; he watches. He is unable to resist feminine power. His identity is formed in reaction, rather than action. When action is forced upon him, such as in the prison, when he kills the *cuchillero,* his guilt is debilitating. When Alejandra tells him she must leave him, his reaction is fatalistic: "He saw very clearly how all his life led only to this moment and all after led nowhere at all" (McCarthy 254), mirroring his loss of identity when he loses the land of which he feels he is a part.

John Grady is unable to oppose the female will, in Texas or Mexico. Nor is Gawain able to oppose the feminine, but for different reasons. Geraldine Heng has argued,

> There, at the limit of the masculine narrative—in the repeating moments where masculine command slips and misses—appear the sedimentations of feminine desire . . . signaling its presence through a medley of practices, figures, and signs. (501)

In *Sir Gawain* these figures and signs of feminine desire are readily identifiable. The very exchange-of-blows game which the plot hinges upon is the result of Morgan le Fay's desire to upset Guinevere, rather than a test of valor. Throughout the poem, Gawain is always the servant of the feminine. Initially Morgan le Fay, through the Green Knight, controls his actions, or rather reactions. Further, during his journey to the Green Chapel, Gawain is the supplicant of the Virgin Mary, whose image he carries on the inside of his shield, and to whom he appeals when he wishes to find a safe haven in which to hear Christmas Mass. The fact that Gawain then immediately finds Bertilak's castle, with its duplicitous Lady, and the evil

Morgan le Fay, seems to suggest some sort of unholy alliance of female powers against him.

Similarly, the Lady's ever more aggressive pursuit of Gawain mirrors her husband's hunting exploits, and the reader sees Gawain as passive prey. In a curious and disturbing passage the lady even invites Gawain to rape her when she states, "Ye ar stif innoghe to constrayne wyth strenkthe, yif yow lykes" (107, line 1496). Here we see poor Gawain scrambling to preserve his purity, and clearly he is in peril, for as we know, the Lady is playing a deadly game with him, one which, if he succumbed, would surely have brought him to his death. Even the gift of the green girdle, the "luf-lace" brings its punishment, the nick on his neck, and Gawain's sense of disgrace. When the Green Knight reveals all to Gawain, his response is an invective against women, beginning with Eve, Delilah, Bathsheba, and the nameless paramours of Solomon. His anger against women is, according to Heng, "a tirade witnessing the belief that women dominate and shape the destinies of men" (501).

In *All the Pretty Horses* the signs of female desire and control are even more evident. What Heng refers to as the "sedimentations of feminine desire" in *Sir Gawain* is less sedimentary and more like geologic substratum in *All the Pretty Horses*. All the major female characters in the novel are adversarial. John Grady's nameless mother is possibly an interesting character in her own right, yet is always seen as simply a negative force through the eyes of her husband and son. She is the Morgan le Fay of *All the Pretty Horses* in the sense that it is her action which sets the ball (like the head of the Knight) rolling. Her decision to sell the unprofitable ranch puts in motion the events of the plot in which John Grady departs, looking for the land which he has lost. Gawain sets off on his journey, looking for honor which he will lose if he does not. Having set in train the plots of the stories, these catalytic female figures then disappear, their motives never entirely clear (can one really believe that John Grady's mother can become an actress in San Antonio, and that her perceived abandonment of her son will outlast his actual abandonment of her? And why, except pleasure in maliciousness, does Morgan le Fay wish to ruin Christmas for Guinevere?).

Although John Grady does achieve part of his desire, that being Alejandra, his victory is pyrrhic. He believes that Alejandra, like Mexico, are his for the taking, but he is proved very wrong. Molly McBride has written,

> John Grady's sexual conquest of Alejandra can be viewed as analogous to his penetration of Mexico. Furthermore, when one considers that "conquest" has both a political and sexual connotation, then these parallel penetrations take on even more significance. (29)

But John Grady Cole in no way "conquers" Alejandra. From the moment she tells him that he is in trouble as she rides away on the horse over which he so naïvely thinks he has some control, to the moment she walks away from him on the train platform in Zacatecas, their relationship is entirely in her hands. Therefore John Grady's non-conquest of Alejandra parallels his own transparently obvious failure to "conquer" in Mexico, and his landlessness in Texas. As a stand-in for the landscape coded as female, John Grady's reaction to the end of his relationship with Alejandra reveals a puzzling passivity in one so apparently avid for land—after all, possession of Alejandra would mean possession of the Hacienda one day. He also accepts the inevitability of Alejandra's refusal to marry him with helpless self-destruction.

When Gawain accepts the Green Knight's challenge, but interprets it as a beheading game, he reveals his immaturity. The trance-like state of Arthur's warriors in the scene is contrasted with Arthur's own angry, childish response to the Knight. When Gawain takes up the challenge and beheads the Green Knight, the other knights seem to awaken from their enchantment, laughing and kicking the Green Knight's head like a football, revealing under the veneer of their chivalry a violent undercurrent. The childishness—"sumquat childgered" as the poet says (54, line 86)—of both Arthur and the court corresponds to the dream of possession which motivates John Grady Cole, who, like the privileged child in the lullaby, feels he deserves "all the pretty horses." Of course John Grady's sense of entitlement ignores the other child in the slave lullaby from which the novel takes its title, who lies in the fields, "bees and butterflies pickin' at its eyes," while its mother looks after the white child. An author as careful as McCarthy cannot have ignored this implication, and John Grady's childish yet implicitly racist assumptions are the root of some of his most serious misconceptions—and the cause of his worst mistakes—in Mexico.

John Grady Cole and Sir Gawain both set off on journeys to unknown destinations due to circumstances created by powerful older females. Both young men have in some way already failed due to their flawed starting points. John Grady believes that Mexico is his for the taking because he is American; Gawain's initial violence toward the Green Knight has tainted his chivalric honor before his journey has even begun. Both John Grady and Gawain find illusory havens peopled by powerful older women, older men who betray them, and seductive but ultimately unattainable young females. Both make a mistake which causes their downfall and disgrace, but both avoid death, though they are wounded. Returning home, John Grady and Gawain themselves feel ashamed and disgraced, but those who meet them do not regard them as such. Both works end ambiguously, leaving the reader to wonder what will happen to these characters, adrift in worlds in which their sense of identity has been posited upon values which, through their stories, have been proven false. In this intertextual reading of *Sir Gawain and the Green Knight* and *All the Pretty Horses* I have tried to show the links, intentional or not, which exist between two texts which are, of their kind, archetypal. That congruencies exist between works which deal with the subjects of idealized heroic figures is not surprising. What has surprised me in this essay is the number of those congruencies, and their complexity. The fact that these congruencies are largely in matters of prescribed "knightly" or "heroic" behavior suggests a subtext in both works of an oblique questioning of those fundamental precepts in their respective societies.

## WORKS CITED

Bailey, Charles. "The Last Stage of the Hero's Evolution: Cormac McCarthy's Cities of the Plain." *Southwestern American Literature* 25.1 (1999): 74–82.

Cowley, A. C., ed. *Pearl and Sir Gawain and the Green Knight*. London: Everyman's Library, 1962.

Ganim, John. "Disorientation, Style, and Consciousness in Sir Gawain and the Green Knight." *PMLA* 91.3 (1976): 376–84.

Heng, Geraldine. "Feminine Knots and the Other Sir Gawain and the Green Knight." *PMLA* 106.3 (1991): 500–14.

Lewis, C. S. *The Allegory of Love*. Oxford: Oxford UP, 1952.

McCarthy, Cormac. *All the Pretty Horses*. New York: Knopf, 1992.

McBride, Molly. "From Mutilation to Penetration: Cycles of Conquest in Blood Meridian and All the Pretty Horses." *Southwestern American Literature* 25.1 (1999): 24–34.

McGilchrist, Megan Riley. *The Western Landscape in Cormac McCarthy and Wallace Stegner: Myths of the Frontier*. London: Routledge, 2010.

Moskowitz, Jennifer. "The Cultural Myth of the Cowboy, or, How the West Was Won." *Americana: The Journal of American Popular Culture* 5.1 (2006). <http://www.americanpopularculture.com/journal/articles/spring_2006/moskowitz.htm> (accessed 15 Nov. 2010).

Weiss, Victoria, L. "Gawain's First Failure: The Beheading Scene in "Sir Gawain and the Green Knight." *The Chaucer Review* 10.4 (1976): 361–66.

# 3 Cormac McCarthy and the American Literary Tradition
## Wording the End

*Jan Nordby Gretlund*

I had thoroughly prepared to write an essay on "Cormac McCarthy and the American Literary Tradition," and I did, but with more focus on Herman Melville than I had planned. Originally, I wanted to show how, from *The Orchard Keeper* up to and including *Suttree*, McCarthy wrote largely in the tradition of the southern grotesque of William Faulkner and Flannery O'Connor. I also wanted to show that to a certain extent southern features remain in his fiction even after he seems to have exhausted his need for "exuberant violence" in *Blood Meridian* (Arnold 31). A book I initially found overestimated. I considered it a spaghetti western in print; and the only redeeming feature seemed to be that the land, the West, survives in that novel. Now, twenty-five years later, I see *Blood Meridian* as an impressive treatment of what is a main theme in American literature from James Fenimore Cooper until today, i.e., man's inhumanity to man.

"Like all novels," Richard Gray explains, "*The Road* is a curious hybrid. It is, like all McCarthy's fiction, haunted by the lives and writings of others; it is densely allusive and yet it is unmistakably the work of a fiercely original writer, swimming against the tide of literary fashion" (260). In the face of the tremendous production of post-9/11 fiction that last point is becoming harder to maintain—personally, I had just hoped to show that Faulkner's "The Bear" and O'Connor's "A View of the Woods" may well have inspired McCarthy's fiction. I planned to continue this line of thinking by looking at Ernest Hemingway's fiction as an obvious stylistic inspiration for McCarthy's best writing so far, which I think is in *The Crossing* (the first 127 pages), where the wilderness dies and is lost forever. I intended to argue that Hemingway's influence goes beyond the unsentimental style, for instance in his emphasis on craftsmanship, ceremony, and ritual to get through life, which is also emphasized in both *No Country for Old Men* and *The Road* (223–24). Everybody has seen "Big Two-Hearted River" as an inspiration, but I argue that Hemingway's story "Fathers and Sons" and above all *The Old Man and the Sea* could now be read in the light of *The Road*.

As I was writing this essay I made a discovery, however, which I want to share: the main stylistic source for the McCarthy trilogy is *not* actually Hemingway's fiction. Hemingway also had *his* source and that was Stephen

Crane. Already in the 1890s Crane had established that men in the present are no less savage than in the past, rather worse. He also made it clear that in life we are driven by both environmental and psychological forces. Long passages in Crane's *The Red Badge of Courage* (1895) look forward to Hemingway and McCarthy. One example is:

> He was being looked at by a dead man who was seated with his back against a columnlike tree ... The eyes, staring at the youth, had changed to the dull hue to be seen on the side of a dead fish. The mouth was open. Its red had changed to an appalling yellow. Over the gray skin of the face ran little ants. One was trundling some sort of a bundle along the upper lip. (41)

Sentences like this also appear in Crane's first novel, *Maggie: A Girl of the Streets* (1893), and in his short stories, such as "The Veteran," "An Episode of War," and in the famed "The Open Boat." I find it noteworthy that Crane and McCarthy share the idea of an "indifferent" God. As McCarthy puts it: "People were always getting ready for tomorrow ... Tomorrow wasn't getting ready for them. It didn't even know they were there" (*The Road* 142).

So what prevented me from pursuing the promising Stephen Crane angle? I simply stumbled over a book that shows the importance of doing something else in trying to place McCarthy in the American literary tradition. The book is Eyal Peretz' *Literature, Disaster & the Enigma of Power: A Reading of "Moby-Dick,"* which I cannot praise enough. I remembered that one of McCarthy's few statements about fiction was that Melville was his favorite writer (Priola), so I read Peretz and the result is that I will now try to read McCarthy's *The Road* inspired by the way Peretz reads Melville's *Moby Dick*. I focus on McCarthy's most recent novel, but I see that many of the elements in *The Road* were in his fiction from the start. In his second short story "A Drowning Incident" from March 1960, a young C. J. McCarthy wrote: "The road angled and switchbacked down the hill until it came to the edge of the woods where it straightened briefly before losing itself in the humming field" (3). And a little later he uses the image of "witnessing the underwater birth of some fantastic subaqueous organism" (4). The vocabulary looks forward to the ending of *The Road*. There is a potential topic there in tracing the development of McCarthy's imagery.

The Road is hard to situate in time and place. Its main event happened ten years before the plot of the book begins, and the toxic disaster is never fully described or explained. But somebody had sought out and murdered "the very spirit and essence of world, mind and wilderness" (Slotkin on *Moby Dick* 25), just as the fallen angels did to the world, taking a third at a time, according to *Revelation* chapters 8 and 9. The two main characters of the novel seem to know as little as the reader about what happened and why it happened, but their unhappy existence is our entertainment. We do not know exactly where the man and his son were living, or where they are headed. We do know they are on the road trying to make it to the ocean. We know they are on the road because something terrible has happened, and yet everything is, and remains, enigmatic. It is the enigma of what happened to the world, to the few survivors that appear, and to us (the readers) that stimulates the narrative. The idea seems to be that as long as the origin of the catastrophe remains uncertain, the story about the event and its aftermath must remain uncertain as well. Much of the extraliterary context of civilization and culture, literature's indispensible props, is *not* in the novel—which makes it challenging reading.

We meet several victims of the disaster, people who are witnesses to IT, because it happened to them; but they remain poor witnesses. Nothing they utter does justice to the catastrophe and its effects. It does not make any sense to ask if they are reliable witnesses telling *the truth*, for there is no point in the narrative where such a question will find an answer, and no authority is present who could rule on the veracity. A distinction is made throughout the novel in the labeling of various survivors as *good* or *bad* by the main characters, the father and son. But the text is apparently *not* about ethics, or for that matter about the law, social problems, historical events, politics, gender issues, etc., which is enough to make today's readers uneasy. All these issues are for once just as orphaned and homeless as the boy and his father. Accounts of the material damage and the historical-political background would fail to document and communicate the dimensions of a catastrophe, as all factual knowledge would, but the effect may be communicated, *aesthetically*, and perhaps best as fiction. It is not a happy story, it is "more like real life," and real life is fairly awful in McCarthy's fiction (Madsen 5). The postdisaster world is a totally changed reality. The difficulty is how to render the otherness of the new in a language locked in the now displaced world.

What McCarthy does, is to communicate to us some of the effects of one particular disaster, so we can all *participate* in the event. When McCarthy is most successful, the reader is convinced that he *witnessed* IT, or at least its aftermath, and therefore can testify about the event; maybe even enact it; as the man in the white fur stovepipe hat does when he "perfectly" reenacts Colonel Sherburn's gratuitous killing of Boggs, the town drunk, in *Adventures of Huckleberry Finn* (chapter 21). "If you don't tell it, honey, it may just as well never have happened!" is a good Southern credo. Without witnesses an event never was. But to be a witness you have to word it, perhaps, as in the Twain passage, *perform* it. Something happened that moves you, so you want to dramatize it. In the translating of the event into words is the transmission of the horrors and the participation in them. The event can only be expressed, which means that, after the fact, it only exists when somebody brings it to life by talking about it. In wording IT, there is also an interpretation of it, and in *The Road* the narrator tells us that something monstrous happened, causing an overwhelming loss of life, and the narrator *interprets* the unspeakable event by choosing the wording.

To investigate the enigmatic event from a postcatastrophe existence would mean to ask questions using a vocabulary not even thought of, in the precatastrophe world. McCarthy bypasses the problem by placing essential images, sparingly, but throughout his story. The emotional response is effected through a steady accumulation of grotesque images, such as: "A corpse in a doorway dried to leather. Grimacing at the day" (10), or: "This is my child. I wash a dead man's brains out of his hair" (63). The images become more and more grotesque: "A human head beneath a cakebell at the end of the counter. Dessicated. Wearing a ballcap. Dried eyes turned sadly inward" (155); and the grotesque is increasingly impersonal: "they began to come upon the dead. Figures half mired in the blacktop, clutching themselves, mouths howling" (160–61). This is an image McCarthy returns to toward the end of the novel: "The incinerate corpses shrunk to the size of a child . . . Ten thousand dreams ensepulchred within their crozzled hearts" (230). The images remain a backdrop, framing the story of the man and the boy on the road, and we sense that at times McCarthy puts his hand not only on the boy's shoulder but also on the reader's and quietly says: "take my hand . . . I don't think you should see this"—which makes it worse. The narrator stages his narrative by focusing on father and son, *not* on what they experience on their way through the "cauterized terrain," *not* on the postdisaster wasteland, but on what they become together as they take their next steps in the gray ashes on the road.

Father and son are the survivors, at least for now, of a disaster. The boy has never experienced any other type of life, but the father has. We learn about the boy's childhood in a few paragraphs and through flashbacks to the father's married life with the boy's mother. But even though Hollywood devoted an inordinate amount of screen time to scenes from the marriage, the point in the novel is clearly that nothing could matter less in the present situation of the survivors. To even think of the past has become meaningless. Memories of the past depend on the survival of people, places, or at least one member of a species remembered. The idea of a Coke—or a green tree, a deer, a dog, and even a little boy—is lost unless there is at least one specimen of these still in existence. Unfortunately, nature has completely lost its regenerative force after IT happened, and without live referents our words become fluid and unreliable.

The novel has narrative problems. On one hand the focus is on an exciting picaresque tale of what happens to a father and son on their road to the sea. It is potentially a sentimental story of the lawless and undeservedly homeless in search of a safe haven. There is even a gratifying Clint-Eastwood scene where the father kills one of the bad guys by firing his pistol "from a two-handed position balanced on both knees at a distance of six feet" (56). On the other, it is about the survivors, and yet victims, of an unspecified disaster, an apocalyptic *conclusion* to everything that happened before the narrative even begins—which is, of course, bad logic, as it is *not* over, not even at the end of the novel. The disaster generates a story that entertains like a traditional biographical road story, giving us exciting incident after exciting incident *and* a father's love for his son. But the novel is also didactic and cautionary. McCarthy does not say what happened but shows it. As readers we have to think of how we can avoid ending up as the last witnesses to life on earth. Now that all meaning and all contexts have been deconstructed and erased by deep layers of gray ashes, we are invited to try to interpret a catastrophe that has interrupted and decentered everything, but still remains incomprehensibly a Wittgensteinesque IT *about which nothing can be said.*

The story is told by a narrator who is *not* a character in the novel. The narrator is *not* mentioned as a survivor of the catastrophe, which detracts from the realism of the novel. So does the fact that he is telling it to us-once they had crawled out of the sea and had only a haunting memory of the total destruction of their ships, both Coleridge's Ancient Mariner and Melville's Ishmael *had* an audience. McCarthy's narrator has his job cut out for him. He has to tell somebody about a disaster that cannot be known, but has to be communicated in order to have some sort of existence. How does he come to know anything about the unexpected catastrophe? It destroyed its own context. And just who is there to listen to him? The articulate person narrating *The Road* is not a suffering victim, so how can he be there *as a witness* throughout? Perhaps the narrator is not reporting, but inventing his narrative of the traumatic event? The constant and unexplained presence of the narrator increases the difficulty of assigning a meaning to the novel. Readers have to build on comments by the bodiless voice of the identity-lacking narrator, whose authority we question, and on a catastrophe that *does* address us but remains an enigma. As mentioned, there are no historical and almost no contextual details to help us interpret the text. The absence of confirmed facts increases our anxiety—which is probably what McCarthy wants to do.

It is a painful realization, of course, that your body can be divided into parts, blackened on the spit, and eaten, as the boy learns when he sees a headless and gutted infant (167). For father and son it is a reminder of their vulnerability. They are exposed to potential extinction any minute, which makes them anguished and gives them a feeling of helplessness. The old truth that life is short, nasty, and brutish—and you can add "arbitrary"—haunts them. McCarthy's "grayness" of absolutely everything, the absence of color, is as enigmatic and as indicative of the presence of evil as the skeleton of a "spectre" ship in Coleridge's poem (Coleridge 88–89) and the undefined "whiteness" of Melville's whale. The grayness will before long have annihilated all values and survivors. By setting up the sea as their goal, and a possible way out of the appalling grayness, the father becomes active physically and symbolically. He tries to give their lives a sense of direction and to make sense of their struggle to survive. Their journey is not just a route picked during a desperate flight; it is also a *quest* for survival *and* for comprehension. It is a willed quest for a meaning with their continued existence, some sort of meaning, any meaning. In the face of the nameless toxicity, their enemies are not just roaming bands looking for food. Their worst enemies as survivors are despair, passivity, and impotence in orienting their journey.

In spite of the inscrutable nature of the catastrophe, *hope* survives. It survives through language, i.e., the father's words that embody his one remaining passion, which is to ensure the boy's survival. In a sense he wants to keep the boy alive to have a witness to what he himself has witnessed. Now that IT has happened to them, his former identity has collapsed. The only remaining part of the man's identity, *not* covered in gray ashes, depends on his being "the father," in which he is successful. At times the identification of father and son is so complete that the reader has a hard time figuring out just who said what (155–56). It is terrifying to speak a language that is losing its meaning as the species referred to are extinct or quickly dying out. The boy indicates that the father's stories become incomprehensible and suspect as they refer to a world that almost is no more, and therefore his stories are "not true" (129–30, 226). The father tries to give their exposure a certain shape through forms, rituals, and language, but when all sense of meaning has to come from you yourself, and "life" is disappearing all around you, it is hard to make an inspiring call for life (63). The loss of anything living leaves only a chasm of dispossession, which language can barely word as the names of things slowly follow the things into oblivion (75). With the loss of even the memory of the world without comes the loss of the world within. Only a restored precatastrophe world and its language could bring back the external referents that would make the language meaningful; but McCarthy offers no hope of such restoration—or does he?

If the narrator, or McCarthy, is addressing anybody, he is addressing the readers. After the father dies, the narrator keeps right on narrating in his usual style. We have volunteered to be his audience and his witnesses. How do we react when we read about the end of life on earth? The event is a shock to us, but can we in our specific historical context comprehend and assimilate the disaster? The worldwide reception of the novel answers that question in the affirmative. We react to this novel because in our present political or environmental state such an unmasterable catastrophe could not impose itself on us as a total surprise; on the contrary we *expect* and constantly predict the radical act and our final erasure. McCarthy is preaching to us "reform and transform your life before it is too late," but the preacher himself seems unable to muster any faith in our doing just that. Writing the ending of a catastrophe novel presents a special problem. Coleridge and Melville wanted their narrators to survive. Unlike Coleridge in *The Rime of the Ancient Mariner* and Poe in *The Narrative of Arthur Gordon Pym of Nantucket*, Melville in *Moby Dick* carefully prepares his readers so Ishmael's escape will appear possible and realistic. Ishmael survives even though it is almost impossible to escape the all-swallowing closing vortex, or, as Poe put it in his only novel, the "embraces of the cataract" circling a chasm thrown open to receive the ship and sailors (239). Melville shows us early in his novel that Ishmael is interested in and accepts Queequeg's native ways (53). In the chapter "Queequeg in His Coffin," Ishmael observes Queequeg's preparation for death and notices that the coffin contains a harpoon, food, water, and a piece of sail-cloth (397). Ishmael was tossed out of Ahab's boat and was too far from the vortex to be sucked in when the Pequod went down. It is convincing that "the coffin life-buoy" shoots out of the ocean and floats by Ishmael, and it appears realistic that he would be saved. After floating with the coffin for about two days, he is, on the last page of the novel, picked up by the Rachel—a ship that is already known to the reader.

Melville had enough on his mind, but he did not have to worry about Hollywood film scripts with inserted love stories, Oprah Winfrey and her loud book club, or anti-Americanism in Stockholm. Melville knew how to end an account and eradicate a microcosm, and he made sure to have a survivor observe the event: "Now small fowls flew screaming over the yet yawning gulf; a sullen white surf beat against its steep sides; then all collapsed, and the great shroud of the sea rolled on as it rolled five thousand years ago" (469). S. T. Coleridge and E. A. Poe ended their narratives suddenly by introducing the unbelievable, the supernatural. McCarthy's ending of the novel is not prepared earlier in the text, and it does not offer much realism. It is, in fact, almost as unbelievable as that by Coleridge, or by Poe. All of a sudden, McCarthy decides to hove old Natty Bumppo (or perhaps it is Daniel Boone or one of Crane's veterans) into view and into the narrative, straight out of the monochrome grey!

> The man that hove into view and stood there looking at him [at the boy] was dressed in a gray and yellow ski parka. He carried a shotgun upside down over his shoulder on a braided leather lanyard and he wore a nylon bandolier filled with shells for the gun. A veteran of old skirmishes, bearded, scarred across his cheek and the bone stoven and the one eye wandering. (237)

To make the scene even less realistic, the Veteran does not stand there alone with both feet planted solidly in the deep layers of ashes, he has with him a woman! And to make you really optimistic about the future of mankind, they claim to have a little girl and a boy! Life is indeed "humming" again, but the only "mystery" is where this happy family comes from. Unless the opening paragraph of McCarthy's next book shows the Veteran, the good woman, and the cute girl feasting on the boy's flesh, the ending is hard to accept—or so I thought, with many others, for some time.

I realized slowly that seen in the light of American literary history the Natty Bumppo character's sudden appearance makes perfect sense. In

"Tradition and the Individual Talent," T. S. Eliot saw it as a crucial principle of aesthetics that in the artistic process a writer is compelled to write "with a feeling that the whole of the literature of Europe from Homer and within it the whole of the literature of his own country has a simultaneous existence" (49). The Anglo-American poet and critic goes on to explain that the presence of the new work of art slightly alters the whole existing order. We are therefore invited not only to read McCarthy in the light of Cooper's achievement, but also to read Cooper's Leatherstocking novels in a slightly different way now that *The Road* has been published. If you read Cooper's Leatherstocking series in the order they were written, you will find that the five novels move from the realistic to the romantic, or better, from personal experience to myth. It is the myth of Leatherstocking, or Natty Bumppo, who first appears in *The Pioneers* as a man in his early seventies, then he is Hawkeye in 1826 in his mid-thirties, but then the year after, as "The Trapper" he is in his eighties and dies in *The Prairie*. After that realistic novel, Cooper may have thought that he had buried the figure of the veteran marksman, but thirteen years later the myth had grown so powerful that Cooper had to bring him back to life, first as Pathfinder, and then in 1841 as Deerslayer, and notably, in this, the last novel of the series, as a young man in his early twenties. In other words, first the Natty Bumppo figure is pushed into vulnerable old age, then forward into legendary youth. D. H. Lawrence was among the first to realize the significance of the publication chronology of the five novels: "The Leatherstocking novels . . . go backwards, from old age to golden youth. That is the true myth of America. She starts old, old, wrinkled and writhing in an old skin. And there is a gradual sloughing of the old skin, towards a new youth. It is the myth of America" (60). Is this why McCarthy sends the Veteran bumping into the last scene of *The Road*?

Surely Cormac McCarthy's America has efficiently sloughed off its old skin; you can argue that we have seen the old wrinkled skin "writhing" from the very beginning of *The Road*. Is the boy and his newfound "family" the first step toward "a new youth" and thereby a confirming of the "myth of America," as Lawrence put it? For the simple myth we do not need the background, nor do we need a hero with a rich and detailed psychological life, and just like Cooper, McCarthy does not offer psychological insight into his hunter's mind. He is just, it seems, a self-sufficient backwoods man, a man of action, who demonstrates moral integrity when he does what he promised to do for the dead father. Just like Bumppo, McCarthy's Veteran character is elusive and almost anonymous, and his origin is also shrouded in mystery; when all the original frontier values have been repressed, both characters are present in their time as a witness to the end of a way of life. The lack of a real threat of cannibalism at the end of the movie and the optimism of the sound track allow moviegoers to read a tone of sentimentality and religion into the ending. In general cannibalism is skirted very quickly in the film, both in the baby-on-the-spit scene and also in the scene with the men and women who are kept alive, so they can be eaten a bodily part at a time. This is *beroeringsangst* or fear of touching a specific topic. Who wants to frighten the moviegoers away? The movie also plays down the ecological catastrophe; the holy American interstate highway, where millions of grimacing skeletons are ensepulchred in their rusting cars, is shown only in the shortest of glimpses. In the film there is even a beetle that is allowed to fly away, which is a source of totally unfounded hope, it would have been dead under the ashes long ago, and its presence and the music used belie McCarthy's text. The novel is secularized and does not offer a moralizing tale at this level, whereas the whole is, of course, a prediction that should frighten us into awareness of what we are doing to ourselves and our surroundings.

John Hillcoat, the director of the movie, does a reasonably good job in matching most of McCarthy's text, but at the end he fumbles the ball twice and finally drops it. McCarthy gives his Leatherstocking character a woman companion, who in herself is surprising company for old Natty Bumppo. Several fellow critics, mostly of the Flannery O'Connor persuasion, see the woman as a heaven-sent mother figure, mainly because she mentions "God" three times in the short paragraph, of eight lines, devoted to her. But as readers we know nothing about her. She obviously knows the hunter, who told the boy that he and the woman have both a boy and a girl. It is important to keep in mind that these children *never appear* in the novel, and that we have no proof they exist; nor is there proof that the woman and the hunter are parents to anybody. In my reading of the novel, we do not know whether the hunter and the woman will eat the boy as soon as they need food. The threat of cannibalism and the dehumanization must remain present throughout. The director of the film makes the mistake of not being satisfied with the number of characters in the novel and, only he knows why, gives us an ending where the surviving boy sees not only the hunter and the woman, but *also* the two children mentioned by the hunter. This image of the family, which seems to imply that humankind will survive even this disaster, has proved so effective that even veteran McCarthy readers and critics will swear that they: hunter, mother, boy, and girl, are all in the novel! But they are not.

It adds to the grotesqueness of the movie ending that there is also a dog in the picture. How this dog should have or could have survived ten years among the starving is not explained. This is a simply ridiculous attempt to totally rewrite McCarthy's ending. It is true that the boy much earlier in the narrative has seen another little boy and has heard a dog bark, but this is long ago and far away from the ending. Only a deliberate attempt to impose a Christian ending on the film can explain their presence there. But the novel does not justify an optimistic interpretation, as McCarthy lets both the ecological and the spiritual catastrophes stand in all their threatening gray reality. If we are looking for any hope in the ending of the novel, we must go to the final paragraph where McCarthy talks of the brook trout that now are no more and cannot "be put back." In his final sentence on the last page the novelist opens the possibility that life, not necessarily human life, may survive: "In the deep glens where [the trout] lived all things were older than man and they hummed of mystery." The humming is obviously a "Hail Mary" that is thrown to us by McCarthy, but Hillcoat drops the ball on the goal line. He does not even bother to try to render in any image the last paragraph of *The Road*. McCarthy's Veteran in the ski parka does seem to be a figure of potential perfection and seems to embody pioneer values that the postcatastrophe hero will need to start a new world; now that civilization is not only encroaching on the wilderness of the world, but has finally managed to destroy it. *The Road* demonstrates the individual talent that T. S. Eliot said could change the literary tradition. But deep in gray ashes, how long will there be any tradition to change?

## WORKS CITED

Arnold, Edwin T. "Naming, Knowing and Nothingness: McCarthy's Moral Parables." Arnold and Luce 31–50.

Arnold, Edwin T., and Dianne C. Luce, eds. *Southern Quarterly* 30.4 (1992).

Coleridge, S. T. "The Rime of the Ancient Mariner." 1798. *The Portable Coleridge.* Ed. I. A. Richards. New York: Viking, 1950. 80–105.

Cooper, James Fenimore. *The Pioneers.* 1823. New York: Holt, Rinehart & Winston, 1967.

———. *The Prairie: A Tale.* 1827. New York: New American Library, 1964.

Crane, Stephen. *The Red Badge of Courage.* 1895. New York: W.W. Norton, 1976.

Eliot, T. S. "Tradition and the Individual Talent." 1920. *The Sacred Wood: Essays on Poetry and Criticism.* London: Methuen, 1972. 47–59.

Gilmore, Michael T., ed. *Moby-Dick: A Collection of Critical Essays.* Englewood Cliffs, NJ: Prentice-Hall, 1977.

Gray, Richard. "Cormac McCarthy's *The Road*: Writing after the Fall." Gretlund, *Still in Print: The Southern Novel Today,* 260–74.

Gretlund, Jan Nordby, ed. *The Southern Novel Today.* Columbia: U of South Carolina P, 2010.

———. "The Past and Present Significance of James Fenimore Cooper's *The Pioneers*." *Pre-Publications of the English Institute of Odense University* 10 (1978): 1–19.

Lawrence, D. H. *Studies in Classic American Literature.* 1924. London: Penguin, 1971.

McCarthy, C. J. "A Drowning Incident." *The Phoenix* (March 1960): 3–4.

McCarthy, Cormac. *The Crossing.* New York: Knopf, 1994.

———. *No Country for Old Men.* New York: Knopf, 2005.

———. *The Road.* New York: Knopf, 2006.

Madsen, Michael. "From the Outer Dark to Mainstream: Cormac McCarthy. *No Country for Old Men* and *The Road*." *Pre-Publications of the English Institute of Odense University* 151 (2008): 1–13.

Melville, Herman. *Moby-Dick; or, The Whale.* 1851. Ed. Harrison Hayford and Hershel Parker. New York: Norton, 1967.

Peretz, Eyal. *Literature, Disaster and the Enigma of Power: A Reading of "Moby-Dick*. Stanford, CA: Stanford UP, 2003.

Poe, Edgar Allan. *The Narrative of Arthur Gordon Pym of Nantucket.* 1838. Harmondsworth: Penguin, 1980.

Priola, Marty. Nd. <http://www.cormacmccarthy.com/Biography.htm> (accessed 4 July 2009).

Slotkin, Richard. "*Moby-Dick*: The American National Epic." Gilmore 13–26.

Twain, Mark. *Adventures of Huckleberry Finn.* 1884. New York: Random, 1996.

# 4    Cormac McCarthy's House

*Peter Josyph*

In paintings, as in dreams, all houses are self-portraits. One reason to paint a house—any house—is to find out what a house looks like.[1] On the street there is too much light. In the studio, under the glare of the bright floods, a painter can close his eyes, let a house build him. Houses are part of the natural history of a landscape, remnants of a remote civilization of which I have only the sparest clues: its dwellings, its people, its bones, and its business. Spare because they betoken so little that means anything to me. The house of a hardworking writer signifies something I understand. A great poet's house is something to celebrate. But a motif—which is only an impulse for dreaming in paint, an organizing principle for visual improvisation—does not derive out of admiration, likes, or dislikes. It is hardly a choice at all. Nor is it an intellectual process.

Walking across Paris, looking to find the house in rue de Villa Seurat in which *Tropic of Cancer* begins, I was walking toward a new series: Henry Miller's House. In my apartment in rue Ravignon, diagonally across the cobbled stone from where, in the shipwreck known as the Bateau Lavoir, Picasso painted the inaccroachable Gertrude Stein and the razorous death-dealing harlots of Avignon, there was handmade paper from Moulin de Larroque—thick, coarse, impossible to violate—like working on a slice of tree—the finest in the world. Not that I needed to prove *a Paris paint-er*—it was enough to be writing novels there, assuming the identities of the city and my narrator-adventurer Matisse, for whom I devoured the streets greedily in eighteen-hour days. On the other hand, why *not* do in Paris what I do back home—breathe in and out between painting and writing—and why not Henry Miller? For that, all I needed was a sketch in brown ink or a couple of snapshots. But Henry Miller's house, number 18 in a cobbled cul-de-sac named after Georges Seurat, ranked among the dullest of any dwelling in the city. Located a few blocks south of rue d'Alésia in the 14th arrondissement, this *maison* belonged in a suburb of Buffalo, or Cincinnati—anywhere but Paris. This was anti-Paris, a Paris mistake by which the trustful alliance of the city was taken from me, with the consequence that I was alone—a feeling that is almost impossible in Paris. I took a few perfunctory pictures the way one mechanically completes a self-assignment, knowing I'd be bringing back the image of a failed day. On another of these excursions I tracked down a location that was less than disappointing or uninteresting, even less than *not there any more*, for along with the building the block itself had been demolished, and in Paris you can lose an entire street that way, for some of them are barely a block long. But even that rue of nothingness had more of an impact than what was left of the house, or had been done to the house, in which *Tropic of Cancer* begins so powerfully. Even the subterraneous Villa Seurat of my dreams was closer in spirit to *Tropic of Cancer*. Didn't help to know that Salvador Dali or Anaïs Nin had lived here too . . . didn't matter that Miller had lived here twice, and wrote *Tropic of Capricorn* and *Black Spring* in it after *Cancer* was published in 1934 . . . didn't matter that this was the door at which Blaise Cendrars—that mythological creature I have tried, in my work, to mythologize further—came aknocking (with his only hand) to introduce himself, congratulate Miller on his knockout punch of a book, and toss down a few in celebration . . . no, it didn't matter from what perspective I examined that mournful building, trying to conjure up some intimation of magic. *Dead end* was right: this was not a place where anything could begin. *Henry Miller's house was contraceptive!* Intellectually, temperamentally, the idea was perfect. But painting is more an issue of the hand than of the mind—or of the feet.

How was I to know? I had had an idea, but ideas are a dime a dozen. McCarthy's house, too, might have been a dead duck. A house that is more architecturally interesting is not necessarily more of a motif. I am not *Brideshead*'s Charles Ryder. The look of what Poe, in "The Fall of the House of Usher," calls *the mere house* has to at least say, however quietly, even esoterically, the name of the author or his book. This is all by way of saying that an image arrives and assigns itself to the brush. When that happens it is not for you to argue. When it does not—forget images: paint a picture about paint.

One of McCarthy's namesakes, King Cormac MacAirt (third century CE), recommends a cheerful face and a warm welcome to poets who visit the alehouse—as well as silence during their poems. I applied that advice to the visit of this poet, through the medium of his house, to my Long Island studio. As for the silence—no; but I wonder whether a third-century alehouse, Irish or not, with or without a king, would have followed that part of the rule either.

Cormac McCarthy's house—I didn't ask for it. I, who have never owned a house, not even in my sleep, have now got over a hundred in my name. Why so many?

I would ask that. Having a sandwich in the studio or tweaking a manuscript, I would look up at the walls thinking: *All these fucking houses!* But I might have an answer, at least the beginning of one. Returning to the same motif—relentlessly, drunkenly, somnambulistically—helps me to inhibit imagination. Imagination is essential to me as a writer but destructive to me as a painter. So is cleverness, facility, polish, anecdote, respect for one's materials. Without contempt for one's materials one is lost to professionalism.[2] In my approach to painting, truth is elemental. Elusive, too. Fortunately one can lie to a picture a thousand ways but it will never lie back. Thus painting *can* be a path to a kind of virtue.

It was my Florida friend Rick Wallach who asked me to make a poster for the second El Paso conference of the Cormac McCarthy Society. He was in the midst of a gladhandle—"I'll see if I can throw some money in your direction" (Gladhandle #6)—when I interrupted him. "*This* is what I want," I said. "I'm going to do a series of variations. A lot of them. I want *walls*. I want a show." I would choose the best image after painting the exhibition, then handletter the poster directly on the piece. Thanks to an open and imaginative museum administrator, Florence Schwein, an exhibition was arranged for the Centennial Museum, which is part of the University of Texas in El Paso. The fact that the Centennial, a three-story building with an 1857 Breese & Kneeland locomotive and tender in front of it, was not an art museum but dedicated itself to the history—natural and cultural—of the Chihuahuan Desert region, and that an exhibition of spiders had to be bumped to make room for my houses, did not bother me. Walls—lots of walls there—and I could have some. I went to El Paso, I stood on the street with a Nikon instamatic, and I took a few shots of McCarthy's small white house on Coffin Avenue in a popular neighborhood known as Kern Place, the city's first suburb, an area that bordered on the desert when it went up during World War I. There are parks and a busy strip for college nightlife, but Coffin Avenue shows no hint of that. On one side of the house were a pickup and two cars, including McCarthy's old purple Barracuda. When a red and white pickup on the street in front of the house started up and drove away, I averted my gaze out of respect for her privacy, I took a few more shots and I disappeared. I had not come for anecdote, had not come to spy or to rummage. When I was introduced to McCarthy's sisters at the Manhattan premiere of Harvey Weinstein's version of Billy Bob Thornton's *All the Pretty Horses* (what McCarthy referred to as "his little project," about which I was making a documentary), one of the sisters said: "You're not the guy who goes through his *garbage*, are you?" "That's someone else," I said. I have spent enough of my life sorting through my own garbage.[3]

The Coffin house is about a dozen blocks from the Centennial, and closer to the Village Inn, a kind of luncheonette where, in January 1992, Dale Walker, then director of Texas Western Press (which published Rick Wallach and Wade Hall's *Sacred Violence: A Reader's Companion to Cormac McCarthy*), encountered McCarthy proofing the galleys of *All the Pretty Horses*. I had dinner with Dale one night in El Paso but I don't remember a thing that he said about McCarthy, a lapse that leads me to wonder whether we talked about him at all. But in the *Rocky Mountain News* of April 1992, Dale gave a description of his encounter which is a glimpse into McCarthy's public life in El Paso:

He was alone, working, bent over his task in his booth, and I went over to say hello, as I've done many times before—in restaurants, bookstores, outside movie theatres. He has a squarish welterweight prizefighter's face which lights up in a broad and good smile, is casually dressed in open-collared cotton shirt and chino trousers. We traded some friendly words . . . and I left him alone, which is what I always do. Leaving McCarthy alone, in fact, is a sort of unspoken conspiracy of El Paso writers and his local admirers. He is not a recluse or inaccessible or unfriendly; he is simply a very private writer who perhaps came to El Paso for privacy.

One afternoon, in a Barnes & Noble on El Paso's Sunland Park Drive, I shared in this leave-alone conspiracy, although *conspiracy* is too strong a word: confraternity or cooperative might be better. McCarthy passed a foot in front of me, returned an automotive magazine to the rack, and left the store unencountered. In fact it was Rick Wallach, who had stood next to me, reading, obliviously, about model airplanes, who shifted into gear as soon as I said: "That was McCarthy."

"Who?"

"The guy who was just here."

"Just now?"

"A minute ago. McCarthy. He was three feet from you."

"Where'd he go?"

"He went out to the parking lot. Someone picked him up."

After a moment of disbelief, this mountain of indifference to the Cult of Personality, this professor of Ur-text and the primacy of The Written Word, moved as fast as I've ever seen him in a Jackie Gleason shuffle out the door. "*What* kind of car? What *color* was it? Which *direction* did he go?" I began to fear a chase such as you see in *The French Connection*, and this endearing display only hardened my belief that the Sanctity of Text In and Of Itself is to be taken with a grain of salt, even—perhaps especially—among its most vocal adherents.

On another field trip to Kern Place, by which time McCarthy had moved, or was moving, to a house on Franklin Mountain by the Coronado Country Club overlooking the border and, across the Rio Grande, the godforsaken town of Juarez, I returned to the Coffin house after the cars and the pickups had departed with McCarthy, and I took better shots with a better lens, shots I can tell that I never used because there isn't a smudge of paint on any of them. This time, as I recounted in an essay called "Older Professions," I walked the grounds a little. There was not much to look at: a two-step stoop at the street with a private lamppost, a weedy hay-colored lawn lost to dirt, a cast-iron fence on the stoop in front of the door, bars on the windows, a few rugged cacti at the entrance to the drive leading up where the fleet had been parked (an area that was hard to distinguish from the "lawn," making it look as if you could drive clear around to the front stoop). But in the essay I thanked McCarthy's play, *The Stonemason*,

> for helping me to nose my way, with no map and no working knowledge of El Paso, to the house of which I have painted a hundred pictures, and to nudge me across the front yard, abandoned now to political handbills and soda bottles, to crouch under a low tree and to kneel in front of a few yards of freestone wall, a modest little wall that I had not noticed before, a wall with a rusty pipe and an open bag of trash behind it, a wall such as a man might make in his spare time just to keep his hand in, a wall McCarthy built while constructing one of the sturdiest reputations in America ... and to put down my pen, my glasses and my paper and to lean my brow against it, not to tribute the man, the work, the wall, or this play that has led me to it, but to ask myself what in hell do I do now that I'm here ... and to answer that by easing myself down from the pressures of life and to feel myself kneeling on McCarthy's old land and to realize *this is the point of reading*: to be brought to a place you wouldn't have thought mattered, to touch something you never expected to find, to kneel in dirt you are happy to have beneath you, to follow an indefensible impulse as if your life depended on it, to dream the world back that insists on dreaming you, to make an ass of yourself and to get yourself arrested or chased off or shot in the head or healed for being a trespasser on property not your own. (135–36)

Yes ... but with regard to these houses, that visit made no definitive imprint. McCarthy's house? This is *it*—*now* what? Paint. Good paper. Audiobook to keep my head away from the brush. Those good metallic pushpins to tack up the work. The novels the novels or reverberations of them in the underground precincts of mind. That was enough.

When I hung the exhibition during the summer of 1998, a swell spunky reporter named Betty Ligon, who used to see McCarthy around town and chat with him cordially but never was able to wrangle an interview ("Sorry, Betty—I just can't do it"), wrote a very nice plug for the show in a local paper. "If Cormac McCarthy doesn't go by the Centennial Museum to see Peter Josyph's stunning exhibit of paintings based on the writer's former home on Coffin Avenue," she began, "then he deserves to be called a misanthrope. It's one thing to keep an indifferent attitude about worshipful devotees who hang on his every written word, or about the phalanxes of journalists panting for interviews, but this is something he, of all people, should appreciate." Had McCarthy read Betty's headline promotion— "Even McCarthy Should Appear at This Show"—the author could not have wanted to rush on over. Quite the opposite. The reason is obvious. And if he has any taste, he would have to have expected the show to be bad— most exhibitions are. When I was working on a film about a movie that was shown on PBS's Visions series called *The Gardener's Son*, which was directed by Richard Pearce and written by McCarthy, I wrote to McCarthy asking a few factual questions, and one afternoon he called me at home. During the conversation, McCarthy said that they faced an important choice in making *The Gardener's Son*: to shoot it in 16 millimeter color, or in 35 millimeter black and white. Seen in retrospect, the choice of the former was, he said, perhaps the one big mistake they had made. To compliment the fact that, despite an inferior film grade, *The Gardener's Son* exhibits a high level of integrity—I used the word *austere* to describe it—I told him that whenever James Cagney played a bad guy, he liked to invent a way of *dropping the goodies* as he called it—a gesture, a shrug, a little something to soften the character, make him more sympathetic, memorable. This, I said, is something *The Gardener's Son* as a movie never does: it never drops the goodies. On hearing the Cagney quote, McCarthy chuckled. To the degree that I pictured McCarthy at the Centennial, taking a few minutes to walk those gallery walls that were strung with his former home and workshop, I liked to think that they might, at least, have raised a similar chuckle: brief, quiet, avuncular. But whether he came or whether he didn't, McCarthy, a brilliant man, would have known that this was another McCarthy's house. If these houses are my own artifacts, my own El Paso, then the man of the title has to be my own McCarthy.

Still . . . these houses, painted in New York . . . formed out of the madness of my life there . . . inspired by seemingly uninspiring snapshots . . . taking the light from color made in Switzerland, Japan, Germany, France . . . carved, clawed, scroddled, scraped . . . stabbed, scrubbed, blotched, brushed . . . draggled, flung, teased, glued, and pounded into very expensive paper molded by dark hands in a one-horse hamlet outside of Mexico City . . . while they might not have been McCarthy enough to lure him into a gallery, are, after all, reverberations of his achievement, and so too are they, in their own small way, a part of the history of Texas. And it's a proud thing indeed to have the author of *Suttree* . . . *Child of God* . . . *All the Pretty Horses* . . . making his home in the town of El Paso . . . in Texas, in the US, where there are few such houses because there are few such poets. In writing about *Blood Meridian* and *All the Pretty Horses*, Harold Bloom has said: "I speak of McCarthy as visionary novelist, and not as a citizen of El Paso, Texas" (539), and Bloom does so nobly. Pictures, though, can speak of him as both in one breath. That is at least the ideal. Of course by now McCarthy has moved several times, and for years he has lived in Santa Fe. But as a result of these engaging little vignettes—decorations, really, which is what all paintings are—McCarthy can move to the ends of the earth: this is his house forever.

Standing before McCarthy's house, it has struck me that if an enthusiast, setting out with no information—no address, no description—were to walk the streets of El Paso with the intention of finding it, he or she could point to it and say, with certainty: "There it is." When I first found the house on my own with rather spotty directions and no map to follow, I did not so much look for it as smell for it, or listen. I was impressed, but not with any skill on my part. The house had marinated, with the right amount of grit, the right amount of seed, in Thoreauvian simplicity. At one time the neighborhood of Kern Place was introduced and advertised by ornamental arches spanning North Kansas Street. Commissioned by its enterprising developer, Peter Kern, the gate was full of esoteric symbols reflecting Kern's interest in matters mystical—symbols that surely Judge Holden could explicate around the campfire—and it was lit by more than four hundred bulbs, a touch that made it even harder to miss, and reminded the world that this new neighborhood had been electrified. Now, with the gate gone, the glow in Kern Place was from McCarthy's house, in which the neighborhood had been electrified by placing one word, the right word, in front of another.

At the time McCarthy was there, Kerners might not have agreed about *the glow*, and a friend of McCarthy's neighbor told me that his tenure of property was considered an eyesore. That's okay: so are some of my pictures. With the curator of the Centennial, Scott Cutler, I was hanging the exhibition when one of the volunteers at the museum had a conversation with Scott about McCarthy's house, which she only knew from seeing the Josyphs going up.

"Does it *really* look like that?"

"Well . . . more or less."

"No wonder he moved."

Shortly after the exhibition opened, a woman looked at a few of the pictures and said: "I wouldn't want to live in *that* house." Which is a way of saying she wouldn't want to meet *me*. I can relate to that: I try not to meet me either. For me, every house is an attempted suicide: without annihilation, nothing is revealed. When another visitor said, about the artist, "He must have been in Viet Nam," it didn't sound strange to me. For that viewer, the houses themselves were Viet Nam—not the one you contemplate for a vacation, *the one with the war.*

Artists and students live in Kern Place, but it isn't a poor neighborhood: one of the city's mayors lived here; the president of the university lives here now; and on the streets around McCarthy the houses are generally well manicured. In other words, like most American neighborhoods, it looks like Squaresville. And so if you wish to argue that a way to have found the house was to look for the one that was the least manicured, I will agree to drop this issue of *the glow* if you will agree that there is more to McCarthy's house than a frumpy front yard. There is a similar syndrome with Hawthorne's place, the Old Manse, on the Concord River; or Samuel Johnson's in Gough Square; or Delacroix's *maison* in rue Furstenburg; or Poe's little whitewashed morgue of a lovenest in that shitheap the Bronx. Feel it, you'll find it. This is not lyricism, this is more like birdtalk: *homing*, sort of the way old uncle Bill Burroughs could radar his way through a world of hygienic facades to score the nearest piece of H or larcenous old croaker who could write him a ticket to the mainline. It is by homing that, out of hundreds of streets and thousands of dwellings in the large Long Island town of Great Neck, I found the one house designed by Frank Lloyd Wright, found it without a map or any references at all—I just closed my eyes, drove around, and there it was—the best, really the only house on Long Island, and one of the few real houses in New York. And McCarthy's is really the best house in El Paso, not because it is funky—there is plenty of that elsewhere in town—but because of *the quality of the funk*, a funk that was made more perfect and oddly beautiful because of its inhabitant.

One more word about the frumpy front yard on Coffin Avenue. Gardening has its own fateful turns, as McCarthy suggests in *The Gardener's Son*, in which the son of the title shoots his and his father's boss in heated cold blood and is hanged for it. There have been gardener-authors, even some who have written about their gardens, but in McCarthy's case you have to chose which of the two you want of him—a yard or a novel, in the same way that you have to choose interviews or a novel, a memoir or a novel, photographs of him at New York parties or a novel, speeches at awards ceremonies or a novel, attendance at your conference or your grandson's bär mitzväh or anything else or a novel. This might be heresy in England, where gardening even makes its way onto the radio, but given a choice between the garden or *The Gardener's Son*, I'll take the screenplay and the film—fuck the flowers. The landscaping in *Blood Meridian* more than makes up for the lack of it on Coffin Avenue. Still, along with the people in their fiction, novelists open another portfolio, one that is less in their control and, in some cases, less in their favor; a cast of secondary characters, some sentient, some not—the houses in which they live and work, the 2-inch pictures on their dust jackets, their wives, their lovers, their stimulants of choice, the films that are made from their books and so forth—any or all of whom might be scrutinized or analyzed with a level of attention or enjoyment that could seem out of proportion, and beyond any meaningful connection, to the work on the page. Don't be stupid about it: *it can't be stopped*. Did you imagine you could wrap it all neatly in a book? When you write that well you end up writing with everything you are, everything you do, everyone you know, everywhere you go, everywhere you won't, everything you say, everything you don't.

There is a lyrical brutality to much of McCarthy's work that may be seen to lend itself to my own rather crude, often hostile line . . . and with respect to McCarthy's compassion for the downtrodden, the outsider, one could say of my style as a painter that it is downtrodden, outsider . . . but this is incidental. The traits in McCarthy's work to which I am most attracted–the masculine lungpower of his prose and its trapdoor phrases that, as in Shakespeare, drop you into the infinite . . . his diabolical sense of humor . . . his vocabular affluence . . . his indifference to popular trend and its boring menus of narrative confections . . . his refusal to write a novel as if he were

writing *a grant* to write the novel . . . his Dickensian authority in populat-
ing the worlds of his invention (and, even, his need—also Dickensian—to
represent the world as an insane asylum) . . . his ability to synthesize, even
to imitate authors who were geniuses before him without self-consciousness
(so that, like Picasso, McCarthy could say: *I don't borrow—I take*) . . . the
undauntable willfulness of his protagonists and the sociopathic (or, better
to say, sophistopathic) strain which informs them—are beyond my capacity
to tribute in paint—which is to say, in verse. And if a picture is painted in
prose there is no point painting it. Picasso told a story of painting a side-
board in a *bistro*. Next day it was gone. This made sense to Picasso (as it
might have done to the Judge in *Blood Meridian*): once he had painted it,
it was pointless for it to exist elsewhere. Can it be that once a house has
hosted a great piece of writing, it may as well dilapidate? If so, perhaps it
vanishes into painting.

Although I walked the property on Coffin Avenue, I never cared to see the
inside of McCarthy's house. Anyway, I knew what was there: cotton fiber . . .
gesso . . . oil pastel. I am not being clever. To know the inside of a house you'd
need to know the inside of the inside, and who knows that? Easy to see McCarthy moving into it through that unadorned doorway. No need to imagine
what poured out of it: one can read that. But there are no blueprints, neither
before nor after, for the profoundly pandemonian assemblage that is the artist's life. Can you say what happens, truly, to a ship as it crosses the ocean,
even in the calmest of seas, let alone a *Bounty*, a *Bismarck*, a *Lusitania*? Cof-
fins are at the start and the finish of *Moby-Dick*—one of them is Peter—and
without both of them, we wouldn't have heard from Ishmael. Who is to say
how much the house on Coffin Avenue had or hadn't to do with McCarthy's
workday—or, to put it another way, while McCarthy was writing *All the
Pretty Horses*, do we know to what degree the house on Coffin Avenue was
writing McCarthy? At least one can say that they bore that fruit together. And
that every architectural façade has its own tale to tell. In some instances everything is facial: exterior is all—or all for now. In *The Fall* Camus' protagonist
says that after the age of forty every man is responsible for his own face. If
it is true of a man, it must be true of his house. But I do insist that a picture
is as much a part of the landscape of a town or a country as a tree or a river.
All right, then—go ahead: walk in it. To the ugliness of Chartwell, Winston
Churchill responded with the view *from* Chartwell, which he regarded as one
of the best in England. But during the rise of the Third Reich the view from
Chartwell, aided by documents smuggled out of the Foreign Office, included a
view of Germany—and of the future—that few Englishmen could, or would,
share with Churchill. We can all see it now, as we can all see the view from
Coffin Avenue of what, at the time, McCarthy called "my 'western',," that
little patch of pulp sensationalism that became *Blood Meridian* (*Guide* 14).

While I was painting the first hundred of my McCarthy houses, I wrote
my fictions about Matisse and I painted pictures of Paris. In an energetic and, I hoped, muted concession to the Paris picturesque in which I

attempted to do something *un*original and yet, in some way, my own, I painted a lonesome corner of St. Eustache . . . the primordial tower of St. Germain des Prés . . . bocce ball along the Canal St. Martin . . . a cobbler's in rue Lamarck . . . a guy reupholstering a chair on the sidewalk in front of the Elie-Fitzo Tapisserie . . . a view in both directions at once along rue St. André des Arts—that sort of thing. And so without a formal invitation, the city of Paris worked its way into "Older Professions"—the piece I was writing about *The Stonemason*, which is set in Louisville—and the city of Paris worked its way into my pictures of McCarthy's house. No one is ever entirely anywhere. Whereness is not that trivial—or submissive, a fact that is understood by David Cronenberg in his film of *Naked Lunch*, where a view of Central Park out of a Tangiers restaurant or, on a narrow Moroccan road (shot in northern Ontario), a businessman with an attaché case smoking under two bright lamps against the rail of an Eighth Avenue subway station, body forth what Cronenberg calls "the hallucinatory duality that Bill Lee lives in, that he is always partly in New York and partly in Interzone no matter where he is." I have painted the playwright Racine's house knowing little about Racine except: *this is his house, it would have to be.* The house *becomes* the man, *my* Racine—and I have noticed a resemblance between some of my Racine houses and my McCarthy houses, which have brought the American Southwest to rue Visconti, that narrow, sunless street in St. Germain des Prés where a community of French Huguenots had lived before they were slaughtered, in the name of French Catholicism, on St. Bartholomew's Day, a street that also belongs to Balzac, Bazille, Mérimée, Delacroix . . . and I have seen Racine's house with a beat-up old Texas pickup beside it. If they are not entirely separate in my mind, why should they be so in my pictures?

When I spent three years writing a piece called "Poe at Ground Zero," I wasn't being smart: Poe was down there with me in Lower Manhattan, with me on Ann Street, on Greenwich and Cedar, on Broadway, on Nassau, on Newspaper Row. When, in 2008, I started a new series of these houses, a pair of monoliths rose up behind McCarthy's low stucco building the way the Twin Towers rose up behind the little four-story Church of St. Nicholas, which had served its Greek Orthodox parishioners, at 155 Cedar Street, for over ninety years before it was crushed by the collapse of the South Tower. Now that those looming Rockefellers have emerged in El Paso, grapplers and dumptrucks and flatbeds and cranes might not be far behind. That will not be inappropriate. All the streets of Lower Manhattan are Coffin Avenue, and I see Ground Zero wherever I look. And when, in the future, I reimagine Dickens' house in Tavistock Place, the beautiful five-story house in which he wrote *Bleak House, Hard Times,* and *Little Dorrit,* don't be surprised to see clocks set to 9:47, or a blown-out bright red doubledecker number 30 London Stagecoach in the foreground.

In the Paris of Flaubert, Zola, Maupassant, bookbinders were not permitted to work in houses of stone because their presses were too tough on them. During the writing of *Suttree,* or *Blood Meridian,* what proseproof substance kept McCarthy from making a ruin of his house on Coffin Avenue? Discussing the Children of Adam cluster of poems in *Leaves of Grass,* Walt Whitman told Horace Traubel: "Children of Adam—the poems—are very innocent: they will not shake down a house" (88), but Whitman was wrong, for such poetry has the power to disrupt or destroy many a house, including his own. Whitman lost a job and a friendship over the poems, and *Leaves of Grass* was suppressed in the city of Boston because of them, because of what they could easily do to a Boston house, and because, as William Burroughs says in *Naked Lunch*—a book that was brought to trial in Boston—*all houses in the City are joined* (90). What's more, the term *stone deaf* is a misnomer. *Stone hears everything.* I wonder at what the stone in or under McCarthy's house absorbed, hearing those books before they were ink on the page? As the Hunchback of Notre Dame, Charles Laughton says to one of its gargoyles: *Why was I not made of stone like thee?* And yet you get the sense that he is halfway there, and he might as well speak to a statue as to a bell. "Its very nature is stone" (330), the Judge in *Blood Meridian* tells us about the desert in which much of the book is set. It's no wonder. That book is at least as primal as stone—and almost as knowing. For six months I read *Blood Meridian* aloud, distributing its sentences all over the map in places that did not have a choice but to listen.

And yet, as with people, longevity for a house might be less related to what you know than who you know, or who knows you. Remember this: When, in a year to come, McCarthy's house is bought to be bulldozed for something new and cardboard, and the armchair appreciators who did nothing about it when it was there will say: "Why wasn't something done about it when it was there," no one can ask *me* that question, for I traveled, I watched, I vigil'd, I shot, I painted, I hanged, I showed, I sold, I spoke, I wrote, I filmed, I published—and, once having been, I am never not there. That's enough for one provincial scribbler. Now *you* get to work.

A few months after that paragraph was written, McCarthy's childhood home at 5501 Martin Mill Pike just outside of Knoxville, Tennessee, where he spent about ten years of his life, burned to the ground on January 27, 2009. This two-story house of seven gables that had been built by a member of the Knoxville Garden Club and had fish ponds and rock gardens around it when the McCarthy family moved there from Providence in 1941 (when McCarthy was seven), had fallen into a state of extreme disrepair, and Knox Heritage had listed it as the most endangered historic structure in Knox County. Its owner, who hadn't paid his property taxes in two years, was not in the house at the time of the fire and had shown infrequently before that. My pal Wesley Morgan, Professor of Psychology at the University of Tennessee and a McCarthy enthusiast who is writing a great book about Knoxville's relation to *Suttree,* rushed to the scene during the fire.

In Wesley's cellphone pictures, the house is only a frame full of flames that are reaching, fiercely, into the black above the forest. "I was at my office about five miles away when I received the call and ran out there," Wesley told me. "By then the house was fully engulfed. It was the first cremation I have attended. There were four fire trucks, but they had decided, by then, there wasn't any saving the place."

"Two floors. So it wasn't a little shack."

"O no, it was a *really* nice house. Five or six bedrooms. I went out next morning and took photos of the remains. I was run off once by the deputy sheriff and was constantly looking over my shoulder. The scene reminded me of the landscape described in *The Road*. I guess houses have a mortality of their own. This place, although special to many, had, in truth, been on its last legs for some time. I had hoped that Knox Heritage might have been able to provide life support—but, alas."

Wesley called me the following day from the site. He was alone in the rubble.

"It's still smoldering," he said. "There's a wet, charcoal, burned wood smell. I can see smoke drifting up around an old sewer pipe that's sticking up in the air. There are four chimneys still standing. One of them has partially collapsed. It was a *huge* house."

"Are there any walls up?"

"There's one wall that goes almost all the way to the roofline. The roof is all collapsed, except for one gable. You can see a second floor radiator. There's a chimney just sticking up in mid-air that has an old television antenna still strapped to it."

"So, if you're seeing a radiator, there must be some flooring?"

"Well, it's actually stuck *on* the wall—kind of suspended. I don't see a stick of furniture. There's an electrical meter right in front of me, but it's certainly not running any more."

"If you were passing on the road, could you see that a house had burned down?"

"You *can't* see it. When the house was here you couldn't see it from the road, either. Although you could sure see it when it was burning."

"So," I said, "the house is now even more of a house that belongs in *The Road* than the house that's *in The Road*?"

"That is *exactly* what I was thinking," Wesley said.

"I realize I'm just kind of chatting with you," I said, "but I'm upset."

"I am too," Wesley said. "In my work in psychology, I've specialized in fetishes—special things—and among the kinds of special things are the attachments that people build up to objects and places. Even though I've never lived here, and didn't have much contact with it, I feel it's a significant loss in some strange way."

"It's consoling," I said, "that someone who feels that way is there amongst the wreckage. I felt that way at Ground Zero—that the place needed people who could appreciate the details *within* the ruined neighborhood, and to preserve that phase of the event. There was a guy whose job was to tag the ruins for what was *not* to be grappled and dumptrucked away—a twisted bicycle rack, a beam, a sign—and I think of you in that capacity, except that you have to both tag them *and* take them away in your car, because no one else will."

"I think once I get to muck around in these ashes," Wesley said, "that's what I'll do."

Afterward, I couldn't shake an ordinary phrase that Wesley had used: *when the house was here*. Already, the past! These things we take for granted we one day wake up to find have disappeared.

Disappeared . . . but not entirely. Once the property had been legally investigated, Wesley returned to it and took more pictures. "Then a funny thing happened," he told me. "When I got home a few minutes ago, I noticed a yellow firebrick sitting on the passenger seat of the car. Wonder how *that* got there."[4] Over the following two weeks there were further developments. When Wesley suggested that I adapt an old song about a fire to the McCarthy situation, I responded by writing a fresh tune that I recorded and sent to him. A week later I received a manila envelope from Knoxville. Within it was a Ziplock sandwich bag in which Wesley had placed a piece of burnt wood from the house. The odor was strong. This, to me, was more than a gift: this was an assignment, as much an assignment as the Knoxville trolley token that Wesley had given me in 2002 and that I wrote about in a piece called "Suttree and the Brass Ring." All right, so I had put the old McCarthy house into a song—that was easy enough. How to get the ruins, the fire, the odor into the new McCarthy houses going up in my studio? Some things are easier to do literally than any other way . . . so, for starters, I ground up some of the charred and stinking wood, stirred it into my paints (which are often house paints in every respect), and I brushed it into some of the new houses with an old-century sash brush. If the Amazons could have their *terra preto*—anthropogenic soil made of mulch, charcoal, shards of pottery—*and ash*—surely I could have mine. I also stirred the ash with my moist, gluey fingers and fingerpainted a little, so that it entered the pores of my skin as it entered the pores of the paper. Thus did the conflagration in Knoxville directly contribute to the building of a brand new home for Cormac McCarthy on Coffin Avenue in El Paso, Texas.

## NOTES

1. I am not alone in this feeling of needing to paint something in order to see it. In his delightful book about painting in watercolors, *The Waters Reglitterized*, written in Paris in 1939, Henry Miller says:

   . . . you can look at things all your life and not see them really. This "seeing" is, in a way, a "not seeing," if you follow me. It is more of a search for something, in which, being blindfolded, you develop the tactile, the olfactory, the auditory senses—and thus *see* for the first time.

One day, odd as it sounds, you suddenly see what makes a wagon for example. You see the wagon in the wagon—and not the cliché image which you were taught to recognize as "wagon" and accept for the rest of your life as a time-saving convenience. The development of this faculty, for an artist in any realm, is what stops the clock and permits him to live fully and freely. (38)

2. In early April 1888, Van Gogh wrote from Arles to his friend Emile Bernard: "I don't keep to any one technique. I dab the color irregularly on the canvas and leave it at that. Here lumps of thick paint, there bits of canvas left uncovered, elsewhere portions left quite unfinished, new beginnings, coarsenesses; but anyway the result, it seems to me, is alarming and provocative enough to disturb those people who have fixed preconceived ideas about technique" (24). In June, still in Arles, he summarized the approach this way: "It's more the intensity of thought than the tranquility of touch we are after." In the same letter, Van Gogh commits an interesting linguistic inversion in which the painter himself, not the canvas, is the victim of attack. "After all," he says, "it's rather like being suddenly assaulted by a rapier" (50). That Henry Miller understood the balance of respect (even reverence) and contempt for one's media is suggested by a passage in *The Waters Reglitterized* in which he refers to his crayons as "the axe," an axe with which he "swung into" a picture "with all my muscle and will" to produce "a terrifying piece of insanity" that is nonetheless "a very tender piece of portraiture" (40–41). Sometimes a shift in a painter's style evokes a response that assumes the use of new and more elemental materials, when in fact there is only a shift in the painter's attitude. When Cecil Beaton went to photograph Picasso at Notre-Dame de Vie in Mougins after an absence of thirty years, Beaton, whose photographs are pristine, was disturbed by the new Picassos, telling his diary that Picasso's work "seems to have lost exactitude. The line is not good, the brush stroke so coarse and rubbed" (44), so that he wondered whether Picasso were painting with a cork. "I noticed no brushes" (44), he says, judging that much of the work was unfit to be seen "and probably will never be exhibited" (47).

> Some were wild blobs and smudges of a ruthlessness that was really very unpalatable. Sad that someone who can draw with the exactitude of Ingres and the freedom of a Japanese master now does thick smudges that have no apparent drawing. (47)

And yet Beaton is open enough to question his own evaluation. "But no doubt I am wrong again" (47), he says—and of course he was.

3. In the Wittliff Collections at the Albert B. Alkek Library of Texas State University at San Marcos, the Woolmer Collection of McCarthy materials contains a letter from McCarthy to book collector Howard Woolmer that sheds light on McCarthy's use of the term *little project*. In referring to the Border Trilogy, McCarthy writes: "Anyway I'm still at work on my little projects I've finished rough drafts of 2 novels and started a third. They are all three connected" (14).

4. During a recent walk around McCarthy's Knoxville in which Wesley and I drove to the site along Martin Mill Pike, where only the top of a chimney can be seen above the trees, we had this exchange:

> JOSYPH: You feel strongly that the route of *The Road* reaches the Knoxville area.
>
> MORGAN: It's from McCarthy's descriptions that I've been able to have a mental picture of these places and drive the route myself. The first place that touches on his early novels is when the man and the boy go through Knoxville. They cross the

Henley Street Bridge. The ragpicker in *Suttree* lives under that bridge. Then the man goes out to McCarthy's house, which is not linked with any of the earlier novels but is certainly linked with McCarthy. I think *The Road* is the only novel in which it appears.

JOSYPH: It never occurred to me to make the connection. You've trained yourself to pin these places down.

MORGAN: That's why I was so interested in the yellow fire brick.

JOSYPH: This is the artifact that found its way onto the seat of your Volvo. What was the significance of the yellow brick?

MORGAN: It's a heavy yellowish facing brick for the outside of the fireplace under the mantlepiece, facing the room. So it's kind of a fancy brick. In *The Road*, McCarthy describes a yellow firebrick, but I don't know whether he means the actual high-temperature hardened brick for inside the fireplace. Those I couldn't get to: they were still cemented in, holding up the chimney.

JOSYPH: Either way, you have a piece of the novel now. This has been one of my themes as a reader of McCarthy: how do you touch a novel beyond the book that's in your hand—how do you walk it, live it, beyond the armchair experience, enacting or reenacting it as a way of savoring it, absorbing it, understanding it beyond the verbal or the conceptual.

MORGAN: I also have some charred oak flooring I'd like to work into frames for some of my pictures of the fire and the remains.

See "A Walk With Wesley Morgan Through Suttree's Knoxville."

## WORKS CITED

Beaton, Cecil. *Beaton in the Sixties: The Cecil Beaton Diaries As He Wrote Them, 1965–1969*. New York: Knopf, 2004.

Bloom, Harold. *Novelists and Novels*. New York: Chelsea House, 2005.

Burroughs, William S. *Naked Lunch*. New York: Grove, 2004.

Cronenburg, David. DVD of *Naked Lunch*. Criterion Collection, 2003.

*Guide to the Woolmer Collection of Cormac McCarthy: 1969–2006/Collection 092*. Wittliff Collections, Albert B. Alkek Library, Texas State U at San Marcos.

Josyph, Peter. "Blood Music: Reading *Blood Meridian* Aloud." *Adventures in Reading Cormac McCarthy*. Lanham: Scarecrow, 2010.

———. "Older Professions: The Fourth Wall of *The Stonemason*." *Adventures in Reading Cormac McCarthy*. Lanham: Scarecrow, 2010.

———. "Suttree and the Brass Ring: Reaching for Thanksgiving in the Knoxville Gutter." *Adventures in Reading Cormac McCarthy*. Lanham: Scarecrow, 2010.

———. "A Walk With Wesley Morgan Through Suttree's Knoxville." *Appalachian Heritage: A Literary Quarterly of the Southern Appalachians* 39.1 (2011): 21–49.

Ligon, Betty. "Even McCarthy Should Appear at This Show." *El Paso Inc.* 23–29 Aug. 1998.

McCarthy, Cormac. *Blood Meridian or the Evening Redness in the West*. New York: Random House, 1985.

Miller, Henry. *The Waters Reglitterized: The Subject of Water Color in Some of its More Liquid Phases*. Santa Barbara: Capra, 1973.

Van Gogh, Vincent. *Letters to Emile Bernard*. Trans. Douglas Lord. New York: Museum of Modern Art, 1938.

Walker, Dale. "'Best Unknown Major Writer' Seeks and Receives Privacy in El Paso." *Rocky Mountain News* 26 Apr. 1992.

Whitman, Walt. *Walt Whitman's Camden Conversations*. Ed. Walter Teller. New Brunswick: Rutgers UP, 1973.

# 5 The Painterly Eye
## Waterscapes in Cormac McCarthy's *The Road*

*Dianne C. Luce*

Much of the interest in *The Road* lies in the startling imagery chronicling the main characters' exploration of the world they find themselves in. For the father and son are new American explorers, charting a new world founded on the ashes of our America. In one of the novel's deep ironies, they reverse the westering direction of American exploration, heading instead for the eastern shore and for death. On their journey, they perform the artist-explorer's essential act: that of taking a look—to discover what is life-sustaining or of interest in this alien terrain. Disappointed pilgrims, they find no new Eden, no earthly paradise, and the father sometimes retreats in memory and dream to the lost antecedent world to recover a more nurturing landscape. Unlike the artist/explorers of the American west, they leave no record of what they discover, but it is etched within their minds, and landscape representation plays a prominent role in this work both as content and as one of the man's consistent acts of consciousness. McCarthy represents the land almost entirely through the man's gaze, and his vision tells us as much about his state of mind and spirit as it does about the ravaged land. Indeed, as is often the case with McCarthy's handling of imagery and indirect discourse, the landscapes represented in the book comprise one of our richest means of access to the inner life of the main character.

That is, his landscapes fulfill not only narrative and allegorical but characterizing functions, for the man's gaze organizes and constructs the landscapes we read as much as does the topology before him. His eye takes them in; his concerns provide the emphasis, focus, and interpretation. Thus in his mind's eye as he explores this transformed land, he "paints" landscapes. And the landscape imagery of the novel, mediated by the man's gaze, often evokes the iconography and compositional strategies of the American landscape tradition—especially, but not exclusively—those of nineteenth-century luminists.[1] Because of what they tell us about the man's meditations on past and present, on the finite and the infinite, on his own mortality and possibilities for transcendence, an especially interesting subset of the novel's landscapes is its interrelated scenes of ocean, lakes, and streams. These include not only the postapocalyptic waterscapes of the ocean and the waterfall in the mountains but also the more visionary ones of the lost past—the lake where as a child the man once worked with his uncle on a perfect autumn day and the trout stream remembered at intervals and finally re-visioned in the novel's lyrical coda.

Many instances of landscape representation in McCarthy's works are of scenes framed within a static and clearly defined vantage point approximating a painted landscape. One thinks of Suttree's view of Knoxville from the bluffs across the river (238), or some of the striking vistas of *Blood Meridian*. Such scenes hold special status as still moments of contemplation, but McCarthy's evocation of landscapes also occurs in less temporally condensed and spatially fixed scenes, where the essential in a place is dispersed across several paragraphs and angles of perspective. Such instances are somewhat analogous to the viewer's thoughtful contemplation of the details of a larger composition over time, accumulating impressions that will inform her interpretation or, in other scenes, to the cinematic camera's moving through time over the features of the land, creating a more panoramic view than the landscape painting allows. These are advantages the writer of landscape has over the painter, but it is remarkable how often McCarthy chooses to "frame" his landscapes from a temporally and spatially defined vantage point, creating painterly landscapes just as he has created painterly still lives in *The Road*, as Randall S. Wilhelm has shown. His waterscapes in the novel are of both types, the shifting or panoramic landscapes partaking of more narrative content as the characters explore the terrain, and the framed ones primarily calling for iconographic readings.

McCarthy inscribes the seascape of the eastern shore through a series of scenes that have a cumulative effect in that imagery from the earlier scenes is retained through time in the reader's eye and continue to inform the later scenes. That is, he establishes through accretion the details essential to the landscape through which the characters move, so that when we arrive at the iconic image of the stranded *Pájaro de Esperanza*, the scene takes on the already delineated details of the place and achieves what phenomenologist Edward Casey calls the "all-at-once character that a landscape painting . . . is well suited to convey" through the composition of the represented objects "as simultaneously present to each other in a literal compresence" (61). The man and his son first view the ocean from a fixed vantage point when they come upon it abruptly from a turn in the road and halt to take it in. Their first impression is of low light and sound:

> Out there was the gray beach with the slow combers rolling dull and leaden and the distant sound of it. Like the desolation of some alien sea breaking on the shores of a world unheard of. Out on the tidal flats lay a tanker half careened. Beyond that the ocean vast and cold and shifting heavily like a slowly heaving vat of slag and then the gray squall line of ash. (215)

Consistent with the other landscapes of the present time of the novel, this seascape is depleted of color and light. The boy is disappointed that the ocean is not blue. It is seen through a grainy screen of ash, and though it may thereby gain a certain quality of diffused light, it manifests none of the transcendental quietism of the luminist painters (see Barbara Novak, *Nature* 28).

What it partakes of the Sublime is of the older gothic kind rendered in landscape paintings that impress the viewer with something overmastering and inhuman in the world of nature. It displays Burkean qualities of "power, obscurity, privation, vastness, infinity, difficulty [all of which] suggest experiences that rob us of control" (Andrews 134). This is the ocean one would logically expect to experience in a world reduced to bedrock: no cradle of life but a cauldron vaguely animated by something alien. Here the essential elements of any landscape painting—light, water, and earth—dissolve into one another, a dark gray mineral slag in a vast ocean, suggesting the un-Creation, the un-differentiation of the world, and dissolution back into the pre-Genesis void without form. Nolta points out that the most crucial element in the Sublime is the "presence of a Creator, acting through, or interchangeable with, the powerful forces of nature" (860). But in McCarthy's seascape the Creator is figured as an Un-Creator, a destructive force that overmasters not only humanity but all forms of life. At the same time, the vat image dialogically suggests the work of some inept latter-day Gnostic artificer—an alchemist laboring over the vast vat to re-create a world out of formless base minerals.[2]

As Novak has shown, many of the Transcendentally influenced nineteenth-century American landscape painters worked under the assumption that light is "the alchemistic medium by which the landscape artist turns matter into spirit" (*Nature* 41). Luminists strove to capture the "atmospheric realisms" of light and through them to suggest "its spiritual equivalences" (*American* 122). Tellingly, the seascapes of *The Road* are nearly bereft of light, water's characteristic of capturing and reflecting light deadened in the absence of any unshrouded light source. The ocean the father and son have so laboriously struggled to reach is no tranquil glass mirroring an ethereal realm; the breakers no bright sea foam. In the background a squall line of ash vaguely looms or retreats. In its dark formlessness, this scene might suggest a seascape by England's J.M.W. Turner such as *Snow Storm* (1842), in which a barely visible vessel struggles within a gray and violent sea and sky. But the overt violence and stormy energy of Turner's ocean and weather, which form "a near-abstract diagram of force fields" (Andrews 197), are only implied agents in McCarthy's. A profound sense of aftermath reigns here, suggested by the absence of sunlight and organic life, the sullen, slaggish movement of the water, and the stranded tanker in the middle distance. David C. Miller argues that the shipwreck-in-progress in nineteenth-century American landscapes frequently evokes the foundering ship of state, calling for energetic human action, but the already wrecked and decaying boat conveys this feeling of aftermath as it "looks back to the heroic and morally tendentious moment of shipwreck" (195).

Shipwreck paintings might bear allegorical titles, such as Francis Augusta Silva's *The Schooner "Progress" Wrecked at Coney Island, July 4ᵗʰ, 1874*, or German painter Caspar David Friedrich's *Wreck of the Hope*, the latter title resonating especially with McCarthy's stranded *Pájaro de Esperanza* or *Bird of Hope*. And as Alicia Faxon concludes, "The symbol of the shipwreck . . . stands as a warning of human limitations and frailty, and as a sign of the mutability of human life and fortunes" (831). As the only human artifact in the scene contemplated by the man, the minimally evoked stranded tanker is emblematic of the wreckage not only of his hopes to find a more livable existence at the shore, but also of human culture as a whole—intimations that are reinforced in two later scenes of stranded boats. As a tanker it also evokes the ways in which American national interests and security in the first years of the twenty-first century are bound up in the oil industry and its suppliers in the Middle East, warning that the ship of state may founder on just such issues.[3] Like the stalled locomotive the boy finds in the once-pastoral countryside, the utilitarian tanker also rings changes on the machine-in-the-garden motif explored by Leo Marx. Both suggest that human technology may ultimately destroy itself along with the natural world it challenges and on which it depends.[4]

In many paintings of stranded vessels, active ships sail on in the background, going about their business, suggesting the thriving of other states. But here no such vessel contextualizes the tanker's disaster. Such absence on the vast gray plane of the ocean's surface, like the absence of the dolphins, pelicans, and other sea life associated with the south Atlantic coast, drives home the global wreckage of the human enterprise, intimating within this focused seascape the totalized destruction of the organic world on which human culture depends. Finally, as an allegorical element in the scene's composition the distant, ashen squall line emblematizes the impersonal force of destruction that has left the tanker foundered and gone on. Novak argues that the luminous background characteristic of mid-nineteenth century American landscape painters typically evokes a spiritual or transcendental realm against which the foregrounded objects are depicted with realistic ultra-clarity, but Miller adds that the diffuse light in luminist seascapes sometimes creates a foreboding rather than a numinous atmosphere and that such paintings tend to "deemphasize the presence of human concerns and artifacts." Further, "[i]nstead of mountains connoting spiritual aspiration, waterfalls giving rise to thoughts of purity and resolution, or forest interiors offering sanctuary to the religious devotee, such landscapes incline toward the flat and unprepossessing . . . [T]hey are deserted, forlorn, at times even blank or eerily elusive; . . . [T]hey belong under the traditional rubric of 'desert' places" (194–95). He continues, "To take the largest perspective, in the image of the stranded or wrecked and decaying boat we witness a transition from a traditional view of the world that is God- and human-centered, historicist, and dramatically conceived to one that could be characterized as radically impersonal, primitivistic . . . and atmospherically conceived. The latter is a world in which God no longer clearly presides" (196). Indeed, McCarthy's wrecked boats in *The Road* are analogous to the wrecked and abandoned wagons and stagecoaches broken on the desert floor and which he compares to "the bones of ships on the sea's floors" in *Blood Meridian* (220), his earlier apocalyptic novel depicting landscape in terms of hard geological facticity and mineral waste, a landscape where the Judge argues in good nineteenth-century manner that one can read God's word in stones and bones (116), but where His presence seems no creative force in the world.

The desert emptiness of the scene with stranded tanker, like many of the landscape scenes in both *The Road* and *Blood Meridian*, partakes of the apocalyptic Sublime. Andrews writes that "Among the circumstances contributing to the terrifying Sublime, according to [Edmund] Burke [*Enquiry into the Origin of our Ideas of the Sublime and Beautiful*], are obscurity, vacuity, darkness, solitude and silence, all of which bewilder the senses of sight and sound, and more generally stress the absence of any determined forms" (146). These characteristics are abundantly evident in Turner's seascapes such as *Snow Storm* and *Morning After the Deluge* (c. 1843)[5] and perhaps even more eerily so in Friedrich's proto-expressionistic *Monk by the Sea* (1809), in which the painter literally effaced two storm-driven ships, and twice painted over the sky, eliminating the night coloration, waning moon and morning star now detectable only in X-ray photographs (Koerner 119). In the final version with its flat, leaden sea, darkened horizon, and blankness of forms, the dark and dwarfed figure of the solitary monk, an image of the artist himself,[6] is nearly swallowed by the immense featurelessness of the scene.[7] Andrews finds it "a portrait of near-nothingness, its power residing in its accumulation of negatives, absences" (146), and Helmut Börsch-Supan observes that the "decisive factor about the [painting's] background is not its physical size as such but its immeasurable quality. Man is unable to orient himself in the infinity that confronts him and makes him painfully aware of his own insignificance and powerlessness . . . Through this experience of endlessness Friedrich [expresses] man's experience of his own inner depths when threatened by death" (84). Much the same aura prevails in McCarthy's first representation of the sea in *The Road*, a seascape largely defined by a vast absence metaphysical in import and portending the death of the man at the very brink of the world.

The death of the organic world is, of course, the dominant theme of all the landscape representation in the novel, but in this first seascape it is suggested through absence rather than explicitly presented in imagery of the ashen remains of plants or the skeletal remains of creatures. Such details soon follow, however, as the father and son continue their exploration of the shoreline, where they sit in the sand to share a meal and observe another focused seascape with "windrows of small bones in the wrack" and "the saltbleached ribcages of what may have been cattle" (216). And the next morning, a scene of "Charred and senseless artifacts strewn down the shoreline" emerges in the "cold and rainy" light (220). This sequence of vistas prepares for the discovery of the *Pájaro de Esperanza*, which McCarthy describes without explicitly evoking again the imagery of the vast bowl of slag, the gray light, the rubble, and the dead organic forms. The reader remembers these images as essential to the sense of place already established, and in her mind's eye she supplies them as ancillary background and foreground to the wrecked sailboat.

Again, the scene is introduced from specific vantage points. Finding their path blocked by a headland, the pair climbs higher up the dunes, and from that rise they see "a hook of land shrouded in the dark scud . . . and beyond that lying half over and awash the shape of a sailboat's hull." The initial seascape was metaphysically threatening in its vast and terrible vacancy, but the exposure of this vantage point from which they might be seen makes it threatening on a more human and practical level. Crouching down for safety, their vantage point shifts lower and brings within their field of vision a stratified seascape of sand and dead vegetation prominently in the foreground, the stranded artifact of human culture in the middle ground, and the leaden sea and sky in the distance: the natural, the cultural, and the metaphysical realms, all in ruin (221). Because the unframed horizontal and planar organization of the scene suggests the compositional strategy of the luminists, it simultaneously emphasizes the absence of their typical deployment of light "as an iconic symbol of Godly immanence" (Novak, *American* 105, 59).

Once the sense of immediate threat has been dispelled, the implications of this stranded sailboat, the middle frame of McCarthy's triptych on the theme of wrecked boats, become even more personal and intimate than those of the tanker, where the destruction of the ship of state is the foremost association. The father's aesthetic response to this well-crafted and thoughtfully provisioned vessel, the vehicle of a single family and its guests, suggests his identification with the boat owner's quest to navigate the world within the context of a secure domestic life. (The sailboat recalls John Western's vessel the *Albion* in McCarthy's unpublished screenplay "Whales and Men").[8] With its allegorical naming, the stranded *Pájaro de Esperanza* is an emblem of the foundering of the individual hopes of the boat's owner, and by extension the dashing of the father's comparable hopes. Beyond that, it suggests the death of both men.

McCarthy's representation of the *Pájaro* keeled over in a gray sea from a closer vantage point as the man approaches it recalls Fitz Hugh Lane's remarkable luminist *Dream Painting* and its historical and biographical contexts. Executed in 1862, Lane's painting of a wrecked boat expressed his and his countrymen's fear for the fate of their nation in the first years of the Civil War, and thus it stands in the tradition of stranded boat iconography. But the painting also had a deeply personal genesis and associations for Lane. The image came to him fully realized in a dream of a framed painting hanging on the wall of a beautifully decorated room, a dreamed painting which he strove to reproduce.[9] Art scholars have interpreted Lane's vision not only as an expression of anxiety for the war-torn nation but also as a premonition of his own death, which came near the end of the war in 1865 (Miller 196–97). A shipwreck's implications could certainly extend to the wreck of the human him- or herself, and for Friedrich, too, the endangered ships in his early work on *Monk by the Sea* were emblematic of the end of life.[10] Created as a companion for *Monk by the Sea*, his desolate *Abbey in the Oakwood* (c. 1809) depicts a funeral procession, presumably that of the monk (Friedrich) himself, in a ruined abbey surrounded by bleak, deadened trees (Börsch-Supan 84–85). McCarthy's studies of stranded boats similarly function not only as expressions of post-9/11 anxiety for the health and safety of a nation at war and newly perceiving its vulnerability to terrorism at home, but also as the father's and perhaps McCarthy's own premonition of impending death and the resulting defeat of the domestic in personal terms.

Such readings coexist with more Biblical implications of the cycles of divine creation and destruction that arise throughout the novel in allusions to Job, Sodom and Gomorrah, and the Flood. Through her name the foundered *Bird of Hope* recalls the dove Noah sends out over the land, whose return with an olive leaf and then her failure to return at all are signs that the flood waters have receded and that human life descended from the line of Noah is to resume (Genesis 8. 8–12). Here the *Bird* is arrested in her flight, signaling not the renewal of hope but the ongoing course of destruction, the dashing of all hopes for a restored earthly paradise.

That the lovely Spanish sailboat is from Ténerife in the Canary Islands emphasizes the scope of the earth's destruction and the power of the forces that have driven her from the coast of northern Africa to the southeastern coast of North America—roughly the course of the slave ships' Middle Passage. In even more explicitly evoking America's colonial past, the seascape that completes McCarthy's triptych of wrecked boats reinforces this delicate suggestion of America's historical European and African associations. After the father recuperates from his wound in a coastal town, he and his son make their way back to the beach, where they make camp and gaze at the land and sea before them:

> Downshore the weathered timbers of an ancient ship. Gray and sand-scrubbed beams, old handturned scarpbolts. The pitted iron hardware deep lilac in color, smeltered in some bloomery in Cadiz or Bristol and beaten out on a blackened anvil. (271)

The broken remains of this antique sailing vessel torn from her moorings at some coastal maritime museum, and which the father infers was launched centuries earlier from a Spanish or English ship-building port, add a historical dimension to the iconography of the wrecked ship of state introduced in the modern tanker. They evoke the imperial hopes of Spain and England in the new world, linking them through the tanker with America's latter-day "imperialism" in the Middle East. The father's attention is caught by the fractured and decaying timbers and by the impervious antique hardware, "good to last three hundred years against the sea" (271). More than the earlier two stranded boats, this one conveys a sense of ancient ruin, a historical perspective that takes us back to the colonial aspirations for America, now reduced to rubble—scraps of timber—and the mineral scarpbolts, defying time and decay, persisting as a national *memento mori*. By calling to mind the thriving European sailing vessels of the past, these remains suggest McCarthy's characteristic theme of the endless process of one culture's supplanting another, or Thomas Cole's painterly theme of *The Course of Empire* (1836), realized in a series of five landscapes depicting the same scene from its original state of nature to its final state in *Desolation*, in which the stone artifacts of a great city stand in ruin and reclaimed by nature—a series in which only the geological features of the land persist unchanged through the ages.

McCarthy's bleak triptych of wrecked and stranded ships is prepared for and dramatically counterpointed by the father's memory of the "perfect day" of his boyhood, when he and his uncle rowed a boat across a lake to an island to gather firewood. Here too is a sense of aftermath, but with none of the apocalyptic sublime of the seascape with tanker. The aftermath is suggested in the "twisted stumps, gray and weathered, the windfall trees of a hurricane years past," the "dead perch lolling belly up" in the lake, and the "[y]ellow leaves" of fall (13). Though superhuman force has felled the trees, here the sense of aftermath is brought into the realm of normalcy, domesticated. The hurricane is long past, no threat to the boy and his uncle, and the images of death are contained within natural cycles and processes, thus conveying through negative strategy the promise of renewal. This is no desert space, but one defined by the apparently ceaseless and abundant processes of nature, and the silence and calm of the scene contribute to the man's sense of it as an ideal day.

Far from the sense of exposure to the raw elements that we take from McCarthy's description of the seascape with tanker, this waterscape depicts a sheltering *locus amoenus* or pleasant place, a place of provision, even providence. As a "topos of landscape description," the *locus amoenus* has been traced back to Arcadia and Elysium in ancient Greek poetry and the works of Virgil, and it was revived in Renaissance literature, art, and landscaping (Curtius 194–200; quotation Curtius 198; Andrews 53). The features of the topos changed over the centuries, and even in the classical world they varied by the taste and preference of the writer (Giamatti 34–47). Thus the *locus amoenus* might include the wild, as in ancient descriptions of the river gorge in the Vale of Tempe (Curtius 199) or as it did more frequently in the eighteenth century (Andrews

69). Or it might be more rustic, a *rus amoenum,* as in the works of Horace (Giamatti 41). Kenneth Myers shows that in sixteenth- and seventeenth-century descriptions of the American land, the topos was rather consistently employed as a generic, geomorphological identification of "naturally fertile places" (65–66).

According to A. Bartlett Giamatti, what all these idealized landscapes share "is a sense of satisfaction and completeness, both for the poet who created the scene and whatever character is involved in the scene . . . a sense of individual, personal harmony with a garden, this ideal of some kind of fulfillment in a landscape." Always it was a place where "Nature most nearly approximates the ideals of harmony, beauty, and peace which men constantly seek in some form or other" (39, 34). The *locus amoenus* was a lovely natural place, but also vital to the designation was that there must be "[—a] sense of insulation from the harsher aspects of the natural world" (Andrews 57) or from the city (Giamatti 45–46). In *The Road* the man's *locus amoenus* is certainly less self-consciously classical, more American rustic, than the scenes of many Renaissance landscape artists, but it shares some of the usual motifs—human figures in relation to sheltering trees, a calm body of water or gentle brook, and a sense of the beautiful in the organic forms, here the yellow leaves and the white birch trunks highlighted against the darker evergreens.

The lake of the man's memory is not, however, a place of resort for pleasure to the exclusion of utility, as in the old cultural tradition (Curtius 192). Much of his enjoyment of this perfect day derived from his companionable work beside his uncle grubbing out a decaying tree stump, tying it to their little boat, and rowing it across to fuel their domestic fires. It is a day not of leisure but of physical labor, even some discomfort, rewarded by the welcoming reflection of the window-lights of home in the "dark glass" of the lake (13)—images of light that suggest the transcendental luminism of nineteenth-century American painters, in which "pockets of still water" evoke "a contemplative idea, a refuge bathing and restoring the spirit," and function as "a compositional device marrying sky and ground by bringing the balm of light down to the earth" (Novak, *Nature* 40–41). [11] Even under a darkening sky, the lake's luminescent tranquility delicately conveys these old ideas of spiritual sustenance, associated here with the refuge of home. The man's *rus amoenus* is an American rural genre scene of life close to challenging but provident nature. As the locus of the man's perfect day, it reveals his character, his Horatian "distrust of the luxurious and a respect . . . for the virtues of a small, private landscape whose rugged and noble simplicity reflects the ideals of the inhabitant or beholder" (Giamatti 45). A specific ideal of the man and his uncle is their harmonious and nonexploitive relationship with nature. Far from the cut stump that appears in many American landscapes as an icon "of progress and destruction" (Novak, *Nature* 161), the tree stump they salvage derives from natural processes.

McCarthy's narrative strategy in creating contrastive scenes of lake and ocean may owe something to E. B. White's essay "Once More to the Lake" (1941) written in the early years of World War II, in which, largely through implication, White contrasts his childhood excursions to a lake in Maine with his adult experience on the ocean. For White the lake is an emblem of changelessness and American peace, the ocean one of turmoil and mutability. But in scenes of his return to the lake with his son, White deconstructs his own illusion that such perfect days are timeless, "indelible" (249). His essay expresses both the charm and the futility of the human impulse to recapture an innocent past. McCarthy may have had reason to identify in a personal way with White's essay, and it may have been very much in his mind when he first composed the lake scene. In a draft in a page of "*Old* Road Notes" with the heading "*Dreams*," McCarthy specified that the events took place at the summer residence of the man's grandfather in Maine. The year of the hurricane is identified as 1938, and a notation at the top of the page suggests that this passage is autobiographical: "(Wm McGrail obit) get date (letters)" (Cormac McCarthy Papers, Box 87, Folder 3). McCarthy's mother's maiden name was Gladys McGrail.

In its published version McCarthy's scene of autumn lake with rowboat expresses the father's deep regret and nostalgia for this lost world of peace, innocence, and shared domestic labor from the temporal vantage point of its total destruction, its irrecoverable loss—loss insisted on in all the present-time landscapes of the novel. Like White's descriptions of the lake in Maine, McCarthy's scene encompasses its own subversive emblems of change and decay; but nothing in the scene prepares for the wholesale destruction of the organic world that the man now witnesses. Indeed, the adult man's designation of this autumnal scene as perfect (the *locus amoenus* of classical and Renaissance Europe more frequently was vernal) stands as his postapocalyptic affirmation of what Novak calls the "paradigm of vitalism," cycles of "bud, bloom, decay" once inherent in the organic system now utterly disrupted (*American* 135).

The relatively small scale of McCarthy's lake scene and its amniotic containment by the shoreline and the surrounding trees contrasts the agoraphobic emptiness of the later seascapes. There the insistent motif of stranded and wrecked boats comments retrospectively on the little rowboat successfully maneuvered by the young man and his uncle, juxtaposing this humble vehicle of their rural and domestic life against the wrecked hopes for human enterprise on individual, national, and global scales. It is as if we have *The Arcadian or Pastoral State* of Cole's *The Course of Empire* juxtaposed with its abrupt *Desolation*, but stripped of classical references in favor of American rustic motifs. The man's memory of this pleasant scene with a boyhood mentor brings added poignancy to his attempts to create such moments with his son, moments of mentoring and shared work to advance their common domestic well-being. He cannot take his son once more to the lake even in a nostalgic and illusory attempt to recapture a perfect past, the memory of which still nurtures him alone. But the icon of the twisted tree stump that fueled the fires on his family hearth connects this remembered landscape with the father's endeavor to pass the cultural and spiritual fire from father to son in unbroken line, to teach his own son, and to maintain a human cultural and ethical continuity from one generation to the next.

"This is a good place" the boy announces to his father when they have explored the waterfall in the mountains (41), and although it does not share even those qualities of the *locus amoenus* that inhere in the father's remembered lake scene, it is indeed as pleasant a place as the pair ever locate in their postapocalyptic world. Wesley G. Morgan has identified the spot as Dry Falls, on the Cullasaja River in western North Carolina, between Franklin and Highlands (43). The spot has been much photographed, and judging from the images available on websites, the preferred vantage points are from below the falls, looking up to the shelf of rocks from which the river cascades, or from the side at fairly close range, illustrating the ledge behind the falls on which one can walk and "remain relatively dry" (Morgan 44). McCarthy orients his characters to the waterfall in less obvious ways, putting less emphasis on its novel or picturesque qualities. As the two approach through the dead woods they hear the cataract, the somewhat ominous sound of heavily moving water that also prefigures their approach to the ocean late in the novel. When they see the falls, the scene is implicitly arranged much like a traditional European painterly composition, the pale water falling in the middle distance framed by the dark, skeletal trees:

> A low thunder coming from the river. It was a waterfall dropping off a high shelf of rock and falling eighty feet through a gray shroud of mist into the pool below. (37)

Astonished by the scale and power of the falls, the boy exclaims aloud and can't tear his eyes away from it—the typical response to the perception of the Sublime. [12]

But the father, through whose focalizing point of view we experience the scene, does not share his son's awe. Having viewed Dry Falls as they once were, in the context of living woods, living water, he experiences a diminishment of the Sublime. His vision of the falls takes in the relative luminosity of the gray mist, a component that contributes to the boy's aesthetic response, but the father sees the vapor as a shroud—suggesting the death of the falls he remembers, even the death of the divine Immanence in nature. His view gives more weight to the mineral architecture of the landscape, the sheer drop from the rock shelf to the stone-rimmed pool. Moreover, his brief attention to the cascading water immediately gives way to his contemplation of the pebbles on the rim of the pool:

Polished round and smooth as marbles or lozenges of stone veined and striped. Black disclets and bits of polished quartz all bright from the mist off the river. (38)[13]

For Novak, "the sharply focused foreground and hazed distance represent . . . the unique polarity of luminist vision" (*American* 159). In McCarthy's scene, the bright clarity of the black and marble stones in the foreground of the man's vision, backed by the mist of the falls, comprising the hazy "radiant wall . . . characteristic of luminist distance," briefly and dialogically suggests the Immanence so common in nineteenth-century American landscapes (*American* 136). In a work such as Lane's *Dream Painting,* for instance, "the light emanating from the core of the picture becomes palpable, uniting matter and spirit in [a] single image" (Novak, *American* 106). But the man's sharper focus on the geological grounding of the landscape also recalls the importance of geology to these painters of the nineteenth century, when, according to Rebecca Bedell, many educated Americans shared an interest in geological collection and study, and when critics and artists alike came to believe that geology was as fundamental a study for the landscape painter as anatomy was for the figure painter. This popular interest in geology antedates our current understanding that natural forces such as glaciation, erosion, and volcanic action have shaped the contours of the land. Before Louis Agassiz propounded his ideas about glaciation and the ice age and Charles Lyell formulated his uniformitarian theory, which argued that change in the earth's surface "occurs slowly over great periods of time, and that the processes that have shaped the earth in the past are essentially the same that we see operating in the present" (117, 125), earlier geologists subscribed to the catastrophist theory and interpreted the earth's history in terms of alternating periods of creation and destruction (36). Catastrophists "found evidence of God's shaping hand in the fabric of the earth." Theirs was "a geology that could draw moral and spiritual lessons from stones" (xi). Artists and geologists of this period shared an interest in illustrating "the diversity and order of God's creation" (ix). Geologists "searched for proofs of order and design in the geologic record and tried to furnish scientific evidence for the biblical account of creation" (4), and artists embodied this geological thought in their works. For example, in Thomas Cole's *The Subsiding of the Waters of the Deluge* (1829), a human skull and the mast of a ship lie broken on the erratic or "diluvial" boulders in the foreground, evidence of the Biblical Flood and its aftermath, while the ark sails safely on in the background (see Bedell 29–33).

Although the man entertains the idea that "in the world's destruction it would be possible at last to see how it was made" (274), and he often ponders the blasted world before him as evidence of divine destruction, he also is versed in twentieth-century science, and he holds the two modes of viewing the world in tenuous balance as he interprets the changed landscape through which he travels. The latter mode assumes ascendancy as he reads Dry Falls. Bedell points out that in a geological reading of landscapes, the waterfall is "a perfect symbol for the forces of erosion" (83). For the father, the smooth, mist-glazed lozenges of stone and the stone pool at the base of the waterfall are reminders of the slow changes wrought by water and gravity, of geophysical cataclysm, and this, rather than the rush of the roaring water per se or its shrouded luminescence, comes close to facilitating in him a perception of sublimity in the presence of geophysical power and deep time. Unlike his son, the father can appreciate this landscape only through his geological understanding of its stony features. Thus the landscape depiction shifts focus from the falling water to the foregrounded rocks, placing the cataract in the distance, as in John Kensett's *Niagara Falls* (c.1851–52). Bedell observes that Kensett's view of the much painted American natural icon from this atypical vantage point follows the convention of scientific illustrations and naturalists' paintings such as those of Audubon in placing "a sharply focused specimen against a more sketchily defined background that indicates the environmental origins of the specimen" (103). McCarthy's economically sketched scene employs a similar strategy. Confronting the destruction of the natural world, the man's attention focuses on bedrock origins, processes of change, and the transience of life. The waterfall is a causative agent but is relegated to the background in the man's contemplation of geological change.

Inevitably for the man, such landscapes also evoke the rueful memory of a different kind of antecedent: the living world now entombed in these mineral remains. For the boy, excited by the power of the waterfall, the awe-inspiring awareness that it is comprised of the "entire river" plummeting from the rock shelf, the shiver of fear he feels as he walks out on the wet rocks secured by his father's firm grip, the place is as sublime as anything he has ever experienced (39). As Andrews observes, the Sublime "is a matter of being taken as close to disaster as is compatible with still retaining the sense that one is not actually in danger . . . [I]t is both destabilizing and reassuring, the two feelings in dynamic tension" (134). The boy's thrill of the Sublime is far different from the pure terror he experiences so often in the novel in the actual or anticipated presence of cannibals and rapists from whom his father may not be able to protect him. But the father does not perceive the same sublimity. Here in this good place, he recalls the better place it was, a wild *locus amoenus* that exists only in the past. Like the scenes of wrecked boats, the waterfall, for all its turmoil, is for him a scene of profound aftermath. In its presence he remembers the "rich southern wood that once held mayapple and pipsissewa. Ginseng" (39). [14] The gnarled and denuded branches of the dead rhododendrons inevitably recall for him, but not for the boy, the luxuriant beauty of the plants in bloom in a spring wood (40). And when he looks into the river flowing away from the falls, it is a vision of absence:

He'd stood at such a river once and watched the flash of trout deep in
a pool, invisible to see in the teacolored water except as they turned on
their sides to feed. Reflecting back the sun deep in the darkness like a
flash of knives in a cave. (41–42)

Like the triptych of stranded boats, a triptych of trout streams contributes to McCarthy's intricate patterning of imagery in *The Road*. The first
of these has already occurred in the mountains when the travelers stop on
a stone bridge, and it explicitly establishes the trout stream as a diminished
thing, contrasting present with past:

[T]he waters slurried into a pool and turned slowly in a gray foam.
Where once he'd watched trout swaying in the current, tracking their
perfect shadows on the stones beneath. (30)

The father's second memory, below the waterfall, further articulates his
image of the trout stream as an emblem of the perfect and now lost past.
With its emphasis on the organically tinted water and the transcendent
flashes of light within darkness, the second scene prepares for the remarkable elegiac waterscape that concludes the novel:

Once there were brook trout in the streams . . . You could see them
standing in the amber current where the white edges of their fins wim-
pled softly in the flow. They smelled of moss in your hand. Polished
and muscular and torsional. On their backs were vermiculate patterns
that were maps of the world in its becoming. Maps and mazes. Of a
thing which could not be put back. Not be made right again. In the
deep glens where they lived all things were older than man and they
hummed of mystery. (286–87)

The narrative stance is ambiguous here. The imagistic links between the
father's recurring memories of the trout and this vision narrated after his
death suggest that the coda is another version of his own memory displaced
in time, or the boy's memory of what his father has communicated to him
about the lost world, or a vision that comes to the boy when he talks to
his dead father, and his father, now internalized within the psyche of his
beloved child, responds to him when he calls, as promised. The final passage also strikes me as more authorial in tone, a blending of the father's perspective with an authorial interpretation that transcends the man's angry
bereavement and celebrates the world as it once was for him—as it still is
for us if we see it rightly. [15] These possibilities do not cancel each other out,
and the ambiguity of point of view seems very much to the point, reinforc-
ing the sense of mystery that McCarthy explicitly invokes in the scene.
    In the coda, the landscape representation progresses from the sensory
to the metaphorical to the abstract and metaphysical, deploying Thoreau's

strategy for reading nature. The color imagery with which the passage begins, the amber water and white fins, extends the father's memory of trout flashing in teacolored water, providing explicit continuity with the earlier scene at the river. Further linking the two are the kinetic images of the flowing water and the trout's torsional turning. To this imagery of light, color, and movement is added the mossy scent of the fish and the implicit sound of the rippling current for a totalized sensory experience of this emblem of the once living world that cannot be restored. The vision of the coda places the trout in a living stream, as has the father's memory, and it places the stream in a glen humming with life and mystery. (The glen recalls the "bee-loud glade" of Yeats's own *locus amoenus* far from the gray concrete of the city in "The Lake Isle of Innisfree" (4), a poem to which McCarthy also alludes in *The Orchard Keeper, 55*). The scene then comprises the truest *locus amoenus* of the novel, a place to which the individual may resort in reality, in memory, in a vision, to experience a sheltering, nurturing, and aesthetically pleasing nature.

As Tim Edwards has written, "Such a pastoral coda suggests an almost Emersonian sense of Nature as sacred text, a book to be interpreted" (55). In the pattern of the trout's coloration, the visionary sees "maps and mazes"—a reading that begins to transcend the naturalistic. The two metaphors, maps and mazes, work in tension with each other. The trout's speckles map "the world in its becoming," suggesting that in the world as it should be, the world of constant renewal, nature herself offers a guiding chart to those who can read her properly.[16] These maps recall the boy's desire to locate himself on the roadmap and the father's more metaphysical search for grounding and orientation in a world now bereft of organic nature and thus of a sense of divine Immanence. Readers have found the influence of Hemingway in the trout scenes of *The Road*, and this vision of nature's ability to ground us metaphysically recalls, too, Gerard Manley Hopkins' "Pied Beauty"—his song of praise not for prettiness nor yet for sublime beauty but for all things "dappled" or "frecklèd" (1, 8) in nature, including "rose-moles all in stipple upon trout that swim," as well as all human "trades, their gear and tackle and trim"—varieties of creation that figure forth God's grandeur (3, 6).

At the same time, McCarthy's metaphors imply that such reading of Creation is not a simple endeavor. The trout's speckles suggest not only maps but mazes—a pattern that confuses and disorients but may be navigated with trial and error: perception, memory, and intuition. According to Priscilla Baumann, the mazes or labyrinthine designs associated with many medieval churches not only attest to the ingenuity of their human architects, "but they also reflect the medieval conviction in the artistry of God, symbolizing the complexity and subtlety of His cosmic design" (485), and such religious symbolism continued into the seventeenth and eighteenth centuries, when architectural designs often symbolized "moral or religious dilemmas" (486). These contradictory aspects of nature—the maze and the map—are a part of her mystery, and of God's, McCarthy suggests.

Central to the last two visions of the trout stream triptych is the suggestion of light in darkness, the flashing of the fish like "knives in a cave" (42), the white fins and polished scales gleaming through the darkened water. Both suggest a cutting through obscurity, the sparkling fish as flashes of insight guiding the visionary through the world's darkness through the agency of nature. Again Thoreau's *Walden* comes to mind, and the role of pantheistic nature in platonic and transcendentalist philosophies (see especially his chapter titled "The Ponds"). Through the strange image of knives in a cave, an image that evolved through many drafts of the passage,[17] the father's memory of the trout is linked to his dream of the cavern in which he and his son wander, guided only by the light they carry. Such troubling dreams mark the aftermath of the death of nature. The book's visions of the now extinct trout flashing light through the obscurity emphasize the survivors' loss of nature's guidance, of a world suited to their requirements and made just so to fulfill them. The coda reminds us at the end of the novel that this human pair experience their very selves as remnants of the lost world of nature, wrested from their rich natural context and thrown back on themselves alone for illumination, for the fire they carry within. That fire functions as genuine illumination for them, the highest value attainable within the dark and devastated world of the novel, but the book culminates instead with praise and gratitude for the world that we still stand to lose, a natural world that vibrates with mystery. Pressed by Oprah Winfrey to pinpoint a bedrock moral in his book, McCarthy replied, "We should just simply care about, about things and people and, and be more appreciative. Life is pretty damn good even, even when it looks bad. And we should appreciate it more. We should be grateful. I don't know who to be grateful to, but you should be thankful for what you have" (McCarthy, Excerpts).

Again McCarthy's landscape resonates with a luminist painting, this time John Kensett's *Trout Fisherman* (1852).[18] Somewhat less prototypically luminist, this painting works less to efface the brushstrokes of the painter, especially in the foreground, and constricts any planar organization to the layered path of the stream in the center right of the frame. It employs the glassy surface of the water in the pool where two figures fish and the somewhat diffuse light of the luminists in the background of the work but without constructing them as extensive planes. Instead, these areas become pools of light within the surrounding darkness. Interestingly, the small figures of the fishermen appear to be a man and a young boy—figures that do not appear in McCarthy's coda, but are the central focus of his novel. The juxtaposition of Kensett's work with McCarthy's brings into relief McCarthy's themes of loss and absence: the father will never take his son trout fishing. On the other hand, the trout foregrounded in McCarthy's final landscape are not represented in Kensett's painting. Indeed, the vantage point of Kensett's work places more emphasis on the brightly dressed fisherman than the fish, while McCarthy's coda is focalized through the stance of someone on the riverbank and in the glade—the point of view of the fisherman himself positioned to contemplate the trout flashing in the pool.

Such differences of focus may appear to obviate the fruitfulness of comparing the two works, but it is in their transcendentalist treatments of nature that the two resonate. Kensett's fishermen are embraced and dwarfed by the natural world in which they fish. It encloses and shelters them, seeming to nurture their endeavor. The palpable solidity of the rocks grounds them in nature, while the luminous horizon downstream and above the trees suggests the numinous origin of all within the scene. The foreground elements are evoked with bright clarity (like McCarthy's depiction of the trout), and the rocks reveal the geological realism underpinning Kensett's art, but the distance, both the cathedral-like trees arching above and the background opening in the canopy, blends into indistinctness. Thus the glen in which this man and boy fish seems to "hum with mystery." Finally, the double focus of the painting bears comparison with McCarthy's coda. The physical orientation of the fisherman directs the eye to the pool in which he fishes, while the directionality of the stream and the trees pulls the eye to the transcendent realm above and beyond. This gives the painting a dual sense of inward and outward depth that McCarthy approximates in his dual focus on the trout, with their metaphysical implications, and the surrounding glen. Both Kensett and McCarthy invite us to read the natural world deeply and transcendentally.

In his extended exploration of what makes a landscape painting more than topographical representation, Casey argues that "[i]nstead of being a mere attenuation of earth—its sheer repetition or replacement—[landscapes] carry forward the being of nature-as-encountered into forms of articulation that describe a new order of being, a renewed cosmos" (270). The painter of the Sublime has "so thoroughly experienced and taken in a given place that it has become one with his psychic space, a psychotopia; it has become a place in that space" (51). In the final vision of the trout stream in the glen, the transcendental leap of McCarthy's language moves into the realm of the Sublime, elevating what begins as a pleasant retreat in the father's first memory of the trout stream to a kind of psychotopia for the narrator and for the reader. The place represented here is not just a lovely microcosm, but a realm of being, an awareness of the mystery and plenitude of the natural world and of our blessed and transient place within it, lost, guided, illuminated.

## NOTES

1. See Robert Jarrett's brief discussion of how McCarthy's landscapes "derive from . . . luminism, which extends from Emerson to Frederic Church, then from Church to the landscape painters and seaside photographers of the late nineteenth century and early modernism, and which culminates in Ansel Adams's black and white photographic landscapes" (136–40). Not much has been written about McCarthy's engagement with the visual arts. In addition to Jarrett, see Wilhelm and Lilley.

2. The alchemical implication in this scene is even more explicit in a typescript draft of the novel, in which the man sees the ocean as a "vast cold athanor shifting heavily like a slowly heaving vat of slag" (Cormac McCarthy Papers, Box 88, Folder 1: 185). In this draft, McCarthy's holograph revisions deleted the reference to the athanor, the self-sustaining furnace used in alchemy.

3. The stranded tanker figured in McCarthy's ideas for the novel from an early stage. In a page among his "*Old* Road Notes" is the isolated description: "On the far side of the bay the rusting shapes of tankers, an enormous gantry crane against a sullen sky" (Cormac McCarthy Papers, Box 87, Folder 3).

4. See Edwards for further discussion of the trope of the machine in the garden in *The Road*.

5. David D. Nolta writes that Turner was the "true heir to the genius of [Salvator] Rosa", the seventeenth-century Italian landscape painter whose works were early exemplars of the terrifying Sublime, who depicted "all the properties of the sublime landscape": "dark and threatening skies, windblown and blasted trees, unquiet seas, ruined castles, jagged rocks, and the gaping black jaws of caves. Above all, these scenes evoke an ever-present sense of danger" (859).

6. See Börsch-Supan (83, 85) and Koerner (120).

7. According to Novak, the "solitary meditative figure is the literal trace of man's presence in nature, and a primary unit of nineteenth-century iconography." But in American landscapes, she continues, "the figure rarely reaches the scale where the individual psyche can displace the transcendental void" (*Nature* 184–85). Although the German Friedrich has great formal and philosophical affinities with the American luminists (*Nature* 255), he occasionally departs from their practice when he "emphasizes rather than erases the self, perhaps a prelude to the alienations—from nature and self—of the expressionist psyche" (*Nature* 185–87). This is more evident in his *Traveler Looking Over the Sea of Fog* (c. 1818), where the human figure "enlarges to a point where it begins to occlude nature" (*Nature* 185), than in *Monk by the Sea*. In *The Road* and *Blood Meridian*, the human figures are typically dwarfed by the immense waste through which they travel. Judge Holden is, of course, the notable exception.

8 On pages 8 and 14 of the first draft, the vessel's name is the *Farfetched*, but on page 114 it became the *Albion* (Cormac McCarthy Papers, Box 97, Folder 1).

9. McCarthy's remarks to Oprah Winfrey reveal his interest in the role of dreams in creativity and his knowledge of a number of notable instances. He does not, however, mention Lane (McCarthy, Excerpts).

10. See also Friedrich's *Wreck in the Moonlight* (c. 1835) in which two anchor holes in the wrecked boat subtly lend it the appearance of a face. The dark tones of this painting together with its desolate aura partake of the apocalyptic sublime, but as a symbol of divine Immanence, the moon breaking through the heavy cloud cover is more affirmative than McCarthy's seascapes.

11. See Novak's *American Painting* for excellent discussions of the transcendentalist sensibility of this indigenous tendency in American art, and of its affinities with and divergences from Impressionism. She writes that "luminism was the most genuine answer to the demands of the age for a synthesis of the real and the ideal" (117). In mid-nineteenth-century America "there was a vested interest in the preservation of the fact, behind which we can perhaps identify deeper religious and philosophical attitudes to the substance of God's world, attitudes proscribing the analytical irreverence of Impressionism" (59). She continues, "If we say that Impressionism is the *objective* response to the *visual* sensation of light, then perhaps we can say that luminism is the *poetic* response to the *felt* sensation . . . The American necessity for the ideal,

for 'sentiment,' which needs but a touch of profundity to become 'lyricism,' militated against an objective, analytic dissection of God's world" (91). "The dialectic of luminist sensibility is . . . attested to by the combined concern with the factual certainty of mathematics and the factual unreality, or unfactual reality, of the world of the spirit" (147). Luminists' fusion of the realistic and the ideal or metaphysical, which derived from "fundamental attitudes toward being" (96), is analogous to McCarthy's own sensibility, even taking into account his greater religious skepticism.

12. Although he does not seem to use the term "sublime" as it has been applied to painted artworks, Chris Walsh affirms that the waterfall scene "is perhaps the closest approximation to a pastoral or sublime moment in the whole novel" (53). I would nominate the closing coda as a better example of the quietist, transcendental sublime, while agreeing with Wilhelm that "the entire narrative is swathed in the [more apocalyptic] Sublime, the terrifying vision that rends the veil of physical reality and offers the human mind a glimpse of the absolute" (135).

13. In a page labeled *"The Grail"* and dated 3 September 2004 from a draft of *The Road* McCarthy identified as his first (Cormac McCarthy Papers, Box 87, Folder 6), the father watches his son handle and smell the stones at the rim of the pool, but in later drafts, McCarthy made the attention to the stones a feature of the father's consciousness alone, stressing his geological awareness.

14. See Curtius for discussion of the classical ideal of the "mixed forest" and the catalogue of species that typically occurred in the rhetoric of the *locus amoenus* (194–95).

15. John Cant argues that many a passage in the novel "is initially a representation of the inner voice of the main protagonist, but as the train of thought develops it seems to segue into that of the author" (267–68). I see these passages that move from concrete observation to more abstract or even metaphysical commentary as fully within the father's perceptual sphere, functioning as crucial indices of his inner experience. But the coda strikes me as deploying a different and more ambiguous narrative stance from any other passage in the novel.

16. At the end of *Cities of the Plain*, Betty contemplates the "ropy" veins on the backs of the aged Billy Parham's hands, veins "that bound them to his heart." There she sees "map enough for men to read. There God's plenty of signs and wonders to make a landscape. To make a world" (291).

17. In the first draft, where the trout are introduced in a marginal holograph addition, their glinting is "like swordplay in the deep". On subsequent pages, the passage is reworked multiple times. In the most substantive of these revisions, the image becomes "like a cult of knives in a cave"; then "The flash and parry like some ancient cult of knives choreographed in the dark of a cave"; then "like the parry of knives in some cult of the ancients, echoed in the coals of their fire in the otherwise dark"; and finally "like the parry of knives in a firelit cave. All things of light called out of the dim beginnings. To compose the destinies of which the world is made" (Cormac McCarthy Papers, Box 87, Folder 6).

18. See also the similar *Trout Fishing in the Adirondacks* by Kensett's friend Thomas Worthington Whittredge and *Fishing on the Sacramento River* by Frederick Ferdinand Schafer.

## WORKS CITED

Andrews, Malcolm. *Landscape and Western Art*. Oxford: Oxford UP, 1999.
Baumann, Priscilla. "Labyrinth/Maze." Roberts 1: 483–87.

Bedell, Rebecca. *The Anatomy of Nature: Geology and American Landscape Painting, 1825–1875*. Princeton: Princeton UP, 2001.

Börsch-Supan, Helmut. *Caspar David Friedrich*. 1974. Munich: Prestel-Verlag, 1990.

Cant, John. *Cormac McCarthy and the Myth of American Exceptionalism*. New York: Routledge, 2008.

Casey, Edward S. *Representing Place: Landscape Painting and Maps*. Minneapolis: U of Minnesota P, 2002.

Cole, Thomas. *The Course of Empire: The Arcadian or Pastoral State*. 1834. New-York Historical Society, New York. *The Anatomy of Nature: Geology and American Landscape Painting, 1825–1875*. By Rebecca Bedell. Princeton: Princeton UP, 2001. Fig.19.

———. *The Course of Empire: Desolation*. 1836. New-York Historical Society, New York. *The Anatomy of Nature: Geology and American Landscape Painting, 1825–1875*. By Rebecca Bedell. Princeton: Princeton UP, 2001. Fig. 23.

———. *The Subsiding of the Waters of the Deluge*. 1829. Smithsonian American Art Museum, Washington, DC. *The Anatomy of Nature: Geology and American Landscape Painting, 1825–1875*. By Rebecca Bedell. Princeton: Princeton UP, 2001. Fig. 16.

Cormac McCarthy Papers, Southwestern Writers Collection, The Wittliff Collections, Texas State U, San Marcos.

Curtius, Ernst Robert. *European Literature and the Latin Middle Ages*. Trans. Willard R. Trask. Bollingen 36. New York: Pantheon, 1953.

Edwards, Tim. "The End of the Road: Pastoralism and the Post-Apocalyptic Waste Land of Cormac McCarthy's *The Road*." *Cormac McCarthy Journal* 6 (2008): 55–61.

Faxon, Alicia Craig. "Shipwreck." Roberts 2: 827–32.

Friedrich, Caspar David. *Abbey in the Oakwood*. c. 1809. Nationalgalerie, Berlin. *Caspar David Friedrich*. By Helmut Börsch-Supan. 1974. Munich: Prestel-Verlag, 1990. Oil painting fig. 7.

———. *Monk by the Sea*. 1809. Nationalgalerie, Berlin. *Caspar David Friedrich*. By Helmut Börsch-Supan. 1974. Munich: Prestel-Verlag, 1990. Oil painting fig. 6.

———. *Traveler Looking over the Sea of Fog*. (Also known as *Wanderer above a Sea of Mists*.) c. 1818. Kunsthalle, Hamburg, Germany. *Caspar David Friedrich*. By Helmut Börsch-Supan. 1974. Munich: Prestel-Verlag, 1990. Oil painting fig. 22.

———. *Wreck in the Moonlight*. c. 1835. Schloss Charlottenburg, Berlin. *Caspar David Friedrich*. By Helmut Börsch-Supan. 1974. Munich: Prestel-Verlag, 1990. Oil painting fig. 53.

———. *Wreck of the Hope*. (Also known as *The Sea of Ice* or *Arctic Shipwreck*.) c. 1824. Kunsthalle, Hamburg, Germany. *Caspar David Friedrich*. By Helmut Börsch-Supan. 1974. Munich: Prestel-Verlag, 1990. Oil painting fig. 38.

Giamatti, A. Bartlett. *The Earthly Paradise and the Renaissance Epic*. Princeton: Princeton UP, 1966.

Hopkins, Gerard Manley. "Pied Beauty." *Gerard Manley Hopkins*. Ed. Catherine Phillips. New York: Oxford UP, 1986. 132–33.

Jarrett, Robert L. *Cormac McCarthy*. New York: Twayne, 1997.

Kensett, John Frederick. *Niagara Falls*. c.1851–1852. Mead Art Museum, Amherst College, Amherst, MA. *The Anatomy of Nature: Geology and American Landscape Painting, 1825–1875*. By Rebecca Bedell. Princeton: Princeton UP, 2001. Fig. 55.

———. *Trout Fisherman*. 1852. Carmen Thyssen-Bornemisza Museum, Madrid. Nd. 13 July 2009 <http://www.museothyssen.org/thyssen/ficha_obra/1033>.

Koerner, Joseph Leo. *Caspar David Friedrich and the Subject of Landscape*. New Haven: Yale UP, 1990.

Lane, Fitz Hugh. *Dream Painting*. 1862. Berry-Hill Galleries, New York. *American Iconology: New Approaches to Nineteenth-Century Art and Literature*. Ed. David C. Miller. New Haven: Yale UP, 1993. Fig. 9.7.

Lilley, James D. "Representing Cormac McCarthy's 'Desert Absolute': Edward Weston, Ansel Adams, and the Dynamics of Vision." *Proceedings of the Second Annual International Conference on the Emerging Literature of the Southwest Culture*. El Paso: U of Texas at El Paso, 1996. 162–66.

Marx, Leo. *The Machine in the Garden: Technology and the Pastoral Ideal in America*. 1964. New York: Oxford UP, 1967.

McCarthy, Cormac. *Blood Meridian or the Evening Redness in the West*. 1985. New York: Vintage, 1992.

———. *Cities of the Plain*. 1998. New York: Vintage, 1999.

———. Excerpts from the 2007 interview with Oprah Winfrey. Oprah's Book Club. July 2007. 21 Nov. 2008 <http://www.oprah.com>.

———. *The Orchard Keeper*. 1965. New York: Vintage, 1993.

———. *The Road*. New York: Vintage, 2006.

———. *Suttree*. 1979. New York: Vintage, 1992.

Miller, David C., ed. *American Iconology: New Approaches to Nineteenth-Century Art and Literature*. New Haven: Yale UP, 1993.

———. "The Iconology of Wrecked or Stranded Boats in Mid to Late Nineteenth-Century American Culture." Miller 186–208.

Morgan, Wesley G. "The Route and Roots of *The Road*." *Cormac McCarthy Journal* 6 (2008): 39–47.

Myers, Kenneth John. "On the Cultural Construction of Landscape Experience: Contact to 1830." Miller 58–79.

Nolta, David D. "Sublime." Roberts 2: 857–61.

Novak, Barbara. *American Painting of the Nineteenth Century: Realism, Idealism, and the American Experience*. New York: Praeger, 1969.

———. *Nature and Culture: American Landscape and Painting, 1825–1875*. 1980. Rev. ed. New York: Oxford UP, 1995.

Roberts, Helene E., ed. *Encyclopedia of Comparative Iconography: Themes Depicted in Works of Art*. 2 vols. Chicago: Fitzroy Dearborn, 1998.

Schafer, Frederick Ferdinand. *Fishing on the Sacramento River*. Undated. 28 Jan. 2004. 21 July 2011 <http://ffscat.csail.mit.edu/images/img0488.htm>.

Silva, Francis Augusta. *The Schooner "Progress" Wrecked at Coney Island, July 4ᵗʰ, 1874*. 1875. Richard and Jane Manoogian Collection. *American Iconology: New Approaches to Nineteenth-Century Art and Literature*. Ed. by David C. Miller. New Haven: Yale UP, 1993. Fig. 9.3.

Thoreau, Henry David. "Walden; or, Life in the Woods". 1854. *A Week on the Concord and Merrimack Rivers; Walden; or, Life in the Woods; The Maine Woods; Cape Cod*. New York: Library of America, 1985. 321–587.

Turner, J.M.W. *Light and Color (Goethe's Theory)—The Morning after the Deluge—Moses Writing the Book of Genesis*. 1843. Tate Gallery, London. *Nature and Culture: American Landscape and Painting, 1825–1875*. By Barbara Novak. 1980. Rev. ed. New York: Oxford UP, 1995. Fig. 123.

———. *Snow Storm—Steam-Boat off a Harbour's Mouth Making Signals in Shallow Water, and Going by the Lead. The Author was in this Storm on the Night the Ariel left Harwich*. 1842. Tate Britain, London. *J.M.W. Turner: "That Greatest of Landscape Painters"*. Ed. Richard P. Townsend. Tulsa, OK: Philbrook Museum of Art, 1998. Fig. 7.

Walsh, Chris. "The Post-Southern Sense of Place in *The Road*." *Cormac McCarthy Journal* 6 (2008): 48–54.

White, E. B. "Once More to the Lake." 1941. *Essays of E. B. White*. New York: Harper Perennial, 2006. 246–53.

Whittredge, Thomas Worthington. *Trout Fishing in the Adirondacks.* c. 1862. Hunter Museum of American Art, Chattanooga, TN. Nd. 20 July 2011. <http://www.huntermuseum.org/gallery/11/whittredge/trout-fishing-in-the-adirondacks>.

Wilhelm, Randall S. "'Golden chalice, good to house a god': Still Life in *The Road*." *Cormac McCarthy Journal* 6 (2008): 129–46.

Yeats, William Butler. "The Lake Isle of Innisfree." *The Collected Poems of W. B. Yeats.* 1933. New York: Macmillan, 1956. 39.

# 6 The Silent Sheriff

## No Country for Old Men— A Comparison of Novel and Film

*John Cant*

Like many McCarthy admirers I am also a long-time admirer of the work of the Coen Brothers. I have taught both the novels and the films to students of one kind or another, although I currently concentrate on teaching film more generally. I mention this because I am likely to be making more references (albeit quite modest) to film theory than is usual in essays on McCarthy's work, and I want to convey at least some idea of where I am coming from. In fact I have recently been working on Latin American film and the influence of this will also be apparent. My initial reaction to learning that the Coens were to film *No Country for Old Men* was one of keen anticipation. This is partly because I like the novel a lot, more than many I think; this is no doubt due in part to its evident relationship to genres (the Western, the crime movie) that the cinema has made its own but which some scholars regard as inherently inferior. Many, of course, consider "genre" as limiting by definition. My view reflects an ideological stance that makes one uncomfortable with the dichotomy at the heart of the project of modernity, between what Néstor García Canclini refers to as "democratization" and "renovation." At the risk of oversimplifying Canclini's categories, these imply respectively, and using his words, "the popularization of science and culture" (democratization) and "the need to continually reformulate the signs of distinction that mass consumption wears away" (renovation) (12).

At its most extreme this division exists as an antagonism between utopian avant-gardism and the products of what, after Adorno, we have labeled the culture industry. In terms of the cinema this manifests itself as Art Cinema versus Popular Cinema; to resort to somewhat dated categories this tends to refer to films whose narratives are structured according to the conventions of Classical Hollywood Realism (based on continuity editing) and those which adopt what we might call "alternative narrative strategies." In fact Canclini goes on to point out that the dichotomy is false, and that, like it or not, "the cultured artist cannot avoid intervening in the symbolic mass market" (73). How relevant this now seems in the case of McCarthy; how much more so in the case of the Coen Brothers? In my view the dichotomy is not only false but pernicious. In fact film criticism, or at least one school of it, has, since the 1960s at least, been at pains to point out that the cinema above all the arts produces works that transcend the so-called distinction between the serious and the popular, between Art and Hollywood. Cinema is essentially a commercial medium; filmmaking costs money, lots of it usually. If this does not come from the market it must come from somewhere else. Commercial sponsorship or independent foundations both impose their own restrictions or "standards" on what is produced. Governments are even less likely to foster artistic freedom: at least the market doesn't care too much about the message, provided profits accrue.

Currently many films are funded by a combination of finance capital, independent producers like Spain's Almódovar brothers, large companies such as Petrobras of Brazil, foundations such as the Hubert Bals fund of Holland, and government subsidy through organizations such as INCAA, *Instituto Nacional de Cine y Artes Audiovisuales* (the Argentine government's National Institute of Cinematic and Audiovisual Arts). The IMDB[1] lists four production companies for *No Country for Old Men* (a modest number these days) and twenty-one distribution companies in half a dozen different countries. These figures illustrate why film criticism has led the way in debates on the nature and consequences of cultural globalism. Anyone who thinks that this does not apply to books need only enter the title of pretty well any McCarthy novel into Google to find it advertised for sale worldwide.

The falsity of the Art/Popular dichotomy that Canclini asserts has long been argued in film circles. The *auteur* theorists of the 1950s and 60s found examples of the serious-popular in the persons and works of Hitchcock, Ford, Hawks, and others. Even if we regard the term *"auteur"* as a synecdoche for the creative team whose efforts combine to create a movie, rather than the director as heroic individual creator, it seems clear that the Coens regard themselves as belonging to that tradition, both in terms of their public persona (I use the singular—their way of working has been described as involving two heads on one body—and like Ford and Hitchcock, their listing for directors' credit is one of the ways their films are "sold") and in a number of other ways also.

They tend to write and edit as well as direct, they work with largely the same team of creative and technical collaborators, Roger Deakins (camera), Carter Burwell (music), and so on. Their films have clearly referred back to the Hollywood movies of the past, reviewing them through contemporary, some would say postmodern, eyes.[2] Each of their films features a strong sense of place, and in each case that place is a region of the US. They combine these two tropes in such a way that they could be said to present to us a "cultural geography" of the US, a re-visioning of the US imaginary that the movies of the past have created for us. In each of their films we find money lying at the root of evil. In each of their films we encounter what I have referred to in McCarthy's novels as the "dangerous man" (Kenneth Rattner, The Grim Triune, Lester Ballard, The Huntsman in *Suttree*, the Kid, the Judge, and just about everybody else in *Blood Meridian*, the Cucillero and Blevins in *All the Pretty Horses,* the Manca and maybe Boyd in *The Crossing*, Eduardo, nearly everybody in *The Road* and, of course, Anton Chigurh). Against this catalogue of deadly males the Coens can field their own team: Loren Visser (*Blood Simple*), Leonard Smalls (*Raising Arizona*), Johnny Caspar (*Miller's Crossing*), Charlie Meadows (*Barton Fink*), Sidney Mussburger (*The Hudsucker Proxy*), Gaer Grimsrud (*Fargo*), The Sheriff (*O Brother Where Art Thou?*), The General (*The Ladykillers*); there are others. In the light of these, Anton Chigurh must have been irresistible to the Coens.

My liking for the novel is also partly based on my estimation of the considerable significance of its place in McCarthy's oeuvre as a whole, and of the thematic development that I trace in that oeuvre. The powerful oedipal theme of the novels gradually subsides and has almost disappeared in *No Country for Old Men*, a trend confirmed in *The Road*. However, McCarthy also re-visions his country's imaginary, its literary sources, and the cinematic genre which sprang from them. I guess we all take it for granted that McCarthy revisits the Western genre in the novels from *Blood Meridian* to *No Country for Old Men*, deconstructing the heroic mythology of the frontier. Prior to the second Bush administration this was old news; G. W. revived the simplistic rhetoric of the Western hero to great if lamentable effect. Perhaps the only thing we can thank him for is the return to our screens of the Western genre.[3] Needless to say in the current climate of cultural pessimism this is generally regarded as a somehow diminished form, out of time, like modernity itself—posthumous—the post-Western. In this respect I will refer to the work of Matthew Carter, a postgraduate student at the University of Essex who is specializing in this field and who argues against the implications of this term, suggesting that the Western metamorphoses according to the exigencies of a given time and the visions of individual artists, but refuses any defined pattern of continuous development. He reminds us that some Westerns of Hollywood's golden age challenged the heroic frontier myth, and he locates both McCarthy and the Coens in this anti-mythic tradition. That such texts remain Westerns is attested to by the fact of their physical location, thematic concerns, and iconography, especially the horse, the gun, and, in this case of course, the sheriff.

In fact my reaction to the film of *No Country for Old Men* was one of disappointment; I found that colleagues who, like me, were familiar with the book shared that disappointment whereas those who had not read it reacted much more favorably. There was, you will recall, a general feeling that the Coens had returned to form after the relative failures of *Intolerable Cruelty* (2003) and *The Ladykillers* (2004). This essay tries to analyze the reason for that disappointment, concentrating in the first instance on the differences between the narrative structures of the two texts and the effect that this has on their respective meanings. The novel's narrative structure of parallel discourses is unique in McCarthy's oeuvre. These discourses are given in two distinct voices; on the one hand Sheriff Bell delivers his highly subjective monologue; on the other a detached authorial voice narrates the violent, deathly action. This twinned narrative structure creates both obstacle and opportunity for the screen adaptor. The Coens are known for the detachment with which they present both characters and action in their films. If some see this as a weakness, it is a view I don't share. This detachment has the effect of maximizing the menace and mystery of Chigurh; it emphasizes his allegorical status, transferring it from novel to screen in a manner that preserves this aspect of the book's meaning. Menace and mystery are intensified by silence—or rather by a particular kind of silence—an absence of a particular kind of sound. Cinematic narrative generates diegetic spaces; that is to say the film presents the spectator with a part of its world that can be seen and a part that is implied—on-screen and offscreen.

Both these diegetic spaces may be the locations for sources of sound—realistic and pertaining to the world of the film: the wind blowing across the desert, a police car siren—unseen, but in the street outside—a gunshot in a hotel room. *No Country for Old Men* deploys such sounds sensitively, accurately, and to great effect. Most films deploy other kinds of sound also, particularly to create atmosphere, sound that does not realistically belong to the world of the film—non-diegetic sound.[4] *No Country for Old Men* features no non-diegetic sound at all. It is this aspect of the film that is silent, and it is this silence that reflects the Coens' detachment and Chigurh's cold nonhuman and deathly persona. There is in fact only one brief passage of music in the whole film. This comes when the wounded Moss wakes on the bridge between El Paso and Ciudad Juarez: a street band plays jaunty Mexican style music, but, significantly, it fades to silence when they register his bloody condition. This is of course diegetic sound. It is the other narrative strand that presents the problem: how can a film present the Sheriff's internal discourse? The answer is that it can't. The only device that could correspond to this novelistic structure is voice-over. Voice-over is certainly a valid cinematic device, and the Coens use it here in a brief initial passage that provides us with the clue to the Sheriff's character and metaphysical status within the film, as a man who declines to "place his soul at hazard."

However it is not possible to construct a major ongoing thread of film narrative using voice-over; the very nature of cinematic narrative privileges "show" over "tell" although there have been successful movies that made significant use of voice-over: examples include Wilder's 1944 *Double Indemnity,* in which the story is spoken into an office dictaphone, or, more recently Cuarón's 2001 *Y tu mamá también,* which features several passages in which diegetic sound is muted to allow an omniscient (but unreliable) narrator to impart information that the visible text elides. The Coens regularly make use of introductory voice-over. Examples include *Blood Simple,*[5] *Raising Arizona, The Hudsucker Proxy, The Big Lebowski, The Man Who Wasn't There*; it is true to say that it is a characteristic feature of their style. But even in these cases its use is strictly limited and of secondary importance. Thus most of the content of the Sheriff's italicized internal monologic passages is missing from the film, and it is this that provoked my sense of disappointment. In these passages Sheriff Bell reveals himself to us in a way that is unique in McCarthy; the novels are noted for the manner in which the internal consciousness and psychological motivation of characters is absent: as George Guillemin points out this is characteristic of figures in allegory (24). This alone gives this thread a special significance. Moreover, as the thread extends itself through the novel, passage by passage, we begin to perceive the extent to which the Sheriff himself is an unreliable narrator. To begin with he is guarded in his self-revelations; he speaks in terms of the traditional conservative pieties of his generation, place, and profession. But as the monologue progresses he contradicts himself, reveals his own shortcomings, confesses to the deceptions with which he has been complicit.

He tells us that he campaigned for Sheriff when he came back from World War II: "I had some medals and stuff and of course people had got wind of that" (90). He also tells us that he and his wife had "No children. We lost a girl but I won't talk about that" (90). Later, however, he speaks of his feeling guilt at the fact that in the war his men were all killed in the incident for which he was decorated and that he went along with the army's false valorization of his role in the event (195). He also implies that he allowed the medal to count in his favor in the election for Sheriff. As we near the book's end he admits: "I talk to my daughter. She would be thirty now. That's all right. I don't care how that sounds. I like talking to her" (285). These passages are indeed like an intimate, but one-sided conversation in which the Sheriff begins by telling us what we expect to hear, for his mode of speech allocates to us a subjectivity similar to his own[6]; but it is as if, as our acquaintance deepens and we earn his trust, he tells us at last what he really believes, how his life has really been, and how the world really seems to him. Sheriff Bell does indeed unburden his soul as no other McCarthy character does. And in the film the full breadth and depth of this is lost because its mode of telling cannot be represented cinematically. In my view *No Country for Old Men* is Sheriff Bell's book: but it is Anton Chigurh's film. And since the Sheriff is a complex, rounded, well-realized, and deeply human character whose experience of loss and failure renders him a truly tragic figure, whereas Chigurh is a one-dimensional allegorical figure of no interest beyond his significance as a personification of all that is deathly, the loss I suggest is great.

The film's opening voice-over sequence also introduces us to the desert landscape of West Texas. In this respect I suggest we recall Tim Poland's assertion that "in the literature of the West the landscape imposes itself on the nature of the characters, rather than acting as a metaphor for human qualities" (37). Matthew Carter takes up this idea, suggesting that Chigurh himself is an aspect of wilderness and that Sheriff Bell perceives that committing himself to combating the mysterious killer would indeed "place his soul at hazard." This important aspect of the novel is preserved in the film. Carter points out that Bell's statement regarding his liking for hearing of the "old-timers" can be interpreted as his liking for the myth of the Southwest. Bell, like McCarthy's other Western heroes, gets his image of history and his values from this mythology. But it is a mythology rooted in the notions expounded by Slotkin in his 1973 analysis of frontier mythology, *Regeneration Through Violence*, and even classic Western film mythmakers such as John Ford have pointed out that following this path leads not to redemption but to the wilderness itself, like Ethan at the end of *The Searchers*. If Bell was tempted in his youth by this tale, his experience of war, his growing knowledge of the region's history—"strange and damned bloody too" (284)—and the arrival in Terell County of the consequences of the drug wars has brought him to the same realization as McCarthy's other failed protagonists: "I'm bein asked to stand for something I don't have the same belief in I once did" (296).

The drugs wars are the final straw for Sheriff Bell. Their direct link to international capital (the Metacumbe Petroleum Company of Houston), Army special forces personnel (Carson Wells), judicial, political, and law enforcement corruption, and the wave of unrestrained killing that has currently proved to be all too real in the border area, as Charles Bowden has reported in his "documentary novel" *Down By the River*, are features of a world in which he cannot function, a world that has taken his region's violent mythology to an extreme that he, unlike Llewellyn Moss, must reject. So I am far from suggesting that the Coens' version of *No Country for Old Men* is a failure. But the nature of cinema is such that their focus and McCarthy's are different. For me Sheriff Bell is an important figure in McCarthy's developed work; his silence in the film is an absence, and his absence is a loss. What this means is that the success of the film hinges not on Sheriff Bell, but on his mysterious and implacable adversary, Anton Chigurh. In this the Coens are well served by the performance of Javier Bardem, although as a number of critics have pointed out, the choice of the Spanish actor has led many to assume that he is meant to be read as Mexican. This is understandable given the relevance of Mexico to the location and action of the film but introduces a facet to Chigurh's meaning that is not present in the book, and, I would suggest, detracts from his indefinable, and thus somehow more generalized, in current terms—transnational—metaphorical status.

The name Anton Chigurh does not immediately suggest a Latin ethnicity: it is hard to pin down—it has perhaps a vaguely Eastern European sound, and this extends the reach of the novel's depiction of the extent of the malign effects of the international drug trade. Some have argued, not unreasonably, that the name derives from "ant on sugar" a figural reference to complexity and chaos theory. Chance is certainly a theme of the book, and to some extent of the film, and the assumed randomness and implacability of "chaos" is certainly appropriate to Chigurh although he himself asserts otherwise. These facets of the name connote a geographical generality and nonhuman quality that is captured by the film but weakened by the actor's iconic ethnicity. This criticism must be modified by an acknowledgment of the excellence of Bardem's performance and the way the Coens' deploy his baleful gaze and emotionless behavior. They are filmmakers with a ready understanding of the way in which iconic actors, those whose very physicality expresses what they are meant to convey, are so important to the cinema. One only has to think of their use of such visually meaningful figures as John Goodman, Steve Buscemi, Jon Polito, and M. Emmet Walsh to realize their grasp of this crucial aspect of cinematic language; in this respect we should, of course, add to the list Tommy Lee Jones himself.

Chigurh's nonhuman status is exemplified in his shrugging off of wounds and injuries, his ability to appear at will at the appropriate place and time, his invincibility, his inescapability. His attitude to language is also "inhuman." Mildly challenged by the Sheffield storekeeper regarding the interpretation of a phrase, he asserts that meaning is absolute:

> You married into it.
> If that's the way you want to put it.
> I don't have some way to put it. That's the way it is. (55)

All these elements are expressed cinematically by the Coens in their visual use of Bardem and the actor's interpretation of the "character." Writing in the *Cormac McCarthy Society Journal* I argue that Chigurh is an allegorical representation of Death itself (116). The absence of non-diegetic sound and the aridity of both natural and man-made landscapes as captured on-screen by Roger Deakins' cinematography create a filmic ambience that matches both the deathly violence of the film's action and the mysterious implacability of Chigurh and provides a contrasting background for the humanity of Sheriff Bell. However this would not be a Coen film if some moments of humour did not find their way onto the screen. Only once is Chigurh reduced to impotence: when he demands to know Moss's place of work from the clerk of the Desert Aire trailer park, the redoubtable lady, played by Kathy Lamkin, adopts a bureaucratic correctness that not even Chigurh can challenge: "Did you not hear me. We can't give out no information" (81). Once again the Coen's deploy an iconic actor: Lamkin looks the part to perfection. It is also characteristic of their oeuvre for female characters to face down patriarchal power in this way: even Carla Jean, condemned to die at Chigurh's hand, refuses to "call" the coin toss, denies the terms of his modus operandi. In both the storekeeper and trailer park clerk conversations the Coens reproduce McCarthy's words precisely, a tribute to the author's noted gift for compelling dialogue.

This faithfulness to the novel's dialogue indicates the Coens' respect for the novel as a whole: I have already explained why I think a significant aspect of the book cannot be readily represented in cinematic terms. Other omissions are less significant and are doubtless made out of a need to concentrate on the atmosphere that is so important in this film and also the demands of time. One detail that is a loss, however, is the omission of the Moss-girl hitchhiker episode, not so much for the loss of the character as the absence of their significant conversation at the Van Horn truckstop. In the course of a long exchange Moss tells the girl: "Most people will run from their own mother to get to hug death by the neck. They cant wait to see him" (234). The significance is ironic: this is exactly what both Moss and the girl are doing. The words also reinforce the notion of Death personified, the function of Chigurh in my interpretation.

So what am I to make of my relative disappointment at the Coens' version of *No Country for Old Men*? "Not too much," is the answer: a film can never exactly reproduce a novel, the forms are too radically different. The medium of language, printed language on the page, is both a vehicle for, and obstacle to, representation. Its partial opacity is both the challenge and the opportunity for the writer. Its nuances are inherent in its form and will not necessarily translate onto the cinema screen, where a completely different *kind* of language is deployed, one of moving images and manipulations of time, light, and space. The long history of screen adaptation of literary texts is full of every kind of example. Few major novels achieve equal status as films: some of the screen's great masterpieces are adaptations of minor literary works or even mere potboilers: there is no pattern.[7] Gifted authors write good books: gifted filmmakers make high quality films; talent is all. In any instance novel and film are two different works and should be judged on their own terms. What is most rewarding in this case is to evaluate and interpret McCarthy in the light of his writing as a whole and to do the same for the Coens and their films: in both instances there are rewards enough for even the most discerning interpreter. Most satisfying is the fact that both succeed, on occasion at least, in uniting the categories "popular" and "serious" in a manner of which Canclini would surely approve.

## NOTES

1. IMDB: the Internet Movie Data Base.
2. Whether the Coens' work is to be classified as 'postmodern' is a matter for debate. (The same could be said of McCarthy of course). If the postmodern text quotes a past, the historical context and meaning of which has been lost (Jameson), then this surely does not apply to the Coens who are all too keenly aware of the Hollywood history that they mine so effectively. If, on the other hand, it is a case of postmodern loss of affect, then their ironic detachment perhaps qualifies them as such. The label no longer seems to matter as much as it once did.
3. *The Assassination of Jesse James by the Coward Robert Ford* (Andrew Dominic, 2007) and *The Three Burials of Melquiades Estrada* (Tommy Lee Jones, 2005) are notable additions to the Western genre, indicating its capacity to express contemporary concerns. Of course *No Country for Old Men* must be considered such an addition also.
4. Some additional clarification is perhaps needed here. Three examples:
    (i) A couple drink in a bar; it has a small band that plays a romantic song. This is diegetic sound from the first diegetic space.
    (ii) A couple drinks in an upstairs room, and an explosion is heard from the street outside. This is diegetic sound from the second diegetic space.

       (iii) A couple walk down a lonely country lane; the sound track features a romantic song. This is non-diegetic sound.
       Forms (i) and (ii) are present in *No Country for Old Men*; form (iii) is not.

5. M. Emmet Walsh (Visser) delivers the Coens' first immortal cinematic words in the voice-over intro to *Blood Simple* (1984): "What I know is Texas: down here you're on your own." This could be Llewelyn Moss speaking.
6. Cinematic voice-over has the same effect.
7. Two positive examples (there being little point in listing the many negatives): Hitchcock's masterpiece (or one of them) *Psycho*, was an adaptation of Robert Bloch's 1959 horror genre novel; Bloch had a level of commercial success but was not regarded as a literary heavyweight. On the other hand Orson Welles' *Chimes at Midnight* (1965) is also a masterpiece; the genius (and sheer egotism) of Welles enabled him to take Shakespeare's Henry IV and V and shape them to his own cinematic ends to produce a rare film that is worthy of its exalted antecedents.

## WORKS CITED

Bowden, Charles. *Down By the River: Drugs, Money, Murder and Family.* New York: Simon and Schuster, 2004.

Canclini, Néstor García. *Hybrid Cultures: Strategies for Entering and Leaving Modernity.* Trans. C. L. Chiappari. Minneapolis: U of Minnesota P, 1995.

Cant, John. "Oedipus Rests: Mimesis and Allegory in *No Country for Old Men*." *The Cormac McCarthy Society Journal* 5 (2005).

Carter, Matthew. "The Dismal Tide: Shoring up the Fragments in Joel and Ethan Coen's *No Country for Old Men*". *Icfai University Journal of American Literature.* Vol II, no's 3 & 4 (August & November 2009).

Guillemin, Georg. *The Pastoral Vision of Cormac McCarthy.* College Station: Texas A & M UP, 2004.

Jameson, Frederic. *Postmodernism, or the Cultural Logic of Late Capitalism,*1991. London: Verso, 1996.

McCarthy, Cormac. *All the Pretty Horses.* 1992. London: Picador, 1993.

———. *Blood Meridian.* 1985. London: Picador, 1990.

———. *Child of* God. 1973. London: Picador, 1989.

———. *Cities of the Plain.* London: Picador, 1998.

———. *The Crossing.* 1994. London: Picador, 1995.

———. *No Country for Old Men.* London: Picador, 2005.

———. *Outer Dark.* 1968. London: Picador, 1994.

———. *The Road.* New York: Knopf, 2006.

———. *Suttree.* 1979. London: Picador, 1989.

Poland, Tim. "'A Relative to All That Is': The Eco-Hero in Western American Literature." *Western American Literature* 26.3 (1991): 195–208.

Slotkin, Richard. *Regeneration Through Violence: The Mythology of the Frontier, 1600–1860.* Norman: U of Oklahoma P, 1973.

## FILMS CITED

Coen, Joel & Ethan. *Barton Fink.* Circle Films, Working Title, 1991.

———. *The Big Lebowski.* Polygram, Working Title, 1998.

———. *Blood Simple.* Foxton Entertainment, River Road Productions, 1984.

———. *Fargo.* Polygram, Working Title, Gramercy Pictures, 1996.

———. *The Hudsucker Proxy.* Polygram, Silver Pictures, 1994.

———. *Intolerable Cruelty.* Universal, Imagine Ent, Alphaville Films, 2003.

———. *The Ladykillers.* Touchstone, Jacobson, Mike Zoss Productions, 2004.

———. *The Man Who Wasn't There.* Good Machine, Gramercy Pictures, Mike Zoss Productions, 2001.

———. *Miller's Crossing.* Circle Films, 20th Century Fox, 1990.

———. *No Country for Old Men.* Paramount Vantage, Miramax Films, Scott Rudin Productions, Mike Zoss Productions, 2007.

———. *O Brother Where Art Thou?* Touchstone, Universal, Studio Canal, 2000.

———. *Raising Arizona.* Circle Films, 1987.

Cuarón, Alfonso. *Y tu mamá también.* Anhelo Producciones, Besame Mucho Pictures, 2001.

Dominic, Andrew. *The Assassination of Jesse James by the Coward Robert Ford.* Warner Bros., Jesse Films, Scott Free Productions, 2007.

Ford, John. *The Searchers.* C. V. Whitney, Warner Bros. 1956.

Hitchcock, Alfred. *Psycho.* Shamley Productions, 1960.

Jones, Tommy Lee. *The Three Burials of Melquiades Estrada.* Europa Corp., Javelina Film, 2005.

Wilder, Billy. *Double Indemnity.* Paramount, 1944.

Welles, Orson. *Chimes at Midnight.* Alpine Films, Internacional Films, 1965.

**"A Namelessness Wheeling in the Night"**

Shapes of Evil in Cormac McCarthy's *Blood Meridian* and John Carpenter's *Halloween*

*Michael Madsen*

In Cormac McCarthy's fictional world, there are many characters that can only be described as evil. Moreover, the origin of the evil that runs through most of McCarthy's fiction is complex and problematic to determine. In her 1985 *New York Times* review of *Blood Meridian*, Caryn James is persuasive in her description of McCarthy's oeuvre when she writes that he "has asked us to witness evil not in order to understand it but to affirm its inexplicable reality." Whether it is the gang in *Outer Dark*, Anton Chigurh in *No Country for Old Men*, or Judge Holden in *Blood Meridian*, characters are created that symbolize undying and incomprehensible evil. The fact that they appear in human form makes them that much more terrifying and mysterious. The existence of this incomprehensible evil is one of the many reasons why McCarthy's fiction continues to frighten, thrill, and fascinate us. In order to probe this notion further, this essay compares Judge Holden in McCarthy's *Blood Meridian* (1985) and the character Michael Myers/ The Shape in John Carpenter's horror classic *Halloween* (1978). [1] To some it might seem ludicrous to treat a low budget horror film in the same context as a literary masterpiece. Even if the original premise of *Halloween* was to make a "killer-stalking-babysitters" horror film, the craft of director John Carpenter in depicting evil embodied in Myers/The Shape creates an enigmatic piece of cinema that has endured for over thirty years, and that continues—just as *Blood Meridian* does—to shock and mystify its audience. In the context of McCarthy's impulse toward horror, and especially in his depiction of the Judge, I believe the comparison is productive and posits yet another intertext for McCarthy's work.

*Halloween* (1978) begins with a long point-of-view shot of Myers, whose identity is unknown to the audience. On Halloween night, 1963, he enters a house, picks up a knife, goes to the first floor, and stabs to death a young girl, who is later revealed to be his older sister. As Myers leaves the house, his parents return home, and the killer is shown to be a six-year-old Myers in a clown costume with a bloody knife in his hand. He is locked up for fifteen years and never says a word. Throughout the movie, he is only heard breathing. Myers eventually escapes from the institution, only to return to his hometown to wreak havoc. He ends up stalking a group of youngsters, killing all of them except one. No reason for his murderous impulse is given, and his actions remain mysterious and troubling. Michael Myers is presented, thereby, as the very shape of evil. In fact, the masked character is referred to in the credits and the script as "The Shape" rather than as Michael Myers. The mask serves as an important element in the portrayal of a shape of evil rather than a distinct individual. Due to the low budget of *Halloween*, the Shape mask was a Captain Kirk mask with minor modifications, and so there is irony in the fact that the face of one of pop culture's most legendary good guys, "a man among men and a hero for the ages," became the ultimate face of evil (Erdmann and Block 3). Once privy to this knowledge, *Star Trek's* themes of relentless altruism and optimism seem forever erased as The Shape comes to embody evil and violence as fundamental truths in the world. The mask is white, hairless, and no trace of Captain Kirk survives: it is essentially featureless. One is reminded of the Judge in *Blood Meridian* who has "no trace of a beard . . . no brows to his eyes nor lashes to them . . . His face was serene and strangely childlike" (6). Also, in Samuel Chamberlain's description, Holden's face is destitute of all expression (271). Both The Shape and the Judge have the haunting appearance of the unmarked everyman. Their blank faces become canvases on which it is possible to project any fear.

Of the characterization of Myers, John Kenneth Muir says, "Myers cannot be explained rationally in terms of psychology. He does not suffer from a specific, diagnosable or treatable disorder, and [his psychologist] describes the monster unscientifically, just as one of our ancestors at the dawn of time might have: Myers is purely and simply evil" (76). Furthermore, Muir argues that the concept of evil is dead in modern America. Instead, psychologists and experts on human behavior deem the evildoers to be a "product of their environment" or "disturbed." Thus, motives and well-documented reasons for troubling behavior are presented whenever someone commits an act that would, in another age, be called evil. As a result, we can refrain from dealing with the irrational or inexplicable (76–77). Everything is analyzed and explained, and living becomes more tolerable. Interestingly, Dianne Luce touches upon something related to this subject in her book on McCarthy's Tennessee period, *Reading the World* (2009), when she discusses similarities between Lester Ballard of *Child of God* and Norman Bates of Hitchcock's *Psycho*. She argues that McCarthy's depiction of Lester as a child of God rather than as a psycho might have come as a reaction to Hitchcock's detailed psychoanalysis of Norman Bates at the end of the movie, which "separates Norman from the experiences of a normal human, and finally fails to illuminate in any essential way the universal mystery of the human heart and spirit" (153).

*Halloween* was released at a time when American horror cinema was moving away from its gothic, supernatural elements, which relied on monsters and invaders from outer space. The new horror was given a human face and used familiar settings and everyday events as backdrops. Indeed, *Halloween* owes a lot to Alfred Hitchcock's *Psycho* (1960): in both, the threat comes from within, and in the human form of Norman Bates and Michael Myers, rather than Frankenstein's monster, spacemen, or Dracula. However, the important difference between the evil of *Psycho* compared to that of *Halloween* or McCarthy's novels is that Norman Bates' insanity is thoroughly explained to the uneasy viewer: he has a split personality and events in his past are to blame. Furthermore, the human forms of the Judge and Myers only serve as shells, because they are depicted as entirely inhuman or even superhuman. But their human appearances make us question whether man is essentially evil.

The Judge, and everything about him, remains a mystery: "Whoever would seek out his history through what unraveling of loins and ledgerbooks must stand at the last darkened and dumb at the shore of a void without terminus or origin and whatever science he might bring to bear upon the dusty primal matter blowing down out of millennia will discover no trace of any ultimate atavistic egg by which to reckon his commencing" (310). Robert Morgan, novelist and poet, has said that "McCarthy is a writer who does not *explain* his characters. They do what they do and you can interpret that however you want" (Josyph 150). In the world of *Halloween* and in the world of Cormac McCarthy, the audience is not subjected to a well-structured explanation on the universal mysteries of the dark aspects of humanity, as seen in *Psycho*. Our own interpretations will have to suffice—and will probably be that much more terrifying.

In his study *A Philosophy of Evil*, Lars Svendsen lists four traditional explanations concerning the origin of evil: "1) people are possessed or seduced by a malevolent, supernatural power; 2) people are predisposed, by nature, to act in a certain way that might be called evil; 3) people are influenced by their environment to commit evil acts; and 4) people have free will and choose to act in accordance with evil" (13–14). In the context of the Judge and The Shape, the second option is the most relevant, because the two characters are used to show that it is in man's nature, in his DNA, to do evil things. Richard Dawkins, ethnologist and evolutionary biologist, has said: "DNA neither cares nor knows. DNA just is. And we dance to its music" (133). In the horrific worlds of McCarthy, evil is a strand in the DNA of humanity itself, one that dominates and cannot be defeated. This is a staple of the horror universe as well. Evil just *is*. Considering the final scene of *Blood Meridian* where the Judge dances, Dawkins' music metaphor seems eerily appropriate. However, Svendsen's idea that "people have free will and choose to act in accordance with evil" could also be applied to The Shape and the Judge. Their motivations are never fully explained, and the possibility that they practice evil simply because they choose to do so definitely exists.

The reason, however, why readers and scholars continue in their attempts to decipher Judge Holden's every word and action is, of course, the relentless need to understand him. To the rational mind, it is difficult to accept that he is perhaps simply and purely evil. In Sheriff Bell's monologue that opens *No Country for Old Men*, he remembers sending a nineteen-year-old to the electric chair for killing his fourteen-year-old girlfriend. According to the newspapers, it was a crime of passion. But the boy tells Bell that there was no passion to it, and that he had in fact been planning on killing someone for as long as he could remember (3). By calling it a crime of passion, the unknown and incomprehensible is named, identified, and, perhaps, thus becomes easier to comprehend. One is reminded of the words from *Outer Dark*: "if you cain't name somethin you cain't claim it. You cain't talk about it even. You cain't say what it is" (177). This is also why Holden and Myers are identified, respectively, mainly as "the Judge" and "The Shape"—incomprehensible as they are, you cannot name them beyond these superficial descriptive labels.

Throughout *Blood Meridian*, the Judge preaches his worldview to those willing to listen, and as such gives clues to his bleak vision of where mankind has been and where it is headed. On the subject of war, William S. Burroughs once said: "This is a war universe. War all the time. That is its nature. There may be other universes based on all sorts of other principles, but ours seems to be based on war and games" ("The War Universe"). The words echo those of the Judge: "Men are born for games. Nothing else . . . War is the ultimate game because war is at last a forcing of the unity of existence. War is god" (249). Although McCarthy reveals a little of the complicated reasoning behind the Judge's view on war in these passages, they certainly do not offer any reasoning behind acts such as raping and killing children, or drowning puppies, seemingly for no apparent reason. These might be construed, therefore, as acts of pure evil, or what Svendsen calls "demonic" evil. On demonic evil, Svendsen says: "If we're going to understand an action, we have to understand its purpose—in these cases, however, it's not clear what the purpose could possibly be" (91). Svendsen notes that evil committed for the sake of evil is a central idea in much of the scholarship on the subject. Also, he reminds us that this form of evil dominates horror films (92). Evil for the sake of evil certainly presents itself as a valid cause for Michael Myers in *Halloween*, but does not necessarily function as a full explanation.

Svendsen's discussion of this subject partly centers on the idea that the evildoer obtains some sort of pleasure out of committing evil deeds, such as murdering or torturing someone, and more importantly, seeing and experiencing it (92). Nevertheless, the only pleasure The Shape and the Judge seem to achieve is that of complete control. The Judge is presented as someone who is always in control, and, of course, all-knowing. If something exists without his knowledge, it exists without his consent (*Blood Meridian* 198). Myers, as The Shape, is also in complete control and moves about effortlessly, always knowing where to go and what to do. In *Blood Meridian*, Glanton and his gang do things far worse than the Judge in the pursuit of scalps. But they are motivated by money. The Judge is motivated by something more complex and terrifying, as is The Shape. In this, the Judge is comparable to Anton Chigurh in *No Country for Old Men*, and Rick Wallach notes that the Coen film presents Chigurh as driven by money rather than the supposed eccentric moral code that makes Chigurh interesting and even more enigmatic in the novel (Welsh 80).

Throughout *Halloween* there is never an explanation as to why Myers killed his sister, nor is it clear why he decides to stalk the young Laurie Strode, played by Jamie Lee Curtis, and her friends. Myers' sister had sex prior to being stabbed to death, and the most common interpretation of the film is that young Myers, when he becomes The Shape, goes on to stalk and kill youngsters because they drink and have sex, essentially punishing them for bad behavior. Furthermore, he primarily kills with a large, phallic knife. Laurie does not have sex but is apparently guilty by association. But The Shape sees and stalks these youngsters long before he discovers their bad behavior. The perception the viewer is left with is that if The Shape sees you and consequently learns of your existence, you will die. Therefore, the standard interpretation of the film might be valid, but John Carpenter has always dismissed this analysis, and I find it to be a bit cheap. In fact, *Halloween* is more complex, primarily due to the Shape character. For The Shape, Chigurh, and the Judge, there are no easy answers to the question of what drives and motivates them. *Blood Meridian* and *Halloween* raise the question whether the Judge and The Shape, respectively, can be killed at all. Throughout the film, The Shape is stabbed and shot but always gets back up to go after its target again. Carpenter has said: "This guy is a human, but he's not. He's more than that. He's not exactly supernatural but maybe he is. Who knows how he got that way?" (Smith). The Judge also appears to be "not exactly supernatural but maybe he is" (Smith). As Harold Bloom asks, "is he a person, or something other?" To this question, Bloom adds that the Judge "almost seems to come from some other world" (257). In addition, Samuel Chamberlain's account of the Judge states that no one knew "who or *what*" he was (271, italics mine).

In the narrative, the Judge's mortality is not explicitly tested in the battles he partakes in. Several times the Kid has the chance to shoot the Judge who appears before him both naked and unarmed, but he fails to act every time. McCarthy does not offer a definite answer as to why, and it remains one of the most complex and also most discussed aspects of the novel. It is clear that the Kid represents an opposition to the Judge, but the question of what is the Kid's motivation remains. Shane Schimpf suggests that the Kid does not kill the Judge, because it lies in his nature to be "inescapably merciful" (38). Schimpf bases this on the Judge's ruling over the Kid as someone who reserved some clemency for the heathen (299). If one believes that the Judge speaks the truth, his judgment might just be the answer. But at the beginning of the novel, the Kid is presented as a child in whom "a taste for mindless violence" is already brooding (3). The Kid does, indeed, seem more merciful near the end of the novel and conscious about his wrongdoings. However, as a character he has been virtually unseen until that point and, as a result, almost ends up as a minor character. McCarthy does not concern himself too much with the Kid. If he truly develops from a kid with a taste for mindless violence to a person whose nature, according to Shane Schimpf, it is to be inescapably merciful, the transformation is poorly depicted.

For a different argument, we can turn to Peter Josyph,[2] who argues that "It's almost as if, by not shooting him, the Kid has disproved [the Judge]. The Kid knew that if he shot the Judge, the Judge would then be right, because the Judge is saying: 'That's what we all are, that's what we're made of'" (84). In this interpretation, the Kid is not overcome by mercy, but rather by a need to prove that the Judge is wrong in his worldview. Moreover, it can be argued that the Kid senses that attempting to kill the Judge would be futile. Harold Bloom suggests that it could be "a kind of spiritual fear that maybe you can pump bullets into the Judge and it won't touch him at all" (Josyph 84). Regardless of the Kid's motivation, he pays with his life for the choices he makes. In *Halloween* Dr. Loomis does manage to shoot his nemesis. But after he goes to check on the body, he sees that it is gone. Upon filming the scene, Donald Pleasance, who plays Loomis, asked John Carpenter how he should play the scene. Carpenter asked if Pleasance had any suggestions. Pleasance's answer was that there were two ways he could react when discovering that the body was gone, the first being, "he's gone!", and the second being, "I knew this would happen" (Smith). Carpenter chose the second reaction. Pleasance's haunting expression as he realizes The Shape is gone tells us that Loomis knew exactly what would happen should he attempt to kill The Shape, and it is one of the most chilling moments of the film. Loomis and the Kid are, then, in the same position as they are offered the opportunity to confront and kill evil. Both seem to know that the attempt will be futile. However, Loomis tries, and fails, while the Kid cannot even bring himself to try.[3] Remembering the words from *Outer Dark*, it seems that it is impossible to claim or kill what cannot be named or understood.

Namelessness in the form of evil that cannot be named or described engulfs *Blood Meridian* and *Halloween*. In *The Transparency of Evil*, Jean Baudrillard asks: "where did Evil go?"—and finds that the answer is "everywhere—because the anamorphosis of modern Evil knows no bounds" (81). In *Blood Meridian* and *Halloween*, however, evil does not limit itself to definitions and labels such as "modern". It is an element, a terrifying truth, which, much like war, existed long before the creation of mankind and merely waited for him to arrive—man being its ultimate practitioner. Early in *Blood Meridian*, there is a reference to "a namelessness wheeling in the night" (46). Near the end of the novel, the Judge says, "There is room on the stage for one beast and one alone. All others are destined for a night that is eternal and without name" (331). Moments before his death, the Kid tells the Judge, "You aint nothin," to which the Judge replies that the Kid speaks truer than he knows (331). When the Kid is killed by the Judge, it happens in an embrace. He is literally engulfed by the terrifying reality that is the Judge's omnipresent and all-consuming existence. One of the most ambiguous elements of *Blood Meridian* is this scene in the jakes where the Judge embraces the Kid—in fact, it is so brief that it barely qualifies as a scene, and there is no clear evidence of what happens or if the Kid is even killed. The Kid thus becomes the final symbol of those who are "destined for a night that is eternal and without name." The Shape disappears into the night and the sound of its breathing tells us that its existence is eternal and equally nameless. The reaction of those who look into the outhouse and see the Kid tells us that something horrifying has taken place. But that "something" remains nameless. The Kid, indeed, spoke true, when he said that the Judge is nothing. Ultimately, the namelessness that wheels in the eternal night that is *Blood Meridian* and *Halloween* refer not only to the actions of the Judge and The Shape, but to them as that "something" that cannot be defined.

The Judge is no doubt terrifying and might just be "the most frightening figure in all of American literature" as Harold Bloom has put it (255). But what frightens us the most: his murderous and cruel actions, or the simple fact that he exists and that we cannot fully understand him? It is ironic that a novel written in such vibrant and hauntingly beautiful prose essentially becomes an example of how language fails us. Michael Myers/The Shape never speaks, which naturally adds to the mystery of his being. The Judge speaks—at times, preaches—at length throughout the novel, but also remains a mystery. His views on the omnipresence of war in all of worldly existence are prevalent, but often his actions cannot be explained with reference to war or the game it supposedly invites among men. His words, then, fail us in our attempt to fully understand him. The words of scripture fail as well, as the Kid carries a Bible around which he cannot read. Words—and, to a greater extent, knowledge, logic, and science—fail Dr. Loomis who, as noted earlier, cannot diagnose Myers or even speak about him with words linked to logic and science. The Judge and The Shape remain mysteries. In both works, the question remains whether there is an answer to the mystery. The Judge tells the gang: "Your heart's desire is to be told some mystery" (252). As readers and spectators, we look for the key to unlock the mysteries of the Judge and The Shape. But perhaps the mystery is, as the Judge reminds us, that there is no mystery (252).

There is very little blood or graphic violence in *Halloween*. The film is most effective when The Shape merely observes rather than when it kills. The presence—or shape—of evil and the simple fact that it exists are what terrify the viewer. As a presence it seems omnipresent and is often in the frame one moment, only to disappear the next. A fine example of this is a scene where Annie, one of the victims, is on the phone while she walks back and forth in the kitchen. At one point she walks to the right, and The

Shape is seen in the background through a glass door. Annie then walks left with the camera following her, leaving The Shape out of frame. Less than two seconds later, she walks to the right again, and The Shape is gone. After The Shape vanishes into the night, the film ends with still shots of all the places it has been throughout the night. Meanwhile, heavy breathing is heard in the background. The breathing suggests that it is a forever living organism and fact of life. The final montage of still images confronts us with the places The Shape *has* been, but more importantly the places it still *is*: it is everywhere. Similarly, the Judge appears to be omnipresent. Near the end of the novel the Kid hears rumors of the Judge everywhere, and earlier Tobin says that "Every man in the company claims to have encountered that sootysouled rascal in some other place" (313, 124). The Judge also appears to have intimate knowledge about events that he could not have witnessed. The omnipresence of evil in the form of the Judge and The Shape is the real horror of both stories.

McCarthy's dark fiction rarely, if ever, leaves the reader with a comforting or optimistic ending. Consequently, it is possible to place him in a horror context. Many works in the horror genre leave the audience with an ending where the evil has seemingly been overcome, only to hint or to show that this is not the case. Michael Myers/The Shape is not silenced or killed; the gang rides on in *Outer Dark*, and neither Culla nor Rinthy receive any form of closure—at least not one they can understand or live with; Chigurh might be injured, but he is still out there somewhere, still representing the new kind of evil and violence that Sheriff Bell fails to understand; and, finally, the Judge dances into the sunset, proclaiming that he will never die. The chilling and haunting prophecy of many horror films and fictions is that true evil never sleeps or dies, and this is an enduring element in McCarthy's fiction. In contrast to this, then, it is interesting that McCarthy kills off one of the more sympathetic of his disturbing and violent characters: Lester Ballard in *Child of God*. I have elsewhere[4] argued that Lester evokes a feeling of the uncanny: there is something both completely unfamiliar and disturbing about him, while there is something oddly familiar as well. Lester is a murderer and a necrophile, and as such, one would find it difficult, if not impossible, to sympathize with him. Lester is, however, still a human being—a child of God—shunned by his community, roaming the hillsides looking for a family, looking for love, and more than anything looking for a place to belong. Owing to his "unusual" ways of achieving these things, however—having sex with dead women and starting a family of corpses in the cave that functions as his home—Lester is always abhorrent, but there is a strange or even grotesque sense of dignity and, certainly, humor in Lester's depiction, which ultimately makes him one of the most unlikely of candidates among McCarthy's characters for sympathy. While one might see elements of evil in Lester, he is never elevated to represent universal evil.

But, of course, Lester does not live on. He is captured by the authorities, placed in a cage, and finally succumbs to pneumonia. His body is then sent to a medical school where it is finally "laid out on a slab and flayed, evis-cerated, dissected. His head was sawed open and his brains removed. His muscles were stripped from his bones. His heart was taken out. His entrails were hauled forth and delineated" (194). In the end, the remains are scraped into a plastic bag. If we choose to believe that there is an element of goodness and humanity in Lester—much like we can be led to believe is the case with the Kid—his being is thoroughly and explicitly pulled apart and destroyed, along with any hope of humanity, however disturbing it might appear, surviv-ing in McCarthy's universe. Ultimately, it is relevant to raise the question: is Cormac McCarthy merely out to scare us? Some of the most effective horror works instill a fear of life itself in its audience. *Halloween* was not designed to be followed by a sequel, and the idea was to leave the audience troubled by the enduring existence of The Shape. As noted earlier, The Shape is most effective when it simply watches and is, literally, a mere shape somewhere in the frame, rather than when it kills. How can we live in a world where shapes of evil exist and cannot be destroyed? The same question can be raised in connec-tion with the Judge—or any of McCarthy's evil characters. In a comparison of *Halloween* and *Blood Meridian*, it may be more relevant to see McCarthy rather than the Judge as a counterpart to The Shape. The Shape and the Judge both have disturbing prankster tendencies and make their victims realize that they are ill-equipped for existence. Many of McCarthy's novels are graphic and grotesque in their depictions of violence and havoc, but ultimately, the uncertainty of human existence stands stronger than any gruesome image encountered along the way. At the end of *Outer Dark* when Culla is con-fronted with the "landscape of the damned," he wonders "why a road should come to such a place" (242). As McCarthy readers, we might wonder why he will constantly lead us to such a place and leave us there.

McCarthy's theme of sending his characters out on impossible journeys on roads toward damnation and despair so far culminates with *The Road* (2006)—or so it appears on the surface. Echoing Culla's question, "why a road should come to such a place?", the road in *The Road* is part of the landscape of the damned. *The Road* is also embroiled in nothingness on several levels. First, everything is gone, and the man and his son roam a landscape where practically nothing has survived. Second, there is never an explanation for the predicament the man, the boy, and the world are in. Third, everyone is nameless. [5] The world is finally shrouded in the night of eternal nothingness that McCarthy and the Judge referenced in *Blood Meridian* (46, 331). Whereas the Judge stood as the ultimate symbol of evil in *Blood Meridian*, the landscape and the 'place' as such take on this role in *The Road*. The novel is also, then, a continuation of McCarthy's enduring emphasis on landscapes, both picturesque and dangerous. In the journeys taken by Culla and Rinthy Holme, Lester Ballard, Suttree, Billy Parham, and John Grady Cole, the landscape, the place, becomes a crucial element in their struggles, and a key to their development—and in McCarthy's fic-tion, development rarely presents itself as a positive.

However, *The Road* does leave its reader with a spark of hope in the ash gray world it so beautifully and depressingly depicts. As a result, the novel suggests a turn in McCarthy's dark authorship where light only manifests to show a void, beyond, without hope. The Cormac McCarthy of 1965–85 would certainly not have let the boy survive and let a good-hearted family take him under their protective wing. In all likelihood, the boy would have ended up as a smoking carcass after a feast held by cannibals, like the infant in *Outer Dark*. The boy in *The Road* carries the fire. "Fire" can be read as a metaphor for the light, and thus hope, inside him—he is, after all, the word of God if God ever spoke (3). But "fire" can also be a reference to the gun that he carries, given to him by his father. The boy carries both good and evil, light and darkness, and the question remains which of them will prevail. Since the novel is dedicated to McCarthy's young son, the most popular interpretation seems to be that, of course, McCarthy will let the boy live on and offer hope at the end of the long, harrowing journey, even if McCarthy does not present a happy ending in the traditional sense. *The Road* is, indeed, one of McCarthy's most optimistic novels. My initial reading of the novel left me with a pessimistic sensation after turning the final page. Knowing how well children usually fare in McCarthy's works, and accustomed to the dominating pessimism he usually displays, I did not expect the man and wife, who take in the boy, to be as good as they appear. Surely, the prince of darkness and master of the apocalypse, who once wrote about a bush of dead babies, would end his most overtly postapocalyptic tale without any trace of hope whatsoever. It does become hard to argue, though, that the ending of *The Road* can be read as anything but hopeful. The confusing and problematic mystery of *Blood Meridian* is that perhaps there is no mystery, and thus no explanations or answers to the questions it poses. But in its final sentence, *The Road* hums of mystery (241). If there is a mystery, there must be an answer. Somewhere.

In a quote that could have been about the Judge, John Carpenter has said: "I thought it might be a good idea to raise this Michael Myers character up to a mythic status—make him human, yes, but almost like a force; a force that will never stop, that can't be denied" (Smith). Rick Wallach has called the questions "Who is he? What is he?" about the Judge "open ends that give the novel its force" (Josyph 106). In Cormac McCarthy's world, evil lives on. This is exactly like the world of horror, which in its core sets out to frighten us and make us uneasy about our existence and the world we live in. *The Road* might suggest a new turn for McCarthy, since hope enters the darkened stage at the end. Only time will tell whether he chooses to follow this road in future novels. Throughout most of his career, McCarthy has been a writer of horror without necessarily having been labeled, or marketed, as such. His authorship, however, stands as the most effective characterization of the outer and inner dark of the Americas of past decades. Like so many horror films and stories, his novels confront us with evil, only to affirm its existence rather than explain it. The Judge

and the shape of Michael Myers walk the earth in human form, but ultimately they stand out as shapes of incomprehensible evil—forces that will
never stop and cannot be denied. As such they will continue to both haunt
and intrigue us, much like Cormac McCarthy himself.

## NOTES

1. Even though the film spawned a handful of largely unsatisfying sequels, this
essay only considers Carpenter's original film.
2. I want to thank Peter Josyph for his help in connection with my work on this
essay. He read it numerous times, both in its early stages as a paper given at
the *Blood Meridian* 25th Anniversary Conference held in San Marcos (October 2010), and in its expanded and revised form as found in this collection.
With each reading Peter made insightful and valuable suggestions. The final
result is undoubtedly better because of his influence.
3. Dr. Loomis appears in four of the *Halloween* sequels, and he becomes
increasingly obsessed with killing Myers as the series develops. With reference to *Moby Dick*, McCarthy's favorite novel, the Judge has been compared to both Ahab and the whale. Loomis' relentless hunt for Myers and his
increasing insanity certainly validate a comparison to *Moby Dick* and 'the
hunt', as well.
4. "The (Un)familiar Necrophile: Reading Freud's The Uncanny in Cormac
McCarthy's *Child of God.*" Paper given at the 2009 International Cormac
McCarthy Society Conference, Warwick University, UK.
5. The old man who the man and son encounter says his name is Ely, only to
reveal that it is not his real name (144).

## WORKS CITED

Baudrillard, Jean. The *Transparency of Evil: Essays on Extreme Phenomena.*
1990. Trans. James Benedict. New York: Verso, 1993.
Bloom, Harold. *How to Read and Why.* London: Fourth Estate, 2000.
Burroughs, William S. "The War Universe." 1991. Taped conversation, first pub-
lished in *Grand Street*, No. 37.
Carpenter, John. Dir. *Halloween.* Compass International Pictures, 1978. Film.
Chamberlain, Samuel. *My Confession: The Recollections of a Rogue.* Austin:
Texas State Historical Association, 1996.
Dawkins, Richard. *River out of Eden: A Darwinian View of Life.* London: Basic
Books, 1996.
Erdmann, Terry J., and Paula M. Block. *Star Trek 101: A Practical Guide to Who,
What, Where, and Why.* New York: Pocket Books, 2008.
James, Caryn. "'Blood Meridian,' by Cormac McCarthy." *New York Times* 28
April 1985.
Josyph, Peter. *Adventures in Reading Cormac McCarthy.* Lanham, Toronto, and
Plymouth: Scarecrow, 2010.
Luce, Dianne C. *Reading the World: Cormac McCarthy's Tennessee Period.*
Columbia: South Carolina Press, 2009.
McCarthy, Cormac. *Blood Meridian or the Evening Redness in the West.* (1985).
New York: Vintage, 1992.
———. *Child of God.* 1973. New York: Vintage, 1993.

———. *No Country for Old Men*. New York: Alfred A. Knopf, 2005.

———. *Outer Dark*. 1968. New York: Vintage, 1993.

———. *The Road*. New York: Alfred A. Knopf, 2006.

Muir, John Kenneth. *The Films of John Carpenter*. Jefferson and London: McFarland, 2000.

Schimpf, Shane. *A Reader's Guide to Blood Meridian*. Seattle: BonMot, 2006.

Smith, Steven. "Halloween: A Cut Above the Rest." *Halloween: 20th Anniversary Edition*. Anchor Bay, 2003. DVD.

Svendsen, Lars. *A Philosophy of Evil*. 2001. Trans. Kerri A. Pierce. New York: Norton, 2010.

Welsh, Jim. "Borderline Evil: The Dark Side of Byzantium in *No Country for Old Men*, Novel and Film." In No Country for Old Men: *From Novel to Film*. Eds. Rick Wallach, Jim Welsh, and Lynnea Chapman King. Lanham, Toronto, and Plymouth: Scarecrow, 2009. 73–85.

# 8 "A Novel in Dramatic Form"

## Metaphysical Tension in *The Sunset Limited*

### Ciarán Dowd

> *Oprah Winfrey: You haven't worked out the God thing, or not, yet?*
>
> *Cormac McCarthy: Well . . . It would depend on what day you asked me.*
>
> (Winfrey)

In May 2006, Chicago's Steppenwolf Theatre Company staged the premiere of Cormac McCarthy's stage play *The Sunset Limited*. Five months later, Vintage published the play in paperback. The paperback's textual content remains essentially the same as the staged production: in a run-down tenement, two men debate the nature of existence and the meaning of life, one trying to convince the other not to commit suicide.[1] But while the content remains essentially the same on stage and in print, the published version of the play has one puzzling additional feature: it contains the subtitle, "A Novel in Dramatic Form." How are we to interpret this? I will argue that one particular reading of the subtitle, and of the published version of the play as a whole, points beyond the play itself to a metaphysical tension present in McCarthy's novels.

The characters of this one-act play are labelled Black and White, reflecting simultaneously their respective skin colors and the polarity of their metaphysical worldviews. White is an atheist professor who "yearn[s] for the darkness" (135) and has attempted to kill himself by jumping in front of a subway train. Black is a born-again Christian and ex-convict who happened to be present on the subway platform at the time of White's "amazin leap" (22) and who now believes this whole episode has been fated so that he can save White from his nihilistic path toward self-destruction. As he puts it himself:

> You *know* who appointed me. I didn't ask for you to leap into my arms down in the subway this mornin. (10)

Throughout the conversation which follows, White wants to leave the apartment and be free to kill himself, repeatedly stating "I've got to go," "I'm going home," "I have to go" (6, 8, 43). Each tentative attempt to leave is halted by another stalling tactic on the part of Black, until White resolutely says "No. No more time. Goodbye." as he heads towards the door for the final time (140).

White claims to have reached his suicidal conclusions through intellectual means, having come to see the world as utterly devoid of meaning. He longs for the nothingness of death to release him from the futility of existence in this "moral leper colony" (75):

> I dont regard my state of mind as some pessimistic view of the world. I regard it as the world itself. Evolution cannot avoid bringing intelligent life ultimately to an awareness of one thing above all else and that one thing is futility. (136)

Or, as Black then paraphrases a little more colorfully: "If I'm understandin you right you sayin that everbody that aint just eat up with the dumb-ass ought to be suicidal," to which White agrees (136). White is of the belief that his superior intelligence leaves him "without dreams or illusions" (136) and grants him a realistic view of the world as "basically a forced labor camp from which the workers—perfectly innocent—are led forth by lottery, a few each day, to be executed" (122).

A man, to White, is a "thing dangling in senseless articulation in a howling void. No meaning to its life" (139), echoing the absurdity of the human condition outlined by Camus:

> At certain moments of lucidity, the mechanical aspect of their gestures, their meaningless pantomime make silly everything that surrounds them. A man is talking on the telephone behind a glass partition; you cannot hear him but you see his incomprehensible dumb-show: you wonder why he is alive. (Camus 20–21)

White is thus presented as a nihilist, albeit one lacking either a Nietzschean will to self-creation or a Camusian revolt engendered by Sisyphean acceptance of his lot's absurdity. Moreover, his nihilism has been arrived at through deliberation and a gradual stripping away of meaning and value. Such an elimination of meaning is one logical extreme of an ontologically naturalist position. *The Stanford Encyclopedia of Philosophy* offers a definition of naturalism as the belief "that reality is exhausted by nature, containing nothing 'supernatural', and that the scientific method should be used to investigate all areas of reality, including the 'human spirit'" (Papineau). Philosophers' self-identification as "naturalists", without precisely defining what this entails or reaching consensus on their definitions, is so commonplace—since at least as early as the mid-twentieth century—as to make a comprehensive definition difficult.

A glance at the foregoing definition, however, reveals two separate components: ontological naturalism, concerned with the contents of reality, and methodological naturalism, concerned with the ways of investigating reality. While there are many potential definitions of naturalism, of either the onto-logical or methodological variety, one prominent theme is the relationship of scientific knowledge to, respectively, the ontological contents of reality and the practice of philosophy.[2] Among philosophers, particularly in the analytic tradition, an overwhelming majority would identify themselves as naturalists (de Caro and Macarthur 2). While it is true that few contemporary philoso-phers would claim to be nonnaturalists, a large subset of humanity in general could be uncontroversially designated as such. I'm speaking here of people who believe in a deity, multiple deities, superstitions, ghosts, and/or mind-body dualism, among many other possible examples.

My identification of White as an ontological naturalist, albeit an extreme and nihilistic example of one, is warranted primarily by Black's contrary position as an patent non-naturalist and White's insistence that his reasons for suicide "center around a gradual loss of make-believe. That's all. A gradual enlightenment as to the nature of reality" (120). It is true that a def-inition of the respective metaphysical positions of White and Black could be refined much further, but their positions are nonetheless species of the more inclusive genera "naturalist" and "nonnaturalist." In using these broader terms (rather than, say, "nihilist" and "revelationist"), I am attempting to tease out a more wide-reaching metaphysical tension in McCarthy's work, a tension that does not limit itself to the more specific metaphysical posi-tions instantiated by White and Black. I will return to this tension later.

Unlike White, Black conceives of his world within a metaphysical frame-work which is in direct opposition to naturalism. He is a Christian, albeit a self-admittedly heretical one, whose faith was awoken while he lay on the verge of death in a prison's infirmary: "I'm layin there and I hear this voice. Just as clear. Couldnt of been no clearer. And this voice says: If it was not for the grace of God you would not be here" (49). We might say that black is a *super*naturalist, in contradistinction to White's naturalism. His metaphysical worldview, or *Weltanschauung*, is one in which the world is suffused with meaning, and in which his presence on the subway platform was orchestrated by God in order that Black may save this professor's life, and potentially his soul. White, presenting a metaphysical outlook which takes naturalism to one of its logical extremes, argues his way toward his terminal destination, and Black attempts to convince White of his own supernaturalist position that the world is numinous, that it is not as White sees it but instead possesses meaning and goodness. However, once White awakens from his initial torpor and hits his rhetorical stride, "warming up the trick bag" (121), Black's earlier confidence seems to dwindle, and he fails to find the words to convince this erudite professor of darkness to keep his feet "nailed down to the platform when the Sunset Limited comes through" (95).

The play's dialectic ends with White remaining resolute in his sui-cidal trajectory, leaving the apartment to his presumed death, and Black questioning the justice of a God who would fail to provide him with the eloquence he believes he required in order to convince White of his folly and lead him onto the path of salvation.

> I dont understand what you sent me down there for. I dont understand it. If you wanted me to help him how come you didnt give me the words? You give em to him. What about me? (142)

Black still remains faithful: "That's all right. That's all right. If you never speak again you know I'll keep your word" (142). But the play ends with his unanswered question to God, "Is that okay? Is that okay?" (143), suggesting Black's continuing struggle to accommodate into his metaphysical worldview what Dianne C. Luce refers to as "the mysterious silence of God" (20).

I first encountered *The Sunset Limited* when the Steppenwolf production came to the Galway Arts Festival in July 2007, and much of the overheard discussion afterwards focused on the outcome of the play's dialectic: on which of the two characters "won" the argument; or on which of the two most closely "represents" McCarthy's own worldview. One such judgment might hold that Black is closest in spirit to a perceived spirituality in McCarthy's work. Black cares for his fellow man, he tries to prevent White's suicide, and his self-admittedly heretical Christianity, born of a revelation in a hospital bed, is in keeping with readings of McCarthy's work which see him as an inherently mystical writer, such as those provided by McCarthy scholar Edwin T. Arnold. As Arnold has written: "Deep inside McCarthy's darkest visions is that mysterious and sacred fire, that hidden illumination that bides and binds" ("Mosaic" 182).

White, on the other hand, claims that his nihilism is the result of a gradual stripping away of dreams and illusions, and it could be suggested that he is of a piece with a darkly nihilistic strain in McCarthy's work. A closer look at White's position, however, reveals that his conviction—that the world is meaningless, that any sane, intelligent person would long for the nothingness of death—is just as much founded on faith as are Black's religious beliefs. White may see no evidence in the world for the existence of a deity (or even of meaning), but neither does he present convincing evidence for its nonexistence. His faith is the counterfaith of an atheism which equates lack of evidence with proof of nonexistence, and just as Black's faith in transcendent communion cannot be reasoned away by discussion alone, neither can White's faith in the innate loneliness and ultimate absurdity of existence. Perhaps philosopher F. H. Bradley was right to state that metaphysics is "the finding of bad reasons for what we believe on instinct" (Kaufmann 103), and it could be that the instincts of these two characters are not going to be swayed by words, one way or the other.

The play suggests that neither man is ultimately "right." Neither of them "wins" the argument, because each clings obstinately to his own unreasonable position. Without an appreciation of the antinomial unity of white and black, of existential loneliness and brotherly communion, of ontological naturalism and mystical faith, neither of these characters, considered individually, unproblematically embody McCarthy's complex metaphysical vision. White leaves the apartment, probably to meet the "Sunset Limited" and his end, and he is arguably even more committed to his nihilism than before, seeing only the bare facticity of material matter divested of spiritual agency or ultimate meaning. Black's faith is shaken slightly by the encounter, as he ends the play with his somewhat accusational entreaty to God, finding it hard to comprehend the injustice he sees in God's failure to provide him with the words with which to convince White. When White says "You see everything in black and white," and Black responds "It is black and white" (105), we can see that Black's faith is one which does not accommodate shades of grey, and of course the same can be said of White's counterfaith in nothingness.

As one of the early reviews claims, "these characters are dramatic constructs that enable the author to argue with himself" (Weiss). McCarthy pits the two sides of his metaphysical character against each other and, through the play's ambiguous lack of resolution, indicates that both are equally valid and must exist in a fraught metaphysical *pas de deux*. The epigraph to this paper is taken from McCarthy's only televised interview, with Oprah Winfrey. His response to her question about God suggests a *Weltanschauung* in vacillation, or suspended in a perpetual and creatively fruitful tension. His familiarity, through his occasional presence at the Santa Fe Institute, with the sciences of complexity might have granted him an understanding that an ontologically naturalist position does not necessarily lead to a reductive scientism, or to the abject nihilism of White, but could potentially accommodate a more nuanced, nonreductive naturalism. Such a naturalism maintains that the world has no need for supernatural agency in order to function as it does, but that certain concepts traditionally considered as 'supernatural' could fall within the remit of scientific study, or at least within an ontologically naturalist framework. Furthermore, a nonreductive naturalist *Weltanschauung* informed by complexity science may, as Stuart Kauffman maintains, "help us find anew our place in the universe, that through this new science, we may recover our sense of worth, our sense of the sacred" (4–5).

I will return, then, to the strange subtitle of the published version of the play: "A Novel in Dramatic Form". While it is tempting to read this phrase as an indication that this work is a novel stripped to little more than its bare dialogue, there is another way to read it that extends the play's meaning beyond the confines of the text itself and back into McCarthy's novelistic output. Instead of seeing the phrase "A Novel in Dramatic Form" as a mere statement of genre, we can also read this as the more specific "A *Cormac McCarthy* Novel in Dramatic Form." That is, a dialogue in which a central motif of McCarthy's novels is dramatized, in which an abstract characteristic of his novels is transposed into these concrete dramatic characters. On this reading, the unresolved dialectic of this play would thus represent the metaphysical tension lurking in the heart of all of his novels.Through this debate between White and Black, McCarthy is continuing a debate he has always been having with himself: a debate between ontological naturalism and mysticism, between causal determinism and free will, between a belief in the utter indifference of a coldly mechanical universe and a belief in a universe supported by a meaningful and spiritually significant architecture.[3]

Ever since Vereen M. Bell wrote, with regard to McCarthy's work, of the "irrelevance of the human in the impersonal scheme of things" (10), much of McCarthy criticism has variously agreed with that judgment (with certain qualifications and adjustments) or argued against it for a reading of McCarthy as a profoundly spiritual writer. I would argue that both of these assessments of McCarthy's metaphysics are simultaneously valid. The two polar metaphysical strands—naturalism (or close variants thereof) on the one hand, and supernaturalism, or mysticism, on the other—are apparent throughout his novels. In the "whited regions" (152) of *Blood Meridian* (1985), for example, we can see this naturalism expressed in the "strange equality" of all phenomena, optically democratic landscapes in which "all preference is made whimsical and a man and a rock become endowed with unguessed kinships" (247): the world of man subsumed under the indifferent workings of a godless, mechanical universe. Judge Holden's claim that "[t]he man who believes that the secrets of the world are forever hidden lives in mystery and fear" (199), among his many other similar pronouncements, identifies him as a naturalist in the philosophical sense of the term (whereas the records kept in his ledger and his expansive knowledge of natural processes mark him out as a naturalist in the other sense of "an expert in or student of natural history" ["naturalist," def. 1]).

In *The Road* (2006), images of the universe's indifferent material forces abound: "Out on the roads the pilgrims sank down and fell over and died and the bleak and shrouded earth went trundling past the sun and returned again as trackless and as unremarked as the path of any nameless sister-world in the ancient dark beyond" (181); and, "he saw for a brief moment the absolute truth of the world. The cold relentless circling of the intestate earth. Darkness implacable. The blind dogs of the sun in their running. The crushing black vacuum of the universe" (130). But, at the same time, his novels play against this naturalist tendency in a number of ways. While *The Road* contains many images which suggest the "irrelevance of the human in the impersonal scheme of things," these are counterbalanced by suggestions of a spiritual framework supporting that which remains good in the novel's scorched world. There are repeated intimations that the boy may be a divinity, such as when the man strokes the boy's "pale and tangled hair. Golden chalice, good to house a god" (75), or, during the encounter with the old man calling himself Ely, the man says of the boy: "What if I said that he's a god?" (172). The "fire" which the man and boy are "carrying" also suggests a metaphysical substance or property which must be guarded against the cold wind of nihilism. Crucially, the final sentence of the novel invokes an ineffable quality exhibited by the mysterious processes of life itself: "In the deep glens where they lived all things were older than man and they hummed of mystery" (287).

To cite an example from an earlier novel, Cornelius Suttree's mystical revelations, which lead him to come to some sort of an accommodation with his mortality, are hints of an immanent spiritual order pervading the merely physical world. When he eventually learns "that there is one Suttree and one Suttree only" (461), he appears to have cast aside the body/soul dualism that he inherited from his Catholic upbringing and which has troubled him so much throughout the events of the novel. No longer does he need to view his flesh as a poorly devised "keeping place for souls," a "mawky wormbent tabernacle" (130); he has been granted a vision of the fundamental unity of body and soul, and the understanding that "all souls are one and all souls lonely" (459). Along with the coexistence of metaphysical antinomies throughout McCarthy's novels, another complicating factor is that the most convincing statements expressing naturalist or determinist ideas are often placed in the mouths of his great villains. Judge Holden, to whom "the freedom of birds is an insult" (198), seeks to categorize and thus control all of creation. Anton Chigurh, who insists on the cold, hard determinism of his flipping coin, is another of McCarthy's professors of darkness. The metaphysical claims of Chigurh and Holden are quite convincing in many respects, and are indeed so deeply unsettling to the reader precisely because they are not easy to dismiss outright.

Chigurh and Holden do not embody identical metaphysical positions, however, nor do they share the nihilistic conclusions of White's intellectual "enlightenment." Furthermore, their respective philosophies could just as easily be read as being essentially supernaturalist, but this interpretative ambiguity exhibited by two of McCarthy's most singular characters is in itself another example of the tension I am attempting to unearth. Although I am arguing for the existence of a metaphysical tension throughout McCarthy's novels, and the simplification of this tension into two concrete (if allegorical) characters in *The Sunset Limited*, it would be remiss of me to gloss over the instability inherent in this dynamic. The contending poles of McCarthy's fictional metaphysic are shifting and indefinite, destabilizing characters, individual texts, and intertextual relationships. There is some overlap and resemblance between the various manifestations of the poles, but the one true constant is the tension itself, the refusal to let any given text's metaphysical architecture settle into a stable framework.

Further evidence of the metaphysical tension exhibited in McCarthy's oeuvre can be found by turning to nineteenth-century literary "naturalism"—particularly its American manifestation. Steven Frye has argued that *The Crossing* (1994) exhibits traits of American literary naturalism, which developed as a more romantic strain of naturalism than its deterministic and scientifically informed European antecedent. Enlisting Eric Carl Link's

*The Vast and Terrible Drama: American Literary Naturalism in the Nineteenth Century* (2004), Frye points out that American literary naturalists (such as Norris, London, Crane, and Dreiser) did not employ "scientific naturalism" (a close synonym for the "methodological naturalism" defined earlier) as the strict method espoused by Zola. Instead, "when these writers drew on philosophical naturalism they did so within the generic context of the romance and *in dynamic tension with renewed forms of humanism and mysticism* [emphasis added]" (49). Frye argues that, in *The Crossing*, we are invited to witness to "the tensions implicit in romantic naturalism, the reality of the ineffable and the power of the natural" (57), with these contending forces cohering through the framing context of narrative as that which grants life meaning. After referring to Arnold's identification of a moral parable in *All the Pretty Horses* (1992) that offers "an affirmation of life and of humanity" (Arnold, "Naming" 66), Frye again indicates that the tension in romantic naturalism is generated "between such an affirmation and a pessimistic determinism" (58).

In *The Sunset Limited*, along with a pair of glasses, a pad, and a pencil, two objects sit side by side on the table: a Bible and a newspaper. Black motions with the Bible at a few points throughout the text—"If it aint in here then I dont know it" (75)—but it is significant that when he picks up the newspaper to read an article to the professor, he pretends to read a report of White's suicide:

> Friends report that the man had ignored all advice and had stated that he intended to pursue his own course . . . Meanwhile, bloodspattered spectators at the hundred and fifty-fifth street station . . . who were interviewed at the scene all reported that the man's last words as he hurtled toward the oncoming commuter train were: I am right. (114)

The Bible and the newspaper; the good news and the bad. These two texts on Black's table concretize the opposite poles of McCarthy's unresolved metaphysical tension, just as the two characters sitting at the table personify those same poles.

## NOTES

1. In the endnotes to her paper "Cormac McCarthy's *The Sunset Limited*: Dialogue of Life and Death (A Review of the Chicago Production)," Dianne C. Luce points out a few of the minor dialogical differences between the staged production and the published work.
2. Ontological naturalism, thus defined, would be construed as the belief that reality consists solely of those things available to observation and to the methods of empirical science, whereas methodological naturalism can be thought of as the belief that philosophy and science are both "engaged in essentially the same enterprise" (Papineau).

3. I am not here suggesting that the three binary pairs I have listed are equivalent. However, they share certain family resemblances and overlap sufficiently to consider them as being more specific instances of the broader metaphysical tension I am attempting to identify.

## WORKS CITED

Arnold, Edwin T., and Dianne C. Luce, eds. *Perspectives on Cormac McCarthy.* Rev. ed. Jackson: UP of Mississippi, 1999.

Arnold, Edwin T. "The Mosaic of McCarthy's Fiction, Continued." Hall and Wallach 179–87.

———. "Naming, Knowing and Nothingness: McCarthy's Moral Parables." Arnold and Luce 45–69.

Bell, Vereen M. *The Achievement of Cormac McCarthy.* 1988. Baton Rouge: Louisiana State UP, 2006.

Camus, Albert. *The Myth of Sisyphus.* Trans. Justin O'Brien. 1955. Harmondsworth: Penguin, 1975.

De Caro, Mario, and Macarthur, David. "Introduction: The Nature of Naturalism." *Naturalism in Question.* Cambridge: Harvard UP, 2008.

Frye, Steven. "Cormac McCarthy's 'world in its making': Romantic Naturalism in *The Crossing.*" *Studies in American Naturalism.* International Theodore Dreiser Society, 2007. 46–65.

Hall, Wade, and Rick Wallach, eds. *Sacred Violence: A Reader's Companion to Cormac McCarthy. Volume 2: Cormac McCarthy's Western Novels.* El Paso: Texas Western Press, 2002.

Kauffman, Stuart. *At Home in the Universe: The Search for Laws of Self-Organization and Complexity.* London: Viking, 1995.

Kaufmann, Walter Arnold. *Nietzsche: Philosopher, Psychologist, Antichrist.* 4th ed. Princeton: Princeton UP, 1974.

Luce, Dianne C. "Cormac McCarthy's *The Sunset Limited*: Dialogue of Life and Death (A Review of the Chicago Production)." *The Cormac McCarthy Journal* 6 (2008): 13–21.

McCarthy, Cormac. *All the Pretty Horses.* 1992. London: Picador, 1993.

———. *Blood Meridian or the Evening Redness in the West.* 1985. London: Picador, 1989.

———. *The Crossing.* 1994. London: Picador, 1998.

———. *No Country for Old Men.* New York: Knopf, 2005.

———. *The Road.* 2006. New York: Vintage, 2007.

———. *The Sunset Limited: A Novel in Dramatic Form.* New York: Vintage, 2006.

———. *Suttree.* 1979. London: Picador, 1989.

"Naturalist." *Concise Oxford English Dictionary.* 11th ed. 2004.

Papineau, David. "Naturalism." *The Stanford Encyclopedia of Philosophy.* 21 March 2009. 30 Dec 2010 <http://plato.stanford.edu/archives/spr2009/entries/naturalism/> .

*The Sunset Limited.* By Cormac McCarthy. Dir. Sheldon Patinkin. Perf. Freeman Coffey and Austin Pendleton. Town Hall Theatre, Galway, Ireland. 21 July 2007.

Weiss, Hedy. "'Sunset' debate on faith, salvation grows tiresome." *Chicago Sun-Times* 30 May 2006, Final Edition, Features: 37.

Winfrey, Oprah. "Cormac McCarthy on Writing." *Oprah.com.* Interview. 8 July 2007. 30 Dec. 30 <http://www.oprah.com/oprahbookclub/Cormac-McCarthy-on-Writing>.

# 9 Believing in *The Sunset Limited*
## Tom Cornford and Peter Josyph on Directing McCarthy

*Tom Cornford and Peter Josyph*

*Tom Cornford's presentation of* The Sunset Limited *at the CAPITAL Centre—a staged reading for which he had only a few hours of rehearsal, with Michael Gould as White and Wale Ojo as Black—impressed me with its vitality, intensity, and clarity of vision. No surprise, then, that Tom himself is vital, intense, and clear. With Nick Monk's encouragement, Tom and I decided to have a talk about the play and its theatrical potential, and rather than submerge my reservations about it, I thought it might be interesting to probe them with a director who had recently tackled it and retained his enthusiasm. As with Ted Tally and Billy Bob Thornton when they spoke with me about adapting* All the Pretty Horses, *Tom did not need to trumpet his admiration for McCarthy as a writer: it was evident in everything he said. If directing an author's play is another way of reading him, so, too, is talking about it; and if a production of a play is, ultimately, a kind of dialogue with it, then this is a dialogue about that dialogue, conducted on a stage you can hold in your hands. —Josyph*

## CORNFORD SPEAKS DIRECTLY TO McCARTHY

*Figure 9.1* Michael Gould as White and Wale Ojo as Black. Photograph: Peter Josyph.

JOSYPH: Are you descended from the Cornforths—those dwellers by the ford of the cranes—of Durham? Or are you of the Cornfords of York, or of London? I need to know whether you aren't, by chance, related to the Cornford who famously translated Plato's *Republic*. That would place a weighty pedigree on this dialogue.

CORNFORD: F. M. Cornford's wife Frances was descended from Charles Darwin, and she was a poet and close friend of Rupert Brooke. Their son was John Cornford, a communist and poet who fought and died young in the Spanish Civil War. He looked a bit like me, so naturally I was hopeful of a connection, but they are the Cambridge Cornfords, and we are the London Cornfords, so I hoped in vain, I think.

JOSYPH: Well now we have to face the tribe of Cormac, so, take a leap of imagination that I am Cormac McCarthy come to Coventry, knocking at your door, saying: "Tom—help me out, but don't treat me like a Pulitzer—what I *don't* need is a pat on the ass. If the play is fine, leave it. If it's not, tell me what will make it really sing."

CORNFORD: The Russian actress Alisa Frejndlikh is reported to have said: "When I play a writer like Dostoyevsky, he holds me in the palm of his hand. When I act the work of some of these new writers, I feel as though I am carrying them on my back" (Cox 76). It's a feeling I know well from directing new plays. Often we come across a boggy patch where the dialogue moves awkwardly from one character to the next, or a character's purpose is unclear, and we have to find a way of carrying the play to the next bit of firm ground. It wasn't a problem that we had very often with the dialogue in *The Sunset Limited*. There is a clear movement from line to line, and the voices come easily off the page. In that sense, the play held the actors securely in its palm. The problem was that they didn't always know what they were *doing* there.

When I direct a play, we need to find a score for each of the roles. That score is determined, indirectly, by the dialogue, but it also *precedes* the dialogue. An example would be White's desire to leave, which is expressed in different forms, as a kind of musical theme, throughout the action. His discomfort in his surroundings will therefore be felt in his unconscious and expressed through his physical behavior before it is formulated in language, just as his subsequent decision to stay is expressed without words.

> WHITE. I didnt leap into your arms.
> BLACK. You didnt?
> WHITE. No. I didnt.
> BLACK. Well how did you get there then? (*The professor stands with his head lowered. He looks at the chair and then*

*turns and goes and sits down in it.)* What. Now we aint goin?

WHITE. Do you really think that Jesus is in this room? (8)

This is a clear example of *an event*, a moment when each of the characters changes his intention. Initially, White wants to leave, and Black is going to follow him, then White decides to stay and asks Black if he thinks Jesus is in the room with them. For this short segment, I asked White (a) to persuade Black to unlock the door, and (b) to stop Black from leaving *with* him; and I asked Black (a) to dissuade White from leaving, and (b) to persuade White to take him along. These intentions become the driving force for each character, and their actions will be modified by the given circumstances.

JOSYPH: Where they are, for example.

CORNFORD: Yes, because White is in an unfamiliar tenement, and Black has an unfamiliar guest. Also, the two only met maybe half an hour ago when Black prevented White from throwing himself under a train.

JOSYPH: It's an interesting premise, but it develops a little strangely, no?

CORNFORD: Well that's just it. The beginning of the play is very clear in its structure, and it's lively: both Black and the play soften up their targets with good jokes. It's a conventional opening, and everyone feels secure. The play's development is much less conventional. We begin to realize that it is resolutely anticlimactic and not interested in narrative/rhetorical development. It is interested in *the characters'* rhetoric, *not its own*. The action does not form itself either into a story or into an argument. Instead, it plays with variations on its initial antithesis. The motif of White wanting to leave and Black wanting him to stay will be replayed again and again—almost, as I've suggested, like a musical theme. But unlike a classical theme, it won't develop in the sense of *changing into something else*. Instead, it *deepens*. We see a tension between two mutually conflicting conditions, and that tension is continuous but also shifting. The reiterated statement of that tension allows it to accrue resonance and to uncover complexity, but not *to progress*.

JOSYPH: After the performance, you were asked about Marsha Norman's *Night Mother*—a more famous two-hander about a suicide—and how it relates to *The Sunset Limited*.

CORNFORD: It was a good question, because *Night Mother* does lots of things that we might expect *The Sunset Limited* to do. It explores the psychology of a relationship through a narrative progression toward a climax that is marked by a series of emotional cruxes. *Sunset* deliberately eschews that approach, and with great success. It is more interested in a character's spiritual condition than narratives of his psychology and relationships, and its emotion is indirect, even subliminal. This means that the play will always be flirting with formlessness. The dialogue can move smoothly back and forth, but the actors will still need *to carry* the play without clear changes to follow. Events are like gearchanges. If they aren't there, the actors end up in the wrong gear, and either the engine's screaming or they step on the gas and there's no power. In rehearsals, they will stop and say: "What am I *doing* here?" Then we have to go back and find the missing gear-change.

What the play needs, then, is structural clarity, and its absence is most apparent in the middle. It doesn't need to be overt, but it needs to hold the actors in the palm of its hand.

**JOSYPH:** What if McCarthy were to say: "I understand what you mean about structural clarity. Now, give me *assignments*, Tom. Without completely rewriting the play, what could I, as a writer, do to help the actors and you as a director?"

**CORNFORD:** Whatever you do, your script, if it ends up in my hands, will be turned into a sequence of events and segments of action (sometimes in America these segments are called *beats*). If you were to do that to the play yourself, you'd have to ask two questions. First: when exactly does the change from this segment into the next segment happen? It has to be the same moment for both characters or the structure falls apart. Second: what is driving this character during this segment—what is he trying *to change* through what he does? Most writers find this a waste of time because they are so focused on the spoken words, but experience is not scripted in spoken language. I use a kind of tabular format to score productions, which is derived from the script and then supplements—and at times replaces—the script in rehearsal. In one sense, this is a deliberate wrong move: going *away* from the script in order to return to it with different kinds of knowledge about the characters—knowledge about their pasts, the situation in which they find themselves, their bodily states, their behavioral and gestural languages—knowledge that will allow us to have a more useful attitude to it as a notation of action. If you work on the play in this way, I can foresee at least two outcomes. First, it will sharpen the changes in your characters' behavior. Second—this might prompt a little rewriting—it might encourage you to broaden the range of tactics for each character. Black seems limited in his range of tactical responses. Perhaps that's appropriate if you think of him as having, by the end, lost the battle. I'm not sure about that, though, and I wonder whether he might be allowed more variation and unpredictability. Finally, it would allow us to share a language for speaking about *the whole play* and not only its dialogue.

## CORNFORD SPEAKS BRIEFLY TO KAZAN

**JOSYPH:** It's interesting that you conceive a play in musical terms, but in deeper ways than thinking about sound. As an actor, I have even scored my scripts—doesn't matter whether it's Pinter, Chekhov, or plays that I have written—so that for every line I know my intention, the obstacle to that intention, and how I, as a character, resolve to overcome that obstacle. In this, it's helpful to ask: "What would have to happen if I (my character) got *exactly* what I wanted?" So let me ask you: what, really, would have to happen for White to consider that he's gotten what he wants out of what he's been saying? Does he just want to leave? Does he want to disillusion Black? Or does he want to make some kind of social space in which he can simply exist between the past and the future—extenuating the Now for its own sake, or out of fear, or indecision? For me as an actor, such an answer *might* become a problem. One of my teachers used to say: "No one is going to pay top prices to sit in a theatre to see a play about *the rent*. Your objectives have to be life and death, and they have to be *hot*, and not just *hot—pistol* hot." Is there any such burning objective for White? Or is the lack of it a fault in the play, a reason for its being less theatrical than it might have been?

*Figure 9.2*   Michael Gould and Wale Ojo. Photograph: Peter Josyph.

CORNFORD: The note that I gave Michael that made the biggest difference to his performance is that White is just as evangelical as Black. White wants his vision of life to convince Black. When they sit back down after White's first attempt to leave, White asks Black: "Do you really think Jesus is in this room?" (8) This is to get Black to express a fundamental belief so that he, White, can chip away at it and destabilize the worldview that Black has built on it. It's a rhetorical maneuver that is more typical of Black, as in the debate about the Bible that starts with his question: "Have you ever read this book?" (10) But White is the first to use that maneuver. He also expresses a belief of his own: "I believe in The Sunset Limited" (14).

On one level we thought of White's suicide as a kind of baptism, a solution to his spiritual crisis. The problem, of course, is that it will only be a solution if he's right, and therefore he needs to prove it to himself—and to Black. That's the paradoxical position he expresses in his final speech: "Now there is only the hope of nothingness. I cling to that hope" (59). I think the actor playing White needs to create a character that so desires to find meaning in his life, and whose life has offered him so few opportunities to do that, that he is left *only* with suicide. The first stage in developing such a character is to see that when White is attempting to convince Black, his objective is ultimately turned back on himself.

JOSYPH: Let's revise my question, then, about how the play might have been written differently and ask how Black might better have gone about "saving" White. Am I alone in feeling that the one kind of saving is followed a little too soon with the other, and that he might have had a more positive prospect if he had simply fed White, drank coffee with him, and hoped to see him again? Is there an urgency behind it for Black that we can see as a counterforce to White's urgency? You've hinted at this in saying that they are equally evangelical. Is Black so certain that he can't wait a moment to start converting White—or is he that uncertain?

CORNFORD: Anyone who presents himself as that secure has got to be compensating for something, and we see, when he's alone, that Black is far from resolved. I think part of Black's trouble is that he needs to be right more than he needs to make White's day better. By giving White something to fight against, he makes it easier for White to take the very course of action from which Black is trying to dissuade him. If I were Black, I'd liken myself to White implicitly, I'd try to establish solidarity rather than emphasize the contrast. But in that respect, Black's weakness is the play's strength.

JOSYPH: When I told you I didn't believe that White was going to kill himself again—once was probably enough—you said that you don't speculate on what occurs after the stage is dark, so let me ask a related question: Would it be interesting to you if McCarthy were to write a second act?

CORNFORD: I think it's best as it is.

JOSYPH: I used to love writing one-act plays that you couldn't possibly follow with another—and then write the other impossible act.

CORNFORD: But here the old joke about condensing the action of plays into one short sentence (*Waiting for Godot*: Nothing happens—twice!) comes to mind, because basically this play is existential; it's about the characters' spiritual condition. And I'm tempted by an autobiographical reading of that. When McCarthy was interviewed by Oprah Winfrey, he said that his answers to questions about religious belief would depend on what day he was asked, and the play clearly expresses that tension or movement back and forth. There are also coincidences between the play and McCarthy's life. White's father was a government lawyer, as was McCarthy's. Black is from the South, which is where McCarthy grew up. White has read the great works of European culture, as McCarthy has. Black has no possessions, and McCarthy has lived ascetically. My understanding of the play, therefore, is that it expresses unresolved and even irresolvable tensions.

JOSYPH: Are you're saying that it's built into the play that they more or less finish where they started?

CORNFORD: In narrative, characters have to resolve themselves to a course of action, but that would be inconsistent with this play. There's a similar feeling in *No Country for Old Men*, where the narrative is driven by chance, and in *Blood Meridian*, where events arrive like forces of nature. In both books, the characters' actions are usually procedural and reactive. They're driven by the need to manage a situation that already exists. White and Black find themselves in a similar predicament, so a second act would have to either repeat the first act with variations (as in *Godot*), or imply an agency that they don't possess.

JOSYPH: In the Steppenwolf Theatre production of the play that I saw in Manhattan, White was played by Austin Pendleton, a fine actor whose work I have always admired. But it wasn't a great performance. Part of it had to do with the fact that his partner, Freeman Coffey, did not know his lines well enough and was slowing down the exchanges—literally hanging the play up. I also think that the work you'd have done with your actors to sharpen all the beats was not evident. But there was something else: neither actor seemed to know what to do with himself physically. It's almost as if the director had thought: "Well, they aren't going anywhere, so there's not that much to do." Blocking the play more organically could have improved it by at least twenty percent.

CORNFORD: The problems of pace in the verbal exchanges, of clarifying events, and of movement and physical actions are all intertwined for me. I looked at pictures of the Steppenwolf production. It looked as though the table were stage center with Black and White on either side of it, slightly turned out toward the audience. That concerned me. I don't like seeing things falling on the centerline. It creates a balanced image that will tend to make the play feel settled, decided. It's hard to give characters a strong reason to move in a balanced space and therefore to maintain visual dynamism. Also, it seemed to imply that the characters were having a dialogue for the audience: expressing themselves outwardly, as if they were on a talk show. Both of these factors will compromise the physical/visual dynamic, which is generated, for me, by two things: intentions and the given circumstances.

There is a kind of thread, as I think Anne Bogart says, between the actors, and that thread needs to be kept taut. The situation that you describe is a slack thread. Often this can be caused by a technical difficulty, such as a poorly learned text, but often it's indicative of an attitude *toward* the text. I tend to counter this with an exercise on verbal impulses: picking up on the precise words, or information, in the other character's speech that prompts your reply, repeating that from your own point of view, then continuing with your own text. For example:

> Black. What did he die of?
> White. [What did he die of?] Who said he was dead?
> Black. [Dead?] Is he dead?
> White. [Is he dead?] Yes. (16)

This emphasizes the continual effort of each character (while speaking and while listening) to move the conversation in a direction that suits him. Gradually the exercise prompts gestures and movements in space, so that you have a situation, kind of like boxing, where they each try to work the ring to gain an advantage. After the exchange that I just quoted, there's a stage direction: "They sit" (18). This happens after Black tells White that he can see the light in him and blesses him. What that tells me is that the blessing has to register as a significant event, for it changes the rhythm of the scene. It's one of a series of moments in the play where the tension between the characters is pulled very tight, then allowed to release.

JOSYPH: I see your point, but in this case I think "They sit" means that they continue to sit at the table but without speaking. One could translate "They sit" as "Pause," or "Beat," or "Silence." I use "They sit" that way in my own work.

CORNFORD: Aha. Of course! I hadn't thought of that. Well, in a sense we're on the same page: the stage direction, or rather stage description in your version, marks a rhythmic change rather than functioning as an explicit instruction. I'd say the change can be achieved in any number of ways: sitting down, if they've been standing; sitting in silence if they haven't; but it's not the kind of thing I'd explicitly prescribe. The actors did express concern about all that sitting, though, and I know what they meant, as I'm keen to keep altering the picture. But sitting *can* be very active. It's not one posture. There are infinite ways of sitting.

Speaking about ways of sitting: on page 16, White is described as "Looking around the room." This relates to another reason for wanting characters to move: the given circumstances. White is locked in an unfamiliar place and he feels vulnerable. This gives him reason to be taking in his surroundings, responding to simple stimuli: the locks and his memory of Black fastening them; noises from the street; and—we assumed—the sounds of passing trains heard through a window. I encouraged both actors to reorient themselves toward, or away from, these stimuli at different times, and of course that has a multiple effect. It suggests physical actions, it opens them up to the audience, it changes the picture, and it helps to anchor their imagination of the scenario so that they can immerse themselves more deeply in it.

JOSYPH: Whenever I've acted or directed a one-man show, which are often on a practically bare stage, it has seemed to me that every slightest move and every seemingly insignificant prop (and, as well, every piece of wardrobe) carries that much more weight.

CORNFORD: Physical actions are always my first concern. I don't separate them from the text: I see speech as physical action. When I talk to the actors about what they're doing, I use the same language to describe their speech *and* their movement. Physical actions aren't any more or less important when there are only two characters and a few objects, but I do have to be more imaginative and thoughtful about how I *plot* the physical action. And that's a question of finding variety. Plays with more characters and varied settings can make life easier, but every play has a built-in physical life, sometimes notated in detailed stage directions, sometimes in speech, or in a mixture of the two.

JOSYPH: How tied are you to McCarthy's stage directions?

CORNFORD: You need to have a very good reason to disobey a stage direction, but limiting your consideration of physical action to the action notated by the text (even in, say, Beckett's *Acts Without Words*, which are minutely detailed in their stage directions) is an abdication of responsibility on the director's part.

JOSYPH: You mentioned condensing *Godot* into a sentence. I recall watching Elia Kazan in a director's workshop at the Actors Studio. It was the kind of scene where you wouldn't be surprised to see Norman Mailer across the aisle from you, sitting there with his bag of groceries from Gristedes, just taking it all in. Despite this relaxed atmosphere in which no one was expected to say "Holy shit—it's Kazan! It's Norman Mailer!" I was impressed with how rigorous—one could almost say merciless—Kazan was about the director being able to summarize the theme, the through-line, the spine of the entire play in one compelling sentence. "This is a play about . . ." His view was that if a director couldn't be that clear about the point of it all, and thus to consider every moment as a contribution to that, he wasn't ready to clarify things with his actors.

Not every director works this way, and not every playwright would *want* directors to, but if Kazan were on your case over *The Sunset Limited*, what would you say to satisfy that demand?

CORNFORD: This is a play about two men, in an inhumane environment, trying to make their lives mean something significant.

JOSYPH: Given that I've "played" McCarthy here, I shouldn't balk at "playing" Kazan, so I'm going to say that your initial formulation is too weak, abstract—*wishy-washy*—I can't get my teeth into it. "Tommy, Tommy—you want your actors going on stage reminding themselves that *this is about making their lives mean something significant in an inhumane environment*? I can barely *say* it, let alone *act* it. I need you to send me out into the street in front of the theatre, calling people in to see a play about . . . *what*? 'Best show in town! Get your tickets to the search for significance in an inhumane environment!' No! Give me some meat and potatoes."

CORNFORD: "Search for significance" might be an improbable pitch, but it works for churches—or at least it did this Sunday morning as I drove through Brixton and passed half a dozen minibuses pulled up at the side of the road to collect people for services!

## CORNFORD ADDRESSES THE LOCKS ON THE DOOR

JOSYPH: After the presentation, you said that you might prefer to cast Black with an actor who has a larger, more imposing physical presence. I

*Figure 9.3*   Michael Gould and Wale Ojo. Photograph: Peter Josyph.

understand that that would make Black an outward, visible representation of everything about which White is uncertain in these unusual circumstances, but I refuse to believe that Black represents a danger to White, other than that he wants to save White's life and convert him to Christianity. In the New York production, Freeman Coffey was quite an imposing physical figure, but I never once felt that White was afraid of him, or that the play would have made more sense if he were—in fact, the opposite.

CORNFORD: The casting of Black is more about going with what he tells us (which I see no reason to disbelieve) about his previous life and his time in prison. When he questions White's method of putting on his coat, White asks if he means it's effeminate. White also asks if he's a prisoner, and Black flips the question off, saying: "You know better n that" (16). White *sees* Black as physically imposing. Not huge or really frightening, but stronger and more conventionally masculine. I don't think that's ever the real reason he stays, but it gives him pause for long enough to keep him there at moments when, if they were in a bar, say, or on a park bench, he would just walk away.

JOSYPH: It is too far a stretch for me to believe that a man who has saved my life will not respond to my request that he unlock his door. Perhaps in some other play, but not in this one.

CORNFORD: Given that Black responds to White's direct request at the end, the locks function really as a delay mechanism: they force White to want to leave *enough* to be direct and make Black do something he'd prefer not to do. Since White is almost always indirect, the requirement that he be direct to get the door unlocked helps to give him pause at crucial moments.

## CORNFORD ADDRESSES HIS ACTORS

**JOSYPH:** During the short rehearsal that you had with your actors, what troubled them the most?

**CORNFORD:** The biggest complaint was that they didn't know where it was going. There are long passages that tend to meander if they are not tightly controlled, and everything starts to sag.

**JOSYPH:** Poor White has practically no physical activities, and the play doesn't encourage you to invent many, either. You can't have a guy cutting carrots for the stew after he's just tried to step in front of a train.

**CORNFORD:** Right, and actors instinctively *anchor* themselves with actions—the fight, the kiss, whatever—and there aren't many *at all* in this play. They had no trouble with the sections where speech and action go together, such as Black going to get his coat and trying to persuade White to take him along. Or the conversation about the food as they eat. Or working

*Figure 9.4*   Wale Ojo and the Bible. Photograph: Peter Josyph.

out the sums. Where the speech starts to float *away* from action—like those moments in Chekhov when they all say "let's philosophize" and off they go—they started to get frustrated. I had to say look, this must be *really* significant to these men or they wouldn't go on at such length about it, and I would suggest character-driven reasons for that. Sometimes that means big emotional things—Black clearly feels that he *must* save others to atone for what he has done—but also simple things: perhaps neither of them has had a proper conversation with *anyone* for days or even weeks.

JOSYPH: Black doesn't even have a Coltrane solo—he's like the guy in *The L-Shaped Room* who, when Leslie Caron gives him a jazz record, apologizing for the fact that there's no phonograph, holds it up to his ear and tells her he can hear it. Nowadays, with CD players costing practically nothing, is that believable?

CORNFORD: Occasionally an actor would complain that such-and-such *wouldn't happen*, or they would ask: "Why the heck doesn't he do this or that?" I have no patience with those kinds of questions: the characters do what they do *and that's that*. One of the actors balked at the initial situation—he couldn't accept the premise—so I helped to realign his thinking so that he could believe in it. Often that kind of complaint is really just shying away from doing the hard work. It was telling that that complaint came before we really got started, and it didn't come up again. Later complaints about verbiage that isn't well anchored to action were much more genuine and serious, and that's where clear and tight direction makes the difference.

## CORNFORD COMPARES *THE STONEMASON* AND *THE GODFATHER II*

JOSYPH: Would you like to direct *The Stonemason*?

CORNFORD: I'd love to, but I'd need a fairly long leash. I'm drawn to it because it takes a documentary-realist story and molds and blurs it to explore its mysteries. Papaw, Big Ben, and Ben almost become a part of each other, not reliably distinct selves. Their stories and natures are twined. I was watching *The Godfather II* last night, which does a similar thing. The significant difference, though, is that Coppola has the confidence to do it with very simple montage. He dissolves from young Vito to middle-aged Michael and back again, and he juxtaposes the revelation of Fredo's betrayal with Batista's resignation and the ensuing disorder. McCarthy's staging, on the other hand, seems clumsy.

JOSYPH: To me it's worse than that, as if he never bothered to *think* about theatre. When I read those stage directions, or look at Ben *at the podium*, I suspect that John Grady Cole has seen more plays than McCarthy.

CORNFORD: I see what he means in his note about placing the events in "a completed past" (5) and allowing the drama "its right autonomy" (6), but his double-Ben isn't the best way of achieving that—there is a more elegant solution, although I'd need to try out a few options before I could say what it is. But I think his novelist's eye for actions and images that capture larger stories serves him very well.

JOSYPH: How so—by asking for a real stone wall on the stage?

CORNFORD: I *love* the "wall of actual stone" (9). Next to that, the lectern and the podium and all the other scenic stuff in the stage directions sound like clutter to me. But I think the action in *The Stonemason* is eloquent and economical. Another option is, of course, to film it.

JOSYPH: *The Sunset Limited* is filming as we speak, so it may yet happen.

CORNFORD: Or to make a film about the process of staging it.

JOSYPH: What Pacino did with *Richard III*? It'd be nice to do that with McCarthy participating.

CORNFORD: Yes—let's do it.

JOSYPH: Is there an appreciable similarity between Black and any of the characters in *The Stonemason?*

CORNFORD: Yes, there are a lot of echoes. Black has a good deal of Papaw in him. Ben has learned from him that "True stone masonry is not held together by cement but by gravity. That is to say, by the warp of the world. By the stuff of creation itself" (9–10). If Black were on a building site, he'd be saying that. He'd have been similar to Soldier as a kid. He must have gone through Big Ben's despair. And he has Ben's evangelical urge. Ultimately, he's most like Ben in that Ben feels that he, too, has lived the lives of his family, and he has the demanding, god-like example of his grandfather to live up to.

JOSYPH: In both *The Sunset Limited* and *The Stonemason*, a story is told that is, for me, the best thing in the play. In *The Stonemason* it's Papaw's account of Uncle Selman's murder. I once wrote that this was the true kernel of the play, or of a play that McCarthy didn't write. In *Sunset*, it's Black's story of beating the daylights out of the guy who attacked him in prison. You hear that and you think: "O . . . this guy can really write." For me these bits are especially interesting because they are, in fact, short stories—passages of prose, if you will—set within the context of a play, and yet they both stimulate interesting dialogue—Ben's reaction to Papaw is *very* interesting, and White is most interesting in his reaction to Black's story. It's just that in both cases McCarthy has other fish to fry, and he moves on. You probably don't agree with me that if McCarthy had taken each of those stories and trusted in their power to generate a better play than the one he'd had in mind or the one he thought that he was supposed to write, he might have had a pair of minor masterpieces. But I'm wondering whether those two anecdotes leaped out at you as well?

CORNFORD: Yes, they did. The jailhouse story is particularly good because it is introduced at a time when we've had witty repartee and a good set piece (the sums), and it shocks the play into darker and more revealing areas. And yes: McCarthy is clearly more confident in shaping and editing prose than dramatic action. I don't think, though, that using the stories for other plays is the answer. I think the answer is to allow the characters to tell more stories. The stories mustn't be allowed to *detach* themselves from the drama, but, as you say, both of these emerge from the drama and feed back, deeper, into it.

JOSYPH: Have you seen characters in any of McCarthy's novels who resemble Black and White, or are they unique in kind within the McCarthy cannon?

CORNFORD: I can't think of a close similarity in *Blood Meridian*, although White has a project not entirely at odds with Judge Holden's. I read the Judge—and here I'm borrowing heavily from shooting the breeze with Nick Monk—as a figure of Modernity, as Chigurh is a figure of Chance. [1] That desire to categorize and disenchant the world is similar to White's spiritual attitude, but I don't think that's useful to an actor because they go about it in such incompatible ways. From my knowledge of the novels—I haven't read them all—I can't think of a particularly apt parallel, although both Black and White's relationship to a world that has a palpable but unfathomable presence, and yet is distant and carelessly hostile, is reminiscent of the novels. White jumping in front of the train, and Black praying aloud once White has gone, both remind me of the mules vanishing into the ravine in *Blood Meridian*.

JOSYPH: I have an approach—I'd almost call it a rule—in directing an author's work. It's that I don't believe an author's characters exist in any other author's world. Authors do not write generically: the more one has a sense of Pinter the playwright and the world of Pinter's stage, the closer one can come, I think, to freshly interpreting a play or a part without turning Pinter into someone else. Arthur Miller's characters are in Arthur Miller's world, Williams's characters are in *his* world, Beckett's are in Beckett's and so on. Each of those worlds might suggest unlimited potential and variation, but they aren't interchangeable. On Broadway, I saw John Malkovich as Biff in the Dustin Hoffman *Death of a Salesman*. It was a compelling performance, but it wasn't a Miller Biff, it was a Sam Shepard Biff, and it disrupted the unity and overall force of the production. Of course one could argue that since Miller was involved in the casting, my theory is bilgewater—but I would argue that either the choice was a mistake or Malkovich was underdirected to partake in Miller's world. I mention this because it seems to me that if an actor were to study, say, *Blood Meridian, Suttree, Child of God, Outer Dark*, he could have a sense of what might constitute a Cormac McCarthy character, at least insofar as he would have a strong sense of McCarthy's world—the world of McCarthy's prose. But if he were then to read *The Stonemason* or *The Sunset Limited*, he would see that those characters would never find their way into any of the novels. The two worlds seem set apart. There might be themes or concerns and even literary approaches that cross over, but McCarthy is *a very different writer* for the stage. Do you find that to be true?

CORNFORD: I absolutely agree about directing *within the author's world*, and thank you for clarifying my uneasy feeling about Malkovich's Biff.

Yes, McCarthy is a different writer for the stage. The dialogue is noticeably fuller in the plays, although parts of *The Stonemason* have something like the novels' economy of speech because there is more scope for action and behavior to do the work. The characters in the plays feel softer, less *hewn*. On the page they don't have the piercing other-worldliness of the novels, although I think some of that quality should find its way onto the stage. I often find myself frustrated in the theatre that a novelist's care hasn't been taken to imagine, edit, and creatively distort "reality" to fit the world of the play. Often they have only adhered to the conventions which seem to gather like barnacles on playwrights. I try to avoid that by beginning with simple clues in the dialogue. Black's clothes aren't described, but we know that he was on his way to work, so what kind of job does he do? Apparently the people he works with will know he's not coming if he hasn't turned up and won't be too worried, so perhaps it's a casual kind of work. When I first read the play, I was midway into *The Wire* on DVD, so I pictured the ex-drug dealer Cutty out of jail and doing yardwork before he sets up his boxing gym. Looking like that, Black could conceivably not have met a professor before and therefore be "studyin the ways of professors" (7), and he could conceivably not know what *primacy* means. He also has to reassure White that "Everthing in here is clean" (40), so the apartment must look shabby. After I've gathered this kind of information, I start to think more widely about the kind of world we're in. Here I used the novels as a guide. They have a rich, symbolic texture. Simple things resonate powerfully, like the coin in "A Drowning Incident" that is clutched by the boy while he runs to see the puppies—puppies that he exchanged for the coin—vanish into the water after they have been shot. We can learn from that in designing the plays in the way that we select objects, and in the ways they are handled by actors.

JOSYPH: Can you learn from the novels in creating the mood or the climate of the piece?

CORNFORD: Yes, the novels can be very helpful. While preparing *Sunset*, I thought of the unbearable tension of episodes such as the wolf-trapper in *The Crossing*, the insistence on violence as a natural law, the harsh landscapes, the wind, the rags of plastic wrapping in *Cities of the Plain*, and McCarthy's attraction to other writers who deal with issues of life and death, as Richard B. Woodward reports in "Cormac McCarthy's Venomous Fiction." All of that clarified for me the image of the train coming through a deserted station at 80 mph; it began to reverberate through the characters, and it helped set the stakes for the play. I suspect it sets them much higher than they would be if you hadn't read the novels, and that may be a failing of the play. But the clues for a director are there. "A black ghetto" (5) might be strictly inaccurate and/or out of date, but it communicates the atmosphere. The clues might be clearer if McCarthy had seen more theatre and had consequently gained a more liberated sense of its possibilities, but they are there.

## CORNFORD COMES TO AMERICA

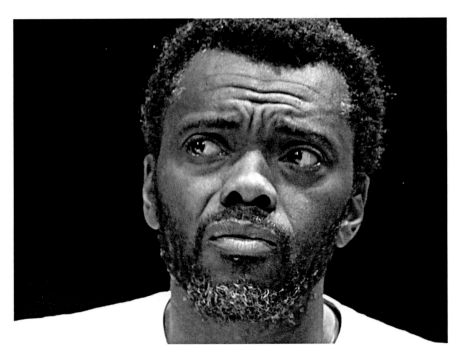

*Figure 9.5*   Wale Ojo. Photograph: Peter Josyph.

**JOSYPH:** When you are using an English actor, how American do they need to sound if the part has been written with an ear for local speech that's as good as McCarthy's?

**CORNFORD:** Very. When I directed David Mamet's *The Shawl* at the Gate in London, I asked an American actor I knew to read for me. It was dumb of me to ask him, because I was never going to get three American actors, and so he was always going to make the others sound inauthentic. I cast an English actor instead. An audience's ear will attune itself comfortably to stage-American, providing it is reasonably consistent. But it's not so simple. The other thing I noticed about my American friend was that he *looked* American. It was unmistakably in his body before he opened his mouth. It drives me mad when the people in, say *The Cherry Orchard*, or *Blood Wedding*, are *so English*. Their behavior just doesn't match the play. I have a similar feeling when we visit my wife's family in the Yorkshire Dales. I'm a Londoner: I do things quickly. People in rural communities have an entirely different pace, and it registers in their accent, their movements, their body rhythms—everything that expresses their relationship with the world. *They fit the landscape.*

Also, it's not simply a case of *how American* my actors have to sound in the sense of their correspondence to "the real thing." That notional "real thing" keeps moving out of reach. White is American, but he grew up in Washington, he's the son of a lawyer, he's a university professor, he's lived in New York for some time—and so on. You can't consciously manipulate that kind of specificity, but you can move toward it by thinking not of *an accent* but of a character's relationship with the world, of which his accent is a part. *No Country for Old Men* is brilliantly cast in this respect. Tommy Lee Jones and Josh Brolin fit the landscape so well, and Javier Bardem is perfectly out of place. So, while I might have to accept compromises with the odd vowel sound, the characters have to *belong to the play*. Learning the accent and finding McCarthy's speech rhythms would be part of the actors' process, but the ability to absorb them deeply into the body is what ultimately counts for me.

**JOSYPH:** Despite a world of reservations about *The Stonemason*, I once offered to direct it in the Kentucky town in which it is set, at the Actors Theatre of Louisville. Would it interest you to direct a full-scale production of either play in the States?

**CORNFORD:** Yes, I'd love to direct them both anywhere, and doing them in America—such as *The Stonemason* in Kentucky—would be a felicity I'd want to exploit. It would allow me to get to the meat of the piece more quickly. I've taught acting to third-year students from the Guthrie/University of Minnesota's BFA program in London for the last five years. We've talked about my going out there to direct, which I'd love to do—I'm waiting for the invitation—especially with the students I've taught. Teaching a system is great, but they can't really get it into their bones until they've felt it in rehearsal and a run of performances. These students are basically Meisner-trained, which I have found to be an enormously helpful foundation, and it's not common in this country. Many English actors are used to being asked to reproduce an effect, and that generates a kind of acting which I find arid, self-conscious and, frankly, distasteful. It often exploits the character to tell us *what the production thinks of them.* And there is certainly more a culture of *practicing* in America. I teach at The Actors Centre in London, which offers marvelous opportunities for actors to develop their craft, but it is scandalously underused by the profession because we've all allowed ourselves to become demoralized by funding cuts and commercial cynicism. My advice to a young actor is to move in with a musician or a dancer and practice as much as they do. Whatever the dangers and excesses of the Method, the Actors Studio is a landmark, and that in itself sends out a message. We don't have that.

JOSYPH: I have speculated that it might help me to solve, or prove unsolvable, the problems of *The Stonemason* if I undertook to play the part of Ben, a character who annoys the hell out of me. Of course as a director one is always, in some sense, playing all the parts, but as a director who also acts, would it interest you to perform as either Black or White? As a heathen and heretic, I'd like to play Black. I'd like to see whether—to paraphrase *Godfather I*—if I used all of my powers and skills, I could convert White to the Good Book so that he, like Billy Bob's character in *The Apostle*, falls to his knees and prays with me at the end! McCarthy, in the audience, would say: "Wait . . . that's not in the script . . . what the hell's happening?"

CORNFORD: That's interesting. Your idea of playing Black to see if you can convert White is actually one of my most common notes: *I want you to go on and make sure that today you get what you want—try to change the ending.* It has the most profound effect on a play if the actors take that idea seriously. So often I go to the theatre and watch a bunch of people auditioning alongside each other for their next job, or trying to convince me that this play is funny or moving or that their character is clever, or a victim, or sexy or goofy—it's like watching a very long advert, and I think: *Don't give me the advert, I've paid for the play.* Part of that play is the continual tension between *what could happen* and *what ends up happening.* My religious instincts, like McCarthy's I guess, move back and forth between Black and White, and I frequently find myself at both ends of a spectrum, so I suppose I should play them both!

JOSYPH: Do you believe that Jesus is in this room with us?

CORNFORD: No, but I believe it could be a useful thought!

JOSYPH: For an all-out production of *Sunset,* would you encourage your actors to improvise, take the play in different directions, in order to come back around to the page?

CORNFORD: Yes. I always ask actors to improvise and continue to do so even at the stage of verbal accuracy and repeating detailed actions. I think of acting like a sport. Rehearsals have to train actors to play instinctively, with shape and intelligence and purpose. Asking an actor to do that without basing the work on improvisation is like asking a boxer to go into the ring having only punched the bag.

## CORNFORD DEFENDS THE UMP IN *THE SUNSET LIMITED*

*Figure 9.6*   Michael Gould. Photograph: Peter Josyph.

JOSYPH: You've mentioned boxing, so, let's go a couple of rounds. Every time that I see the play, or reread it, I have this gnawing sense that it's not really a play. It's called "A Novel in Dramatic Form," but it isn't a novel either, not a McCarthy novel. It's a dialogue, but then so is Galileo's *Two World Systems*. If *Sunset* were submitted to me as an artistic director, I'd say: "Cut it to shreds, and use that as the basis for starting the play again." I'd have said the same about *The Stonemason*. For me, *Sunset* is too much glibness and banter—not enough theatrical *ump*. There's more *ump* in one exchange—*any* exchange—in *No Man's Land* than there is in all of *Sunset*. All the more impressive that you managed so much *ump* into your reading.

CORNFORD: I honestly feel that the *ump* is there. Yes, Pinter is more availably dramatic—usually—and the introduction of two further characters in *No Man's Land* takes that play beyond its initial premise on a trajectory that *Sunset* declines. But that is partly to do with Pinter's chosen themes and with his experience of the theatre and the theatrical. *Sunset* is, in some ways, a challenge to the theatre because it *eschews theatrics*. But it does that with a purpose in mind. That purpose is in some ways novelistic in that watching it is more like sitting down to read a boxing match than to watch it. But in its construction it is nothing like a novel, it's more of a dialogue in the philosophical sense. That doesn't disqualify it from being a play, though. As for the glibness and banter, it is the director's job, as it is in, say, '*Night Mother*, or *The Importance of Being Earnest*, to discover what's *driving* that. I've seen Wilde, tediously, given *the style* treatment (you know—all that *wit*), and, on rare occasions, I've seen that handbag and the name Earnest *really matter*. And I can imagine a '*Night Mother* that fails to deliver *the heart* in the wit of the play.

*Sunset* has the feeling of trying to be long enough to justify the ticket price, but it's a meditative piece and therefore we *need* the time to get into its rhythm. I remember seeing a beautiful production of *Death and the Ploughman* by Johannes von Saaz at the Gate in London. Medieval ploughman argues with Death, who has taken his wife, then he comes to terms with it—*the end*. I was rapt. And I've been bored out my mind by plays you would think could not possibly fail. I'm not saying the script isn't important, it's vital—it's very very hard to be better than your script—but still, it's what you do with it that counts.

JOSYPH: If you were to cast me as White and we had a first reading round the table and you asked us to air our opinions, I would say: "As a New Yorker, I find it annoying that McCarthy, Master of Research, didn't bother to get the fundamentals of New York subways. No New Yorker, Tom, not even someone who came to it from Mars, would refer to a subway station or a subway stop as *a train station* or *a train depot*; and despite the fact that commuters ride the subway, they aren't *commuter trains* (49): that term is reserved for trains coming in from the outer boroughs or from Jersey, Long Island, Connecticut. As for White saying 'There wasnt any post' (13), if there weren't any posts then we weren't in the subway! The fact that White refers to Bellevue Hospital as 'up' (47) suggests that McCarthy didn't even consult a Manhattan map. So I need some help here. I can accept the convention that we both refer to some express roaring through the 155th Street station as The Sunset Limited, but I need to know what happened, physically, in the subway. In Manhattan, if you want to kill yourself, you walk to the edge of the platform, wait until you see the lights of the train, and step down onto the tracks—it's only a yard or two drop—and the train will do the work. It's not pole vaulting, it's not the broad jump—*you just step off the platform*. How did Black save my life? What was this 'amazin leap' (12)? If I were 'haulin ass' (13) and took some mighty leap that sent me 'off the edge of the platform' (14), Black would have to have been down there already if he were going to catch me—and that makes no sense."

CORNFORD: Exactly. The matters of terminology need a rewrite, unless the mistakes are deliberate, in which case I need to know why we are deliberately confusing New Yorkers in the audience but not anyone else. As for the backstory, I got images of trains and stations and laid out things on my desk and tried to work it out and came to the same conclusion. McCarthy can only have intended that either (a) White imagined the leap and was actually caught by Black, who was running behind him down the platform, or (b) Black was on the tracks, or (c) Black is an angel who appeared from nowhere, or (d) the play takes place in a distorted dream-reality (which isn't made sufficiently clear). Or, I suppose, (e) Black *is the train*. My solution with the actors was to ask them, apologetically, to say it as if it made sense, but I did also use it as evidence for the surreal atmosphere that I wanted them to capture. That's the only reason I can think of for McCarthy to present the story so unclearly—that he wants it to come across as mysterious, as not quite right. If that's correct, I think it needs to be done with more clarity. Whether or not it's a lapse, it has the feeling of one.

## CORNFORD PROVES AN UPSTART CROW

JOSYPH: The reading that you directed took place in the shire of Shakespeare, where you are a man of the theatre in residence. As a teacher, writer, and director, you're working on something called The *Hamlet* Project, which entails excavating and tributing the craftsmanship of earlier directors and their approach to that play. I have referred to McCarthy as a Rhode Island Shakespeare, so let's end by connecting the two. You've worked at Shakespeare's Globe on the South Bank of London,

*Figure 9.7*    Wale Ojo. Photograph: Peter Josyph.

a great venue for Shakespeare. When I tried to imagine *Sunset* there, I couldn't—it seemed as if it were the anti-Globe—until I tossed overboard that little apartment and all the stage directions and the actors started *moving* in a much wider choice of personal spaces. That set me wondering. You require a good reason to ignore an author's stage directions. Let's presuppose that a very good reason is to try something fresh and unique to make the play work in ways that the author hadn't imagined. Can you envision a production of *Sunset* in which McCarthy's stage directions would be thrown out the window and there are no locks because there isn't any door and they aren't stuck at the table because there isn't any table? Could a more abstract—perhaps you could say surreal—approach to the play be productive? Or, to go back to what set me off on this, could you find a way of doing it at the Globe?

CORNFORD: Yes. But abstraction takes us *away from action*, and therefore from acting. Surreal is a more achievable goal. We'd end up with a more Beckettian play, but it's an attractive idea. The difficulty with abstraction is that it has to be set *somewhere*. *Waiting for Godot* isn't nowhere; it's by a tree by a road, and there is a clear sense of time, of waiting and hunger and so on. Likewise Hamm's parents, in *Endgame*, aren't notional beings: they are people who live in dustbins and eat biscuits. All drama must be realistic on some level because it is constructed from concrete actions. I can imagine a very bad *Sunset* at the Globe that would cut references to the original setting and turn the play into a philosophical dialogue. A good one would require a new setting and consequently some rewriting. Characters can be confined in huge spaces as well as small ones. I'm thinking of Cary Grant at the crossroads in *North by Northwest*, and of all those McCarthy deserts. Setting *Sunset* in one would open the actors out and it would use the epic dimension of the Globe, as well as giving them something simple and concrete to play. The Coen Brothers do this very well in *No Country*. They capture the way the book yokes the bizarre and the mythic into its uninflected view. It's a testament to their craft as filmmakers—and to their attentive reading of McCarthy—that they can match McCarthy's prose in doing this without self-consciously striving for effect. The encounters with everyday life—Moss and the guys by the border, Chigurh and the suburban kids after the car crash—gently underscore the story's surreality without allowing it to settle comfortably into a genre or divorcing it *from* reality. That would be the challenge at the Globe, but in a sense it's always the challenge—I'm back to talking about the world of the author and of the play. What you'd need to do at the Globe is to match McCarthy's world to the building.

## NOTES

1. See Monk.

## WORKS CITED

Cox, Brian. *Salem to Moscow: An Actor's Odyssey*. London: Methuen, 1991.
Hall, Wade, and Rick Wallach, eds. *Sacred Violence: A Reader's Companion to Cormac McCarthy. Volume 2: Cormac McCarthy's Western Novels*. El Paso: Texas Western Press, 2002.
McCarthy, Cormac. "A Drowning Incident." *The Phoenix*, March 1960: 3–4.
———. *The Stonemason*. Hopewell: Ecco, 1994.
———. *The Sunset Limited: A Novel in Dramatic Form*. New York: Dramatists Play Service Inc., 2006.
Monk, Nick. "'An Impulse to Action, an Undefined Want': Modernity, Flight and Crisis in the Border Trilogy and *Blood Meridian*." Hall and Wallach 2. 83–103.
Winfrey, Oprah. Interview with Cormac McCarthy, June 1, 2008. http://www.oprah.com/oprahsbookclub/Oprahs-Exclusive-Interview-with-Cormac-McCarthy-Video.
Woodward, Richard B. "Cormac McCarthy's Venomous Fiction." *The New York Times Magazine* 19 April 1992: 28–31, 36, 40.

# 10  Cold Dimensions, Little Worlds
## Self, Death, and Motion in
## *Suttree* and Beckett's *Murphy*

*Euan Gallivan*

If there was one point on which a significant number of early reviewers of Cormac McCarthy's *The Road* (2006) were united—that is, other than their near-uniform levels of enthusiasm—it was in their identification of the novel's particularly "Beckettian" quality. In the UK, for instance, the *Times* described it as "written in a stripped-down, but intermittently lyrical, style that recalls Beckett at his most elliptical"; likewise, Alan Warner, writing in *The Guardian*, suggested that McCarthy at times sails "close to the prose of late Beckett" (7). Such comparisons were relatively widespread; indeed, the collection of review excerpts found on the Random House website alone contains no fewer than four other explicit references to the 1969 Nobel Laureate.[1] However, this Beckett-like quality is by no means a new development in McCarthy's work; rather, I argue that Beckett stands alongside Joyce, Faulkner, Twain, and the many others who make up the complex intertextual web of his fourth novel, *Suttree* (1979). But while *The Road*'s reviewers consistently drew parallels with the minimalist Beckett of works such as *The Unnameable* and *How It Is*, and with the absurdist Beckett of the familiar dramatic works such as *Waiting for Godot* and, specifically, *Endgame*, *Suttree*'s affinities lie with a less familiar Beckett: that of his first published novel, *Murphy* (1938).

Of all the references to Beckett in *The Road*'s early reviews, Adam Mars-Jones' comments in the *Observer* are particularly noteworthy. In "Life After Armageddon," Mars-Jones suggests that the novel occasionally comes "uncomfortably" close to Beckett's style—Beckett being the "literary figure who seems to have a copyright on desolation and futility, who wrote about last things almost from the first" (27). Such a view engages with what both Martin Essler and Simon Critchley, writing over thirty years apart, identified as the foremost cliché of Beckett studies: in short, that Beckett is a nihilist, his *ouevre* a celebration of the "meaninglessness of existence." Georg Lukács' chapter on "The Ideology of Modernism" in *The Meaning of Contemporary Realism* (1957) is the most well-known incidence of such an interpretation of Beckett's work. In Lukács' analysis, which takes modernism as almost a synonym for nihilism, Beckett finds himself in the company of Proust, Joyce, Faulkner, and Kafka: a group of writers united, despite otherwise innumerable differences, by an obsession with psychopathology. This obsession takes the form of a "negation of outward reality" (25), which Lukács objects to because he sees depiction of this reality as central to a politically and socially engaged realist tradition. He thus argues that whatever protest exists within such a negation—which he interprets as a "desire to escape from the reality of capitalism" (36)—is merely an empty gesture that "is destined to lead nowhere; it is an escape into nothingness" (29). And while his greatest scorn is reserved for Kafka, Beckett remains high on Lukács' hit list: *Molloy*, the opening volume of his famous Trilogy, is a vision of the "utmost human degradation," and Beckett himself is labeled "perverse" (32).[2]

If one defines nihilism in Nietzschean terms as a "will to nothingness" (66), it is easy to see why Beckett's work would invite such accusations, concerned as it often is with the end of what in his 1931 monograph on Proust he termed the "suffering of being" (19)—and even more so when we consider that one of the philosophers who looms over *Murphy*'s rigorously dualistic vision is none other than Arthur Schopenhauer, the foremost exponent of that nihilistic European Buddhism which in the *Genealogy of Morals* Nietzsche identified as the most sinister symptom of late nineteenth-century European culture (5). In his masterwork, *The World as Will and Representation* (1818), Schopenhauer accepted and elaborated upon the fundamental distinction between appearance and thing-in-itself as set out in Kant's *Critique of Pure Reason*, but gave it a pessimistic twist—taking a "giant step beyond the unknowability of transcendent reality" (Jacquette 72), Schopenhauer identified the thing-in-itself as "Will," a blind, non-individuated, objectless desire or striving which underlies all empirical acts of volition, precipitates all phenomenal competition and discord, and gave rise to his infamous pronouncement that "all life is suffering" (I.310).[3]

As a result of this, Schopenhauer has traditionally been viewed as the arch-pessimist of post-Enlightenment philosophy, whose negativity stands in contrast to the supposedly "optimistic" Nietzschean conception of Will. However, this binary, as Robert Wicks has pointed out (29), has long been overemphasized, and Schopenhauer's pessimism is much more complicated and nuanced than many have given him credit for. The same is true of Beckett, although commentators have been much more forthright in questioning his nihilistic image: Theodor Adorno, Gilles Deleuze, and Alain Badiou are just three of the many influential philosophers and literary theorists who have lined up to defend Beckett against the charges laid by Lukács. One of the most powerful and eloquent defences of Beckett came on the occasion of his being awarded the Nobel Prize for Literature in 1969. Addressing the assembled audience in Beckett's absence, Karl Ragnar Gierow of the Swedish Academy described the worldview of the new Nobel Laureate as one which descends to the very depths of negativity yet simultaneously portrays the human condition in the lights of "fellow-feeling" and "charity." As Gierow pointed out, such a worldview has precedents in the work of Schopenhauer and has its basis in the difference between an "easily-acquired pessimism that rests content with untroubled scepticism, and a pessimism that is dearly bought and which penetrates to mankind's utter destitution." Gierow's distinction between these two forms of pessimism is crucial, for while the former proceeds on the assumption that nothing is really of any value, the latter proceeds from quite the opposite standpoint, from the belief that "what is worthless cannot be degraded. The perception of human degradation . . . is not possible if human values are denied." It is in this context that Beckett's shadow casts itself over what is arguably one of McCarthy's most optimistic works, an exception perhaps to the "gothic and nihilistic mood" (1) which Vereen Bell saw as prevailing in McCarthy's writing up to and including *Blood Meridian*.

As readers of McCarthy will know, a "subtle obsession with uniqueness" (113) troubled the dreams of Cornelius Suttree, and justifiably so. Indeed, so closely does he resemble Beckett's "hero" in this regard that he might well be thought of as the *Othermurphy*. Like Suttree, Murphy is intelligent—college-educated in fact—but has turned his back on academia in favor of a vocational joblessness. Like Suttree, he has a sneaking admiration for the insane; both characters are fixated by order, and both undertake a quest for a life's meaning in the face of death: a quest which is, in each case, jeopardized by a romantic entanglement with a prostitute. Both novels are, of course, characterized by a rich vein of humour, but more significant are the various thematic points of contact between the two novels. In particular, I argue that what William Spencer has referred to as Suttree's "mystical" experiences can be understood in reference to Beckett's description of the "three zones" of Murphy's mind, and as such, discussion of the two novels side by side casts light on many of *Suttree*'s philosophic concerns, particularly as they relate to the human consciousness of death, the possibility of transcending selfhood, and the validity of non- or supra-rational knowledge.

*Murphy*'s dualistic vision is established in chapter 6 of that novel, when the narrator reluctantly reaches the point "where a justification of the expression 'Murphy's mind' has to be attempted" (63). First, the reader learns that Murphy "felt himself split in two, a body and a mind" (64). The body is the locus of outer reality, or the "big world" (8) as Beckett calls it. In this realm, physical needs, bodily desires, and rationality prevail. It is strictly deterministic, as is clear from the novel's opening: "The sun shone, having no alternative, on the nothing new. Murphy sat out of it, as though he were free, in a mew in West Brompton" (5). *As though he were free—* clearly, no freedom can exist in the big world. True autonomy exists for Murphy only in the little world, or the world of his mind. Murphy must suppress the body and curb his fleshly desires, for it is only in this way that entry into the pure interiority of the mind can be obtained—a withdrawal which is, significantly, characterized in terms of a Schopenhauerian "will-lessness" (66). Murphy's mind is not an instrument but a refuge, entry into which is obtained via his bizarre ritual of tying himself to a rocking chair. Quieting his body in this way, Murphy escapes from the material. Certainly, the longing for such an escape is not unfamiliar to Suttree, and there are days in which he too "so wanted for some end to things that he'd have taken up his membership among the dead" (405). Such passages have led a number of critics to suggest that Suttree courts death; that he, like Murphy, would see it as "a relief from the burdens and torments of consciousness" (Shelton 73). But while this sense of respite is occasioned when death is viewed from a purely *subjective* standpoint, there is in Schopenhauer's system another reason why death, considered this time from the *objective* standpoint, should not be feared, and it is this which has a larger bearing on *Suttree*'s metaphysic.

Schopenhauer argues that what we fear in death is not pain, but "the extinction and end of the individual, which it openly proclaims itself to be" (I.283). However, as the blind man tells Billy Parham in *The Crossing*, "*Si el mundo es ilusión la pérdida del mundo es ilusión también*" (283)—if the world is an illusion then the loss of the world is an illusion also. Those who become aware that individuality is an illusion will deduce that death, existing as it does as a fact of the phenomenal world alone, is also mere illusion. Suttree seems to be aware of this, conceding that "[d]eath is what the living carry with them. A state of dread, like some uncanny foretaste of a bitter memory. But the dead do not remember and nothingness is not a curse" (153). However, since both life and death are temporal concepts (in the sense that they indicate beginning and end), neither has meaning in relation to the Will, it being independent of the *principium individuationis* or principle of individuation. Will, of which we are merely objectifications, is indestructible, and we can take solace therefore that there is something within us, the innermost kernel of our Being in fact, which transcends death. It is this very sense of conflictedness over the self's annihilation which Spencer, in slightly different terms, attributes to Suttree. Suttree, Spencer argues, "has dreaded death because it means the annihilation of the self," but later experiences the annihilation of the self as "something rapturous and unspeakably enlightening. He thus comes to view the annihilation of the self as the *transcendence* of the self" (92).

This conflictedness manifests itself for Suttree in something akin to a sublime experience. He wonders at the vastness of the cosmos and on several occasions lies in the grass looking up at the heavens, watching a "star spill across the sky" (159). Later he watches "the cold indifferent dark, the blind stars beaded on their tracks and mitered satellites and geared and pinioned planets all reeling though the black of space" (284). Faced with sights such as these, "[t]he enormity of the universe filled him with a strange sweet woe" (352). The oxymoronic nature of this "strange sweet woe" captures the essence of the mathematical sublime, which Schopenhauer categorizes as the experience achieved by "contemplation of the infinite greatness of the universe in space and time [whereby] . . . we feel ourselves reduced to nothing" (I.205). Yet when—in consequence of our awareness that there is no object without subject, that each individual can rightly say "the world is my representation" (I.3)—we intuitively recognize ourselves as being "the conditional supporter of all worlds . . . our dependence on it is annulled by its dependence on us . . . and [we] are therefore not oppressed but exalted by its immensity" (I.205). All difference, even that between humans and galaxies, is conditioned by the forms of consciousness, the *principium individuationis*, and our feeling of exaltation proceeds from the simultaneous annihilation and transcendence of our individuality, the feeling that we are at one with the universe on a level which is nevertheless inaccessible to consciousness.

If the dualism between thing-in-itself and phenomenon invoked by both *Suttree* and *Murphy* distinguishes between two levels of consciousness— one rationalistic, the other intuitive—Suttree's project might be characterized as an attempt to fathom the relationship between the two. He wonders "how does the world mesh with the world beyond the world" (453) but the answer is beyond the power of, and is in fact obstructed by, reason: as much as Suttree turns his back on the world of order represented by his father, his knowledge remains shaped "by the constructions of a mind obsessed with form" (427). The famous biscuit episode in *Murphy* is typical of such obstruction. Surveying his lunch of five differently flavored biscuits, Murphy laments the fact that his infatuation with the ginger, which he always eats last, and his prejudice against the anonymous, which he always eats first, reduces the number of ways in which he can consume his meal to a mere six. He realizes, however, that if he could overcome both his infatuation and his prejudice, "then the assortment would spring to life before him, dancing the radiant measure of its total permutability, edible in a hundred and twenty ways" (57). Struggling to assert his appetitive autonomy, Murphy is constrained by desire. In like manner, Suttree's obsessions with those "small enigmas of time and space and death" (376) defer his metaphysical insight, and he is drawn back from the edge of knowledge to more fleshly concerns.

In one of *Suttree*'s extended comic sequences, Gene Harrogate descends into the caves running underneath Knoxville in an attempt to dynamite his way through the wall of one of the city's subterranean bank vaults. The incident, while it is imbued with the same vein of humour which attends most of Harrogate's escapades, illustrates symbolically the difficulty of accessing the nonrational dimension. Like Suttree, Harrogate wonders how the world meshes with the "world beyond the world," but he tries to solve his conundrum through the use of maps—maps which, as the ultimate rationalistic abstraction of the city in spatial terms, prove useless. Attempting to establish some spatial correlation, Harrogate pushes markers through cracks in the sidewalks above him, which he never manages to find again on the outside. Eventually, he "began to suspect some dimensional displacement in these descents to the underworld, some disparity unaccountable between the above and below" (262). In the framework of the novel's thematic preoccupations, the caves evoke that world beyond the sensory experience which Suttree courts, and the episode as a whole makes it clear that the relationship between this world and the other cannot be mapped in such terms.

In Schopenhauer's thesis, time and space, the forms of the principle of sufficient reason and of the *principium individuationis*, are only applicable to the world as representation. The underground caverns into which Harrogate ventures, which are analogous to the world as Will, or which lie behind representation, are thus presented as having an unaccountable spatiotemporal relationship with the world aboveground. Lost, trapped, and injured after he mistakenly blows up a main sewage pipeline, the light that Harrogate carries is extinguished and he is enveloped in darkness "so absolute that he became without boundary to himself, as large as all the universe and small as anything that was" (274–75). It is telling that McCarthy's city, the ultimate expression of humankind's drive for form and order, is built on such foundations—Suttree, immersed in that world of form, "had not known how hollow the city was" (276). Such hollowness signifies the naïveté of human faith in the constructions of mind, and just as all phenomena are fated to revert back into that nothingness which is pure, blind Will, so Knoxville itself teeters on the brink of the abyss, as illustrated by a bus which disappears through a crack in the road.

In the face of such difficulties, Suttree courts those whom he believes might be able to teach him something about the true nature of existence and betrays some admiration as he moves among those preachers "haranguing a lost world with a vigor unknown to the sane" (66). Likewise, Murphy takes a job at the Magdalen Mental Mercyseat, the padded cells of which were a "more creditable representation of . . . the little world" (103) than he had ever been able to imagine. He revels in his proximity to the insane, who, due to their complete disconnection from the outer world, epitomize his ideal state. He takes particular interest in one Mr. Endon, who is possessed of "a psychosis so limpid and imperturbable" (105) that Murphy is inexorably drawn toward it. In McCarthy's novel, Suttree visits his Aunt Alice at the asylum and is surprised to find the certified "invested with a strange authority" (431), an authority shared by the boy he passes in the previous chapter who possessed "the most rudimentary brain and yet seemed possessed of news in the universe denied right forms," gibbering "word perhaps of things known raw, unshaped by the constructions of a mind obsessed with form" (427). For Suttree, the insane, like those possessed of genius, are closer to truth because they are able to see more clearly beyond the relations between phenomena to the flux at the heart of existence; they are marked by the knowledge that all life is suffering and that it is our fate to perish into nothingness. Thus he sees madness as an authentic mode of existence, a transcendence of rationality and its attendant obsessions with time and space; it is a window through the transience of phenomena to the universality and timelessness of the Ideas.

I too now find myself, in the interests of further considering the implications of this line of thought, at the point where a justification of the expression 'Murphy's mind' has to be attempted. Beyond his initial Cartesian dualism, Murphy's mind is further split into three zones, the light, the half-light, and the dark (65). In the first, or light, zone "were the forms with parallel . . . the elements of physical experience available for a new arrangement," which is the world of individuated phenomena. In the second zone were forms without parallel, where the pleasure is in contemplation. These forms correspond to the Platonic Ideas, the direct or unmediated manifestations of the thing-in-itself, which in Schopenhauer's system form the objects of aesthetic experience. In the most important zone, the third or dark zone, which is characterized as a state of "will-lessness," there is a "a flux of forms, a perpetual coming together and falling asunder of forms" (65), which captures the essence of the unmediated thing-in-itself. Movement toward Murphy's ideal state involves him spending less time in the light and more in the dark, and he becomes increasingly withdrawn until he is "not free but a mote in the darkness of absolute freedom" (66).

Importantly, the first of Suttree's mystical experiences is attendant upon him too going to great lengths of will-lessness. Having hiked into the mountains, Suttree spends some weeks in a state of deprivation until he feels that

> Everything had fallen from him. He scarce could tell where his being ended or the world began nor did he care. He lay on his back in the gravel, the earth's core sucking his bones, a moment's giddy vertigo with this illusion of falling outward through blue and windy space, over the offside of the planet, hurtling through the high thin cirrus. (286)

Proximity to death leads Suttree to recognize that it is nothing to be feared: it is merely a reversion to that universal anarchic flux from which he, like the rest of the world, was born. Unable to tell where he ends or the world begins, Suttree approaches a metaphysical understanding of his connection with the world by virtue of their common source. Later, in the crescendo towards the novel's climax, he finds himself in a hospital and, no longer caring whether he lives or dies, imagines himself being voided "[i]nto a cold dimension without space without time where all was motion" (452), another evocation of the Will's blind flux. Suttree sees the doctors:

> Phased out to abstractions of color and form that severed in elastic parallax like colorplate ghosts in a printing and parted forever. Whereon new forms arose and wheeled all and along, good carousel of crazies. (453)

The invocation of unceasing movement, the rising and falling of forms, signals Suttree's knowledge of the world's ephemerality; that the "particular things," as Schopenhauer says, "[a]rise and pass away; they are always becoming and never are" (I.129).

The "cold dimension without space without time and where all was motion" also illustrates the paradoxical character of Will: he is in a dimension where there is neither space nor time, yet all is motion, which is nothing more than the movement across space in time. Yet in the previous chapter, when Suttree learns of Ab Jones's death, he likens Doll's gaping ocular cavity to "the pineal eye in atavistic reptiles watching through time, through conjugations of space and matter to that still center where the living and the dead are one" (447). This dimension, taking both references into the account, is simultaneously stillness *and* motion. In Schopenhauer's system, "permanence no more belongs to the will, considered as thing-in-itself . . . than does transitoriness, since 'passing away' and transitoriness are determinations valid in time alone, whereas the will and the pure subject of knowing lie outside time" (I.282). The same can be said of movement. As evocations of Will, Suttree's extra-phenomenal stance invokes both the static *and* the motile, yet is represented adequately by neither. It is akin to Murphy's third zone, in which he is "not free but a mote in the darkness of absolute freedom . . . a missile without provenance or target, caught up in a tumult of non-Newtonian motion" (66).

As numerous critics have pointed out, it appears that as a result of his experiences, Suttree has overcome his dividedness and achieved a sense of unity—the obsession with uniqueness which was exacerbated by the remembrance of his dead twin has been quieted. The twin, his replicated image, which had previously diminished his otherwise exclusive claim to Suttree-ness, weakening the conviction with which he could claim ontological independence, becomes less significant, and he ends up occupying a position similar to that of the novel's other twins, Vernon and Fernon, who display a happy acceptance of their sameness. And just as Vernon and Fernon "despise a wristwatch," so does Suttree's acceptance of his sameness have as its corollary a reconfiguration of his obsession with time. No longer subject to what Mr. Compson in Faulkner's *The Sound and the Fury* refers to as "that constant speculation regarding the position of mechanical hands on an arbitrary dial which is a symptom of mind function" (75), Suttree instead exists in a plane of pure, intuitive temporality, which exists independently of the constructions of intellect, as indicated by the hallucinatory clock-shop sequence which follows his vision of wheeling forms.

If all this sounds too much like the negativistic "flight into psychopathology" so lamented by Lukács, one should take time to remember Gierow's pronouncement on Beckettian pessimism: "what is worthless can not be degraded." As a result of his experiences, Suttree gains an insight into the common source of all phenomena and the collective lot of humanity. He expresses anger at the ragpicker's suicide, exclaiming "You have no right to represent people this way . . . A man is all men. You have no right to your wretchedness" (422). He learns that "all souls are one and all souls lonely," and while Bryan Vescio resists the temptation to read this in terms of Emerson's Over-soul (67), Suttree's statement adequately represents Schopenhauer's stance, to which Emerson's idea bears more than a passing resemblance: the statement both captures the pessimism of Schopenhauerianism and retains its transcendental viewpoint. There is, it seems, some consolation in the fact that the wretchedness of humanity is nevertheless a shared experience, and the sense that participation in it is somehow cathartic—for "even the damned in hell," says Suttree, "have the community of their suffering" (464).

In the end then, both *Suttree* and *Murphy* are strangely affirmative. At the conclusion of Beckett's novel, Murphy resolves to return to his home in Brewery Road, and back into the arms of Celia. Yet if we consider Suttree himself as being the replicated image, or the twin, of Murphy, there is one important way in which he and his story assert their difference. Murphy delays his return, resolving to have one last rock in his chair, and through an unhappy accident, someone inadvertently pulls the wrong chain in the bathroom, and he meets his end in a gas explosion. The bathos of his demise is completed when, his ashes on their way to being scattered, the package containing Murphy becomes the object of an impromptu game of football, and his body, mind, and soul are freely distributed across the ale-soaked floor of a pub (154). The novel concludes with Celia's grandfather, Mr. Kelly, pathetically chasing his kite, which has broken free from its line, as it disappears into the dusk, symbolic of life's departure from this earth. And of course, the image of flying concludes McCarthy's novel too, although in this case it is Suttree flying from the huntsmen and the tireless hounds which have haunted his dreams. Flying from death, Suttree has found consolation and a justification for life in the shared experience of humanity, and in his final affirmation and continuance, he makes a final journey, from *Other-Murphy* to *Anti-Murphy*.

## NOTES

1  For a summary of the reviews, , see Random House inc. *The Road*. Nd. <http://www.randomhouse.com/catalog/display.pperl?isbn=9780307265432&view=quotes> 29 July 2009, and panmacmillan.com. Reviews of *The Road* by Cormac McCarthy. Nd. <http://www.panmacmillan.com/displayPage.asp?PageID=4617>. July 29 2009.

2. I am indebted here to Shane Weller's *A Taste for the Negative* for its extremely useful synopsis of the critical debate surrounding Beckett's alleged nihilism. See particularly "Introduction" (4–23).

3. For more on the possible relationship between McCarthy and Schopenhauer, see my "Compassionate McCarthy?"

## WORKS CITED

Beckett, Samuel. *Murphy*. 1938. London: Picador, 1982.

————. *Proust and Three Dialogues with Georges Duthuit*. London: Calder and Boyars, 1970.

Bell, Vereen M. *The Achievement of Cormac McCarthy*. Baton Rouge: Louisiana State UP, 1988.

Emerson, Ralph Waldo. "The Over-Soul." *Selected Essays*. Ed. Larzer Ziff. New York: Penguin, 1982. 205–24.

Faulkner, William. *The Sound and the Fury*. 1929. London: Vintage, 2005.

Gallivan, Euan. "Compassionate McCarthy?: *The Road* and Schopenhauerian Ethics." *Cormac McCarthy Journal* 6 (2008): 98–106.

Jacquette, Dale. *The Philosophy of Schopenhauer*. Chesham: Acumen, 2005.

Lukács, Georg. *The Meaning of Contemporary Realism*. Trans. John and Necke Mander. London: Merlin, 1963.

Mars-Jones, Adam. "Life after Armageddon." Rev. of *The Road,* by Cormac McCarthy. *The Observer* 26 Nov. 2006. 30 July 2009 <www.guardian.co.uk/books>.

McCarthy, Cormac. *Suttree*. 1979. London: Picador, 1989.

————. *The Crossing*. 1994. London: Picador, 1995.

————. *The Road*. London: Picador, 2006.

Nietzsche, Friedrich. *The Genealogy of Morals*. 1887. Trans. Horace B. Samuel. Mineola: Dover, 2003.

"Nobel Prize in Literature 1969: Presentation Speech." Nd. *Nobelprize.org.* 30 July 2009 <http://nobelprize.org/nobel_prizes/literature/laureates/1969/press.html>.

Schopenhauer, Arthur. *The World as Will and Representation*—2 vols. 1819. Trans. E.F.J. Payne. New York: Dover, 1969.

Shelton, Frank W. "Suttree and Suicide." *Southern Quarterly* 29.1 (1990): 71–83.

Spencer, William C. "Altered States of Consciousness in *Suttree*." *Southern Quarterly* 35.2 (Winter 1997): 87–92.

Vescio, Bryan. "Strangers in Everyland: Suttree, Huckleberry Finn, and Tragic Humanism." *The Cormac McCarthy Journal* 4 (2005): 60–71.

Warner, Alan. "The Road to Hell." Rev. of *The Road,* by Cormac McCarthy. *The Guardian* 4 Nov. 2006. 30 July 2009 <www.guardian.co.uk/books>.

Weller, Shane. *A Taste for the Negative: Beckett and Nihilism*. London: Legenda, 2005.

Wicks, Robert. "Schopenhauerian Moral Awareness as a Source of Nietzschean Nonmorality." *Journal of Nietzsche Studies* 23 (2002): 21–38.

# 11 From Blue to Blood
## Jean Toomer's "Blue Meridian" and Cormac McCarthy's *Blood Meridian* as Intertexts

*John Ferer*

Roland Barthes described text as "a woven fabric" formed by interlacing threads of the "already written" and the "already read" (159). If Cormac McCarthy's *Blood Meridian* is viewed as such a "woven fabric," then McCarthy critics and scholars have spent the past twenty-five years pulling on the loose ends of the garment to untangle its multitude of intertextual relationships. Just the title *Blood Meridian* alone has spawned a litany of conjecture and debate as to its possible connections to previous and subsequent texts. John Sepich in *Notes on Blood Meridian* suggests that the title was influenced by a nineteenth-century novel called *The Scalp Hunters* by Mayne Reid which uses the word "meridian" in its first paragraph (129). Sepich also notes that in 1845 the Commander at Presidio del Norte used two imaginary longitudinal lines (or meridians) to describe "the area of greatest Comanche and Kiowa activities," that same area being referred to by General Ralph Smith as a "bloody corridor" (129). In *A Reader's Guide to Blood Meridian*, Shane Schimpf traces the title to Lord Byron's poem "Stanzas to the Po" which features the line "My blood is all meridian" (28). Other readers have analyzed possible links with Albert Camus, the Book of Moses, and even the lyrics of a Bob Dylan song (*The Official Website of the Cormac McCarthy Society, Forum*).

Moving beyond the title of the text to the whole novel opens the analysis up to an even broader array of possible intertexts including Sam Chamberlain's *My Confession*, Herman Melville's *Moby Dick*, John Milton's *Paradise Lost*, *Beowulf*, the Bible, and the poetry of William Wordsworth to name just a few (see Hungerford, Phillips, Sepich, Wallach). As Michel Foucault wrote:

> The frontiers of a book are never clear-cut: beyond the title, the first lines and the last full stop, beyond its internal configuration and its autonomous form, it is caught up in a system of references to other books, other texts, other sentences: it is a node within a network . . . The book is not simply the object that one holds in one's hands . . . Its unity is variable and relative. (Foucault 23)

Julia Kristeva takes Foucault's statement one step further in her conclusion that authors do not create original texts, but rather compile parts of pre-existent texts to produce "an intertextuality" in which "several utterances, taken from other texts, intersect and neutralize each other" (36). Cormac McCarthy himself appears to have recognized the validity of Kristeva's theory in an interview in 1992. "The ugly fact is books are made out of books. The novel depends for its life on the novels that have been written" (Woodward 36). This essay will drag another "ugly fact" into the light and will pull another loose end of the fabric of *Blood Meridian*. The loose end is Jean Toomer's poem "Blue Meridian." Using Kristeva's theory of intertextuality as a model, this essay will explore the intersections and neutralizations that take place between the two texts that bring the meridian from blue to blood.

Jean Toomer's place in the literary canon and his fame in literary circles are a result of the success of his 1923 novel *Cane*. *Cane*, considered a leading influence on the Harlem Renaissance, is a series of poems and vignettes illuminating the black experience in the South and the quest for African-American identity. After *Cane*, Toomer shifted his focus to issues of national identity and what he called "the new world soul" (Estis-Hicks 1). Over a fifteen-year period, he intermittently worked on a composition that portrayed his vision of a new order of man that was free from classifications of race and class. Toomer's obsession with cultural identity and race is a product of his multiracial ancestry. Toomer was born on December 26, 1894, in Washington DC (Fabre and Feith 31). His grandfather on his father's side was a white Georgia plantation owner and his grandmother was a "woman of mixed blood including Negro and Indian" (31). On his mother's side, his grandfather was the son of a white Virginia plantation owner and a Mulatto slave mother (Fabre and Feith 31). In a 1922 letter to Claude McKay, Toomer wrote that he was composed of "seven blood mixtures—French, Dutch, Welch, Negro, German, Jewish and Indian" (Turner 18). During his life, Toomer formed his own view of racial classifications and (de)categorized himself as follows: "I am at once of no one of the races and I am all of them. I belong to no one of them and I belong to all. I am, in a strict racial sense, a member of the new race" (Fabre and Feith 7).

The "new race" that Toomer referred to would be the subject of his lifework and would evolve in the medium of poetry. The conception of the "new race" began in 1921 when Toomer wrote a 126-line poem that he called "The First American." The poem fuses the best racial characteristics of America's black, red, and white races to form a new "race of races" called the American race. Toomer called himself the first conscious member of this new race. The origins for this new universal race are described by Toomer in his essay "On Being an American":

> Underlying all of the divisions, I had observed what seemed to me
> to be authentic—namely, that a new type of man was arising in this

country—not European, not African, not Asiatic—but American. And in this American I saw the divisions mended, the differences reconciled—saw that (1) we would in truth be a united people existing in the United States, saw that (2) we would in truth be once again members of a united human race. Now all of this, needless to say, did not get into the poem. Years were to pass before that could happen, before the germ of "The First American" could grow and ripen and be embodied in "The Blue Meridian." (Turner 121)

After "The First American" was published, Toomer continued to struggle with the poem and his perspectives on a unified national identity. This struggle led to Toomer's interest in the mysticism of Georges I. Gurdjieff, the Russian founder of Unitism. Gurdjieff's philosophy of Unitism, according to the book *Black Poets of the United States*, "envisaged the reconstruction of man by teaching him to unify, transcend, and dominate himself" (Wagner and Douglas 262). Toomer's concept of a new unified race and Gurdjieff's philosophy of Unitism proved to be a perfect match.

In the 1920s, Toomer became a devoted follower of Gurdjieff and introduced principles of Unitism into his poetry. In 1936, after fifteen years of wrestling with his poem, an 835-line magnum opus emerged with the final title of "Blue Meridian." In "Blue Meridian," black, white, red, and brown racial classifications are cast away in favor of the racially indeterminate "blue man" who represents a unity of mankind that transcends the very nature of race. The poem is divided into three sections or meridians: Black Meridian, White Meridian, and Blue Meridian. The colors of each meridian have multiple layers of meaning. On the surface the black and white refer to racial classifications based on skin pigmentation, with the color blue referring to the amalgamation of all races. The colors also signify a three-step transformation process where black represents darkness, white represents awakening from the darkness, and blue, a mystical transformation into a new order of man. Each meridian begins with a similar three-line stanza that first addresses the Black Meridian as black light, then the White Meridian as white light, and then culminates with the fusion of the black, red, brown, and white races to form the new "Blue Meridian" wherein Americans reunite the primordial life force to achieve actual and aesthetic equality.

"Blue Meridian" and *Blood Meridian* intersect and neutralize each other on three thematic or philosophical levels regarding: (a) the equality of beings, (b) light as a symbol of one primordial life force, and (c) man's ability to transcend to a divine apex. Kristeva described any text as an "absorption and transformation of another. The notion of intertextuality replaces that of intersubjectivity and poetic language is read as at least double" (66). There is no better starting point to apply Kristeva's theory than the diametrically opposed doubles that McCarthy provides in his text: black John Jackson and white John Jackson. The racial composition of the Gang consists predominantly of whites, but also includes an African-American (black John Jackson), American Indians (the Delawares), and a Mexican (Juan Miguel, a.k.a. John McGill) (McCarthy 81, 86, 98). All of the white, black, red, and brown racial classifications referred to by Toomer in "Blue Meridian" and united in the homogeneous "blue man" are represented in Glanton's Gang. Toomer's vision is one of equality. McCarthy's portrayal of Glanton's Gang also holds equality of paramount importance. The activities of Glanton's Gang take place around the year 1850 prior to the commencement of the Civil War and the abolition of slavery. Most free blacks in the US at that time lived in racial enclaves in the northeast in large cities and suffered extreme prejudice. McCarthy's black John Jackson, on the other hand, roams the Southwest as a member of Glanton's Gang side by side with fellow scalphunter white John Jackson.

One night, Glanton's Gang build two campfires, one fire occupied by white members of the Gang, the other occupied by racial minorities. Black Jackson approaches the fire surrounded by the whites, but is warned away by white Jackson. Black Jackson departs only to return to the campfire with a bowie knife with which he decapitates white Jackson in a clear display to the rest of the Gang. In the 1850s, the murder of a white by a black would be met with certain capital punishment, whether administered through court-ordered justice or backyard justice. But, in Glanton's Gang the norms of society do not apply. Glanton does nothing, the murdered "anchorite" is left behind, and not another word is said of the event (107). Black Jackson remains a member of the Gang just like all the rest, and the headless "man" is left behind to sit by the extinguished fire. "Anchorite" is an interesting word choice by McCarthy. The only other time the word 'anchorite' is used in the text is to describe a racist hermit slave trader who has a shrunken heart of a slave as a memento and who believes that "four things can destroy the earth: women, whisky, money and niggers" (18). It is clear that McCarthy groups the ex-slave trader hermit and white Jackson together in beliefs that are anchored to a racial hierarchy that is outside the belief system that holds the Glanton Gang together. The fact that Glanton does not punish black Jackson, and does not say one word of the murder, has been analyzed by John Sepich:

> Glanton's acceptance of his gang member's murder in this scene is a careful demonstration by McCarthy of Glanton's unqualified acceptance of both John Jacksons as equals . . . Only if men had found Black Jackson's act to be abhorrent might Glanton have confronted the killer. Glanton's loyalties seem not to favor Anglos over Indians, or Anglos over Mexicans, but gang members over outsiders. (10)

Just as the "blue man" transcended race in Toomer's "Blue Meridian" through miscegenation, the members of Glanton's Gang have found equality through violence. This dismissal of racial classifications by Glanton's

Gang and enforcement of equality is also evident in their interactions with the "outside" community.

Again, black John Jackson is the central character of this theme. When the Gang arrives at the presidio of Tucson, they enter an eating house, and the owner refuses to serve Jackson at the "white" tables (234). The reaction by the members of Glanton's Gang is confusion. "He thinks we're niggers," one of the Gang members offers in explanation (235). This response shows the unity of the group. If an outsider labels one member with a pejorative label, they all assume the label. Glanton speaks for the whole Gang: "Mr. Owens, if you was anything other than a goddamn fool you could take one look at these here men and know for a stone fact they ain't a one of em goin to get up from where they're at to go set somewheres else" (235). After the owner continues to refuse the men because they are seated at the "white" tables with a black man, the issue is pushed to a quick and deadly resolution by Gang member David Brown. Brown tosses a revolver to the owner and instructs him to "shoot the nigger" (235). The arming of victims before they are killed is a tradition in Western legends. Brown knows that once the owner of the eating house is armed, Jackson will shoot and kill him, bringing the disagreement to an end. Jackson does exactly what Brown expects, nonchalantly passing his hand over the hammer of his revolver, shooting and killing the owner. Then, the Gang serves themselves dinner and eats their meal at the "white" tables with the owner's corpse still warm on the floor.

Even more telling than the obvious display of unity in this scene is the fact that Glanton and the Judge continue to defend Jackson when a lieutenant and a half dozen armed militia come to arrest Jackson for murdering the owner. Glanton denies that the Gang ever even entered the eating house. The lieutenant is incredulous, yet powerless to take action with a group of fully armed scalp hunters backing up Glanton's words. Not only is equality found in *Blood Meridian* in the acts of enforcement undertaken by Glanton's Gang, but it is also present in the text's emphasis of aesthetic equality and its disdain for sociological labels. Just as miscegenation results in the elimination of the distinct skin pigmentations of white, black, red, and brown, aesthetic equality is also apparent in many descriptions of Glanton's Gang despite the gang's heterogeneous racial composition. McCarthy describes the aesthetic unity of the Gang as follows: "The men as they rode turned black in the sun from the blood on their clothes and their faces and then paled slowly in the rising dust until they assumed once more the color of the land through which they passed" (160). This passage shows the members of Glanton's Gang shifting color in unison from black to pale to the color of the land, very reminiscent of the three-step evolutionary process of Toomer's "blue" man: (a) black meridian for darkness before awakening, (b) white meridian for awakening from the darkness, then (c) blue meridian for transcendental unity. The color of the land that McCarthy refers to in the above passage, thus the color of the Gang members, could very well have been blue upon moonrise, as it was earlier in the novel when the moon "overtook them at its midnight meridian, sketching on the plain below a blue cameo of such dread pilgrims clanking north" (88).

McCarthy not only invests Glanton's Gang with aesthetic equality, but he also attacks sociological labeling and nomenclature in the same manner as Toomer. In "The Americans," he states:

> There is only one pure race—and this is the human race. We all belong to it—and this is the most and the least that can be said of any of us with accuracy. For the rest, it is mere talk, mere labeling, merely a manner of speaking, merely a sociological, not a biological, thing. (Rusch 109)

Toomer focuses on the fact that man has categorized and labeled humans emphasizing our differences in order to establish a hierarchy based on sociological observations rather than true biological differences. McCarthy frequently and consistently focuses on the same issue throughout the novel. The following is an example of the narrator endowing the Gang with aesthetic equality and attacking sociological labels and categories that lead to empty hierarchies:

> Specter horsemen, pale with dust, anonymous in the crenellated heat. Above all else they were wholly at venture, primal, provisional, devoid of order. Like beings provoked out of the absolute rock and set nameless and at no remove from their own loomings to wander ravenous and doomed and mute as gorgons shambling the brutal wastes of Gondwanaland in a time before nomenclature was and each was all. (172)

The reference to Gondwanaland furthers the theme. Gondwanaland refers to the fact that for hundreds of millions of years, all of the land of the Earth was joined together in one large mass or supercontinent that scientists called Pangaea. Approximately 200 million years ago, Pangaea split into two pieces: Laurasia and Gondwanaland. Later, Laurasia and Gondwanaland divided into the continents we have today through the process of continental drift. By recalling the concept that all humans originally came from one large landmass, McCarthy is evoking a similar theme to the Unitism that Toomer advocated in "Blue Meridian."

McCarthy goes even further and concludes that not only are all humans equal and devoid of order, but that humans are equal to nonliving nature as well:

> In the neuter austerity of that terrain all phenomena were bequeathed a strange equality and no one thing nor spider nor stone nor blade of grass could put forth claim to precedence. The very clarity of these articles belied their familiarity, for the eye predicates the whole on some feature or part and here was nothing more luminous than another and

nothing more enshadowed and in the optical democracy of such landscapes all preference is made whimsical and a man and a rock become
endowed with unguessed kinships. (247)

McCarthy is stating that humans, animals, grass and nonliving nature such
as rocks are all equals and share the same luminosity. McCarthy's bio-
spherical egalitarianism is a step beyond Toomer's more anthropocentric
view of equality, but nonetheless demonstrates both writers' desire to advocate equality in both aesthetic and biological terms.

The equality achieved by Glanton's Gang and the "blue man" demonstrates the intersection of the two texts. However, McCarthy's version of
equality neutralizes or transforms Toomer's vision in several ways. The
first transformation is apparent in examining the manner in which equality is achieved. In "Blue Meridian," equality is achieved by giving free rein
to man's primitive sexual instincts, which lead to interracial procreation.
Toomer describes the results of miscegenation as creating "the world of the
aristocrat—but not the social aristocrat; the aristocrat of culture, of spirit
and character, of ideas, of true nobility" (Turner 112). In *Blood Meridian*,
a new order of man is also created by giving free rein to primitive instincts.
However, the primitive instincts unleashed in *Blood Meridian* are not sexual. They are violent. And the resulting new order of man is far from noble.
All members of Glanton's Gang are equally violent regardless of race. As
John Cant wrote in his book *Cormac McCarthy and the Myth of American Exceptionalism*, "The scalphunters evince no hint of nobility and their
characters are uniformly homicidal" (Cant 160). As Toomer's "blue man"
climbs the chain of being to achieve almost god-like harmony and nobility, McCarthy's characters descend the chain of being and are equal to all
forms of living and nonliving nature. Dana Phillips makes a similar point
when he writes: "In the raw orchestration of the book's events, the world
of nature and the world of men are parts of the same world, and both are
equally violent and indifferent to each other" (447).

The color blue used in the title of "Blue Meridian" and in the skin color
of the "blue man" represents equality and nobility, akin to blue blood. In
his essay "The Americans," Toomer focuses on the biological fact that all
humans have the same color blood and that this unity will be the basis for
eliminating racial classifications:

> I myself talk merely talk when I speak of the blending of the bloods
> of the white, black, red and brown races giving rise to a new race, to
> a new unique blood, when I liken the combination of hydrogen and
> oxygen producing water. For the blood of all the races is *human* blood.
> There are no differences between the blood of a Caucasian and the
> blood of a Negro as there are between hydrogen and oxygen. In the
> mixing and blending of so-called races there are mixtures and blend-
> ing of the same stuff. [ . . . ] Moreover, it is a mistake to speak of blood

as if it had various colors in the various races. All human blood is the same. (Rusch 109)

Blood in the title of *Blood Meridian* also represents equality and unifies humanity. "Is not blood the tempering agent in the mortar which bonds?" the Judge asks the Man in the final chapter of the novel (329). However, Toomer's "blending of the bloods" to create a new order of man is replaced in *Blood Meridian* with the spilling of blood. Whether through miscegenation or violence, equality is reached in both texts. But does such equality allow mankind to transcend and reunite with our primordial origins? The answer to this question might be approached through an examination of how light is used as a symbol in the texts of "Blue Meridian" and *Blood Meridian*.

Toomer uses light in "Blue Meridian" as a symbol of the primordial source of life, light, and energy. In Onita Estes-Hicks' article "Jean Toomer and the Politics and Poetics of National Identity," she describes the symbolism of light as follows:

> In Toomer's myth of genesis, the light of humankind was initially one life force, as the gods of "Blue Meridian" originally came from one "root religion." In its Wordsworthian falling away, human society broke the wholeness of the life circle, consigning humanity to separate existences seen as half meridians, imprisoning life in categories of race and nationality, abandoning the universal spark which represented wholeness. Neither black nor white meridian can reach a higher point of existence until they partake of each other's nature, by accepting that *teritum quid* which will propel a new fusion, a stronger and higher strain of being because it shares all of nature's bounty and inherits all of culture's gifts. (34–35)

In Toomer's vision, man has experienced a "falling away" from nature whereby he has lost sight of the glories of our origins and has become divided. The "falling away" that Toomer portrays in his poem consists of man distancing himself from his original primordial source of life, light, and energy. Such original life source is dimly recalled in childhood and then forgotten in the process of becoming a man. Toomer's objective in "Blue Meridian" is to rectify the "falling away" and to reunite mankind's racial divisions.

*Blood Meridian* is also very much concerned with man's "falling away" from his origins. The symbolism of a primordial light that is found throughout Toomer's text is also present in several passages of *Blood Meridian*. For example, the Gang enters a barn to spend the night, and each member is enshrouded by light (222). Each member appears to have a vestigial "universal spark," which represents some essence of the primordial life force that man has lost. In "Blue Meridian," humans partake of each other's "animal" nature by giving in to their primal sexual appetites leading to interracial procreation. This miscegenation leads to the recapture of the primordial light that reunites the wholeness of life's circle once again. In *Blood Meridian*, Glanton's Gang partakes of each other's "animal" nature by giving in to their primal appetites for violence leading not to transcendence, but to degeneration, a path consistent with the concept of "falling away." This theme is addressed again in *Blood Meridian* when the gang members circle around the campfire mesmerized at its light:

> The flames sawed in the wind and the embers paled and deepened and paled and deepened like the bloodbeat of some living thing eviscerate upon the ground before them and they watched the fire which does contain within it something of men themselves inasmuch as they are less without it and are divided from their origins and are exiles. For each fire is all fires, the first fire and the last ever to be. (244)

No other passage from *Blood Meridian* captures the essence of a "falling away" as effectively as the above text. This fire describes the same concept of a primordial source of life energy that is described in "Blue Meridian"— the light of humankind as initially being one life force. Men are less without the divine life source, they are lost, and they are exiles from their origins. McCarthy gives the reader the sensation that the fire is divine in the sense that it is proceeding directly from a god not only in the text cited above, but also in McCarthy's subtitle: "The godfire" (241).

The intersection between the texts of Toomer and McCarthy in their use of light as a symbol of mankind's primordial source of life, light, and energy is far from identical, and seeks to communicate a different vision. Toomer and McCarthy transform the concept of a "falling away" for their own purposes. In "Blue Meridian," the separation of the races and man-made hierarchies represent the lowest level of evolutionary progression. The evolutionary progression must ascend beyond plants, animals, and man to reach "The Big Light," as demonstrated by Toomer's repeated refrain of a hierarchy of being that portrays plants at the lowest rung of the ladder, followed by animals, then man, and, finally, featuring the universe and "The Big Light" at the pinnacle. It is clear in "Blue Meridian" that mankind reaches its meridian or apex when the race ascends to the top of the hierarchy to a divine level. When man reaches that divine apex, there still exists a hierarchy, but universal man sits atop that hierarchy. "Blue Meridian" is optimistic that this transcendence and recapturing of the light is possible. This is completely different in *Blood Meridian* in several ways. First of all, the primordial light in *Blood Meridian* is not just for humankind. It is for all of nature, whose living creatures are all equals as McCarthy shows when the Kid encounters a burning tree in the desert surrounded by other animals engaged in a "precarious truce," all mesmerized by the light (215). The burning tree in *Blood Meridian* demonstrates that humans and animals derive from the same life energy and are equal. Man by his nature is a predator existing on a horizontal chain of being where all of nature (living and nonliving) are undifferentiated. Nonliving nature carries the vestigial universal spark as well, which becomes clearer in the epilogue in which a man is "striking fire out of the rock which God has put there" (337). "Blue Meridian" takes a more anthropocentric view—as indeed does the Bible when Moses encounters the burning bush (*New American Bible*, Exodus 3.1–22). The light of the burning bush is not for Moses and his flock; it is for Moses alone.

It is no coincidence that the demise of Glanton's Gang is brought about by the rupture of equality amongst its members. When Glanton is away on a trip to San Diego, the Judge and black John Jackson take control of the Gang and transform it into a cult, raising themselves into positions of divine rule:

> The judge was standing on the rise in silhouette against the evening sun like some great balden archimandrite. He was wrapped in a mantle of freeflowing cloth beneath which he was naked. The black man Jackson came out of one of the stone bunkers dressed in a similar garb and stood beside him. (273)

This passage is reminiscent of the first two sections of "Blue Meridian" in which the Black Meridian and White Meridian represent two separate half-meridians that must fuse together to transport humanity to the apex of divinity resulting in the "blue man." Jackson, being the sole African-American in the Gang, is the Black Meridian, and the Judge, being the whitest member, is the White Meridian. The use of the term "archimandrite" to describe the Judge furthers the theme. "Archimandrite" is defined as a "chief of a monastery, corresponding to abbot or father provincial in the Roman Catholic Church" (*Webster's*). The attempt at divine ascension, however, fails. Jackson is killed at the commencement of an invasion by the Yuma Indians—a four-foot cane arrow shot through his upper abdomen. The remaining members of the Gang that are present on the riverside camp are slaughtered, and only the Judge and his idiot escape. McCarthy's new order of man comes to a swift and violent end. McCarthy's vision reveals an outright pessimistic view of man's ability to reunite and transcend. This philosophical division between Toomer and McCarthy is most apparent when examining the endings of both texts.

Toomer's poem ends with a dance celebrating unity and the transcendence of man (74). The dance in "Blue Meridian" is modeled after the dance found in the fourth and last part of Friedrich Nietzsche's *Thus Spoke Zarathustra* (296): "All the gods are dead: now we want the superman to live," Zarathustra announces at the end of part one of the text

(78). The death of the gods (or the loss of morality) is to be replaced by the life of the "superman." Toomer has combined parts of Nietzsche's preexistent text to produce an intertextuality exploring the same theme of transcendence. Nietzsche's "superman" is the "blue man." Zarathustra's dance is the "dance of the Blue Meridian." Nietzsche's refrain of "Lift up your hearts, my brothers, high, still higher!" repeated three times is similar to Toomer's refrain beckoning mankind to lift its "waking forces" repeated three times in "Blue Meridian" (Toomer 50, 51, 74 and Nietzsche 304, 305, 306). Both dances celebrate life and the possibility of transcendence.

*Blood Meridian* also ends with a dance reminiscent of Zarathustra. Only this dance, rather than celebrating life, can be viewed as a perpetual dance of war and violence and bloodshed. Men can only truly participate in this dance if they have accepted their role in nature and have returned to their primal origins. And it is the Judge, death incarnate, who leads this dance in the end:

> And they are dancing, the board floor slamming under the jackboots and the fiddlers grinning hideously over their canted pieces. Towering over them all is the judge and he is naked dancing, his small feet lively and quick and now in doubletime and bowing to the ladies, huge and pale and hairless, like an enormous infant. He never sleeps, he says. He says he'll never die. (335)

McCarthy, it seems, absorbs Zarathustra's dance and the "dance of the Blue Meridian" into an intricate intertextual network and transforms them into an anti-myth intended to shatter the proposition that the power of reason can conquer nihilism. John Cant describes this example of intertextuality as follows:

> Zarathustra's is the dance of life and the judge's the dance of death . . . In this, McCarthy's most highly wrought text, Nietzsche's myth is inverted and the result is a tale of such all encompassing pessimism that even the glories of its language and the realized ambition of its author's imagination cannot fully overcome the sense of crisis that it seems to express. (174)

"There's no such thing as life without bloodshed" McCarthy said in an interview in 1992 (Woodward 40). "I think the notion that the species can be improved in some way, that everyone could live in harmony, is a really dangerous idea. Those who are afflicted with this notion are the first ones to give up their souls, their freedom. Your desire that it be that way will enslave you and make your life vacuous" (40). McCarthy's quote from this interview, alongside *Blood Meridian*, can be seen as a direct retort and dismissal of the substance of Toomer's "Blue

Meridian." While Toomer's uplifting vision of racial declassification is forward-looking after decades of evolution, McCarthy's dark vision is primitive and paid for in blood. Both texts engage in an intertextual battle of optimism versus pessimism, unity versus divergence, transcendence versus degradation. Who wins this battle is determined by the reader, who is charged with unraveling the intertextual patchwork of intersections and transformations. On one side, Toomer portrays a harmonious future created by humankind's transcendence to the apex of divinity. On the opposing side, McCarthy envisages an endless dance of war and violence and bloodshed caused by a primordial descent to the very base of nature.

## WORKS CITED

Barthes, Roland. *Image-Music-Text*. Trans. Stephen Heath. London: Fontana, 1977.
Cant, John. *Cormac McCarthy and the Myth of American Exceptionalism*. New York: Routledge, 2008.
Estis-Hicks, Onita. "Jean Toomer and the Politics and Poetics of National Identity." *Contributions in Black Studies* 7, 3 (1985). 3 March 2009 <http://scholarworks.umass.edu/cibs/vol7/iss1/3>.
Fabre, Genevieve, and Feith, Michael, eds. Jean Toomer and the Harlem Renaissance. New Brunswick: Rutgers UP, 2001.
Foucault, Michel. *The Archaeology of Knowledge*. London: Routledge, 1972.
Hungerford, Amy. "17. Cormac McCarthy, Blood Meridian." *YouTube*, 21 Nov. 2008. 3 March 2009 <http://www.youtube.com/watch?v=FgyZ4ia25gg>.
Kristeva, Julia. *Desire in Language: A Semiotic Approach to Literature and Art*. Trans. Thomas Gora, Alice Jardine, and Leon S. Roudiez. Ed. Leon S. Roudiez. New York: Columbia UP, 1980.
McCarthy, Cormac. *Blood Meridian or the Evening Redness in the West*. 1985. New York: Vintage, 1992.
"Meridian Blood & Meridian Thought." *The Official Website of the Cormac McCarthy Society*, 1 Jan. 2008. 3 March 2009 <http://www.jadaproductions.com/>.
*New American Bible*. Confraternity of Christian Doctrine. World Catholic Press, 1990.
Nietzsche, Friederich. *Thus Spoke Zarathustra*. Trans. Marianne Cowan. Chicago: Gateway, 1957.
Phillips, Dana. "History and the Ugly Facts of Cormac McCarthy's Blood Meridian." *American Literature* 68.2 (1996): 433–60.
Rusch, Frederik L., ed. *A Jean Toomer Reader: Selected Unpublished Writings*. Oxford: Oxford UP, 1993.
Schimpf, Shane. *A Reader's Guide to Blood Meridian*. Seattle: Bon Mot, 2008.
Sepich, John. *Notes on Blood Meridian*. Louisville: Bellarmine College Press, 1993.
Toomer, Jean. The Collected Poems of Jean Toomer. Ed. Robert B. Jones and Margery Toomer. Raleigh Durham: U of North Carolina P, 1988.
Turner, Darwin T., ed. *The Wayward and the Seeking: A Collection of Writings by Jean Toomer*. Washington, DC: Howard UP, 1980.

Wagner, Jean, and Douglas, Kenneth. *Black Poets of the United States*. Chicago: U of Illinois P, 1973.

Wallach, Rick. "From Beowulf to Blood Meridian: Cormac McCarthy's Demystification of the Martial Code." *Southern Quarterly* 36.4 (1998): 113–20.

*Webster's Online Dictionary*. "archimandrite." 27 Jan. 2011 <http://www.webstersonlinedictionary.org/definitions/archimandrite>.

Woodward, Richard B. "Cormac McCarthy's Venomous Fiction." *New York Times Magazine* 19 April 1992: 28–31, 36, 40.

# 12 Versions of the *Seeleroman*
## Cormac McCarthy and Leslie Silko

*Nicholas Monk*

*Going within . . . takes me beyond.* (Taylor 136)

Charles Taylor's dictum is a reminder that a prerequisite of any spiritual journey is the struggle to reconcile oneself with oneself, and the *Seeleroman*, a variety of the *Bildungsroman*, the genre of the novel that informs the title of this essay, conforms to a similar pattern in terms of its focus on the journey toward the "formation" of its central character.[1] What follows proceeds, therefore, from the assumption that both McCarthy and Silko are at some significant level engaged in the study of ontological crises that may or may not lead to an awareness of something greater than the individual self. What drives these ontological crises, however, and what informs all Silko's fiction, and much of McCarthy's later work, is resistance to a wholly pervasive strain of capitalist modernity that seems to many to be moving ever closer to the point of subsuming the cultures of the world within its economic and cultural imperatives.[2] What is created in this process are spiritual journeys, or *Seeleromane*, in which both authors' protagonists search for a lost or disappearing means of engagement with a world in which that engagement is not determined overwhelmingly by technology and the consumerist imperatives of the globalized capitalist modernity I mention. McCarthy's and Silko's characters drift physically through the frequently unforgiving, often unfathomable, geographical expanses of the Southwest, just as they drift psychologically through the frequently unforgiving, often unfathomable expanses of late-twentieth-century society, searching at numerous levels for a unity of self with self, and self with what lies "beyond"—be that "community," "god," or the "natural" world.

The *Seeleroman* is a version of what John McClure describes as the "narrative of spiritual formation," and which he identifies as a manifestation of the "postsecular" in contemporary fiction.[3] There is much that is common to the work of both McCarthy and Silko in these terms, particularly in the focus on a journey toward maturity that is conceived through the means of the protagonists' philosophical and spiritual development (including the use of the notion of "romance" as a staging post), the pervasive but frequently liminal desire for ontological unity, and the spiritual guides and mentors that appear at various points in the course of their journeys in an attempt to clarify these desires. I want to suggest, however, that, while the novels remain unmistakeably "novels of the soul," the *Seeleromane* of McCarthy and Silko are strongly differentiated from one another. The spiritual journeys in McCarthy are like rivers in the desert, parched almost to nothing in the heat of a overwhelming and spiritually deadening modernity, while Silko's journeys offer paths of spiritual development that seek to circumvent modernity by refuting its primacy and asserting alternative realities that deny its truth claims.

In Silko's *Ceremony*, for example, Tayo returns to the Laguna Pueblo after the Second World War nursing the horror of his experiences in the Pacific theatre. He and his friends have turned from traditional practices and are sodden with alcohol. A response at the immediate psychological level to their trauma, and at another level, perhaps, a reaction to the indisputable evidence that Native Americans such as Tayo have been duped into taking up arms for one version of the modernity that has attempted to annihilate them against another that would annihilate them equally readily. Tayo stumbles toward awareness of the pernicious nature of this modernity via a series of contacts with tribal elders, "medicine men," and figures from the spirit world. He is reintroduced to the traditional stories of his people, gradually rebuilds a spiritual relationship with the land, and begins to repair his damaged life. Ultimately, in his hitherto losing battle with modernity, he is redeemed from the point of destruction by the religious practices and rituals of his community. *Ceremony* demonstrates exceptionally clearly a successful conclusion to the *Seeleroman* as Tayo is "healed" and returns to a spiritual relationship with his inner self and, thereby, his land and his community.

McCarthy's engagement with the *Seeleroman* dates from as far back as *Suttree* (1979), a novel in which his protagonist embarks upon a fraught journey of psychological and emotional development that is triggered by a violent confrontation with his wealthy family, but is informed by a variety of spiritual experiences—both "weak" and strong. Unsurprisingly in a McCarthy novel, however, Cornelius Suttree never reaches an accommodation with the world and its values. To apply the strict terms of the genre from which the *Seeleroman* derives, the *Bildungsroman*, he fails, in most ways, to "mature" or become "formed." His "apprenticeship" remains incomplete. It is certainly possible to argue that something similar happens to Billy Parham in *The Crossing*—and, beyond, into *Cities of the Plain*—as he and his brother Boyd journey into Mexico in search of horses stolen from their parents' ranch. As in *Suttree*, in McCarthy's later fiction, a successful conclusion to the journey is rarely, if ever, reached: death intervenes (Boyd Parham, John Grady Cole in *Cities of the Plain*, or the kid in *Blood Meridian*), the catalytic muse is removed (John Grady Cole in *All the Pretty Horses*, and *Cities of the Plain*), or the possibility of spiritual redemption is tantalizingly close, yet reverts to the secular and the quotidian (Billy

Parham at the end of *Cities of the Plain*). The journey toward spiritual formation is always present, but is never complete. The *Seeleroman* in McCarthy details a host of lost opportunities and failed potentialities as the end point of modernity looms ever closer and then finally arrives, leaving its aftermath in *The Road*. Even this bleakest of novels, however, still manages to posit a spiritual journey beyond its own parameters as, at the end, the newly orphaned boy is welcomed into his new family of "good guys."

For the purposes of this essay my principal focus will be on McCarthy's western fiction, and my argument will be that the development of the characteristics of the *Seeleroman* in the novels begins with John Grady Cole in *All the Pretty Horses*, continues with Billy Parham in *The Crossing*, and reaches an inevitable conclusion in the trajectories of both characters in *Cities of the Plain*. The move is, I believe, from romance to the spiritual.

Many critics have alluded to romance tangentially in McCarthy's novels, but only Steven Frye, to my knowledge, has suggested that romance might be a step along the path toward something greater and more profound in the fiction: "when [Norris, London, Crane, and Dreiser] drew on philosophical naturalism they did so within the generic context of the romance and in dynamic tension with renewed forms of humanism and mysticism" (49). Unlike Frye, however, I use "romance" here in its broad generic sense of a courtly (or quasi-courtly) pursuit, punctuated with adventure, conducted by a hero in a world removed from the quotidian in which the fantastic, the mythic, and the marvellous thrive in the absence of the "real." This realm of the "irrational" allows the supernatural space in which to develop. There are suggestions of such a development in Frederic Jameson's *The Political Unconscious*, in which he argues that modernity (his version is the very similar "late capitalism") has promoted realism at the expense of romance, but he sees evidence of a resurgence of the romantic impulse in fiction, and this impulse offers a direct challenge to modernity:

> [I]t is in the context of the gradual reification of realism in late capitalism that romance once again comes to be felt as the place of narrative heterogeneity and of freedom from that reality principle to which a now oppressive realistic representation is the hostage. Romance now once again seems to offer the possibility of sensing other historical rhythms, and of demonic or utopian transformations of a real now unshakably set in place; and [Northrop] Frye is surely not wrong to assimilate the salvational perspective of romance to a reexpression of Utopian longings. (104)

Although the word "spiritual" is not specifically mentioned, "demonic" has supernatural resonances, of course, and the word "salvational" is telling.[4]

That McCarthy's characters are in flight from a modern, technologically frenzied, eco-destructive US—the "real" world—is a phenomenon widely recognized by McCarthy critics. Dianne Luce, for example, writes of an incident in *Cities of the Plain* in which the truck in which Billy and his companion are traveling strikes an owl, spread-eagling it across the windshield: "the dead owl is an image of the natural world crucified at the hands of man, the truck and the fence manifestations of the imposition of his mechanized world on the world of nature" ("The Vanishing World of Cormac McCarthy's Border Trilogy" 196). The crossings into Mexico are, perhaps, an attempt on the part of McCarthy's protagonists to escape from the mechanization of the modern United States that Luce describes. As Eduardo the pimp makes transparently clear to John Grady Cole in *Cities of the Plain*, he (Eduardo) is keenly aware of this possibility: "[the farmboys] drift down out of your leprous paradise seeking a thing now extinct among them. A thing for which perhaps they no longer even have a name. Being farmboys of course the first place they look is the whorehouse" (249). This "thing" it seems to me, certainly in the case of John Grady Cole, is romance. This is a key notion, and I believe that "romance," as it is described by Jameson, is a stage on the journey toward spirituality as a means of resistance to the realities of capitalist modernity. John Grady Cole's nebulous longings for a world uncontaminated by a "leprous" modernity are manifested in his willingness to plunge into affairs with women symbolic of an older order and represented by Mexico's comparative lack of engagement with the trappings of that modernity.

In all McCarthy's fiction these romantic interludes possess an otherworldy, quasi-spiritual quality that tends to reinforce the notion that romance is, at least partially, detached from the "real" world and exists on the spiritual plane:

> The last time [John Grady] saw [Alejandra] before she returned to Mexico she was coming down out of the mountains riding very stately and erect . . . the lightning fell silently through the black clouds behind her and she rode all seeming unaware . . . until the rain caught her up and shrouded her figure away in that wild summer landscape: real horse, real rider, real land and sky yet a dream withal. (*All the Pretty Horses* 131–32)

If one believes Jameson's argument and accepts realism as a clear literary manifestation of capitalist modernity, and the "unreality" of romance as a movement away from this, then the move to the *Seeleroman* is a level of resistance—or at least, defiance—further. This certainly seems to be the case in the Border Trilogy. What begins with romance in *All the Pretty Horses* becomes dominated by spiritual experience in *The Crossing*, and although reverting to a more equal balance between the two in the main body of *Cities of the Plain*, prevails again in the epilogue, the conclusion to the Border Trilogy.

In *The Crossing* romance and the spiritual have parallel trajectories that become imbricated and intertwined in the elevation of Boyd Parham from romantic hero to near-saint. Boyd's romance with the girl that he and Billy rescue from her abductors begins as just that (a romance), but after Boyd and Billy's separation Boyd begins to take on the role of a Messianic figure. He is celebrated in song as a redeemer; his deeds are transfigured into exemplary myths and legends of the battle of good against evil. Boyd becomes the hero of "the corrido, the poor man's history" (386) as the novel has it. His journey is initially one of romance, but it is mythologized into a journey of the soul through Boyd's "martyring." Boyd, like John Grady Cole, dies for his love of a young woman, but unlike John Grady Cole, Boyd has begun to represent something deeper and more profound—before, of course, his journey is ruthlessly truncated. Boyd's story passes through the stage of romance, beyond which John Grady Cole's never progresses, but before the *Seeleroman* is complete his life is ended by older, darker powers in an older, darker land. Billy, however, whose journey *The Crossing* mostly concerns, cannot read Boyd's elevation, and cannot, therefore, set a trajectory for his own development.

*The Crossing* is compelling in the context of the spiritual in McCarthy's fiction partly for the sheer weight of material, and the number of different sources from which this material comes, but this weight of material appears not to possess the force to change the relationship of its characters to the spiritual in obvious ways. Very early in the novel, for example, Billy consults the old, bedridden Mexican trapper, on the nature of wolves:

> the wolf is a being of great order and that it knows what men do not: that there is no order in the world save that which death has put there . . . if men drink the blood of God yet they do not understand the seriousness of what they do . . . Between their acts and their ceremonies lies the world . . . and all the animals that God has made go to and fro yet this world men do not see. They see the acts of their own hands or they see that which they name and call out to one another but the world between is invisible to them. (47)

Humanity has lost its ability to connect its spiritual needs to its religious rituals and, thence, to a world that it is not merely the empty creation of modernity. [5] These ideas, however, seem to have little effect on Billy. Nor do the weeks in the mountains Billy spends after the loss of the wolf seem to provoke change. We learn little of Billy's inner world during this time of almost Christ-like self-imposed exile to the wilderness. There is no discussion of temptation, temptation resisted, or very much else internal for that matter, other than the fact that Billy returns hungry.

And, of course, as Edwin Arnold has so perceptively suggested, there is the influence of Jacob Boehme on the Border Trilogy:

> Boehme saw humankind existing in three states simultaneously: the external world composed of the natural elements; the world of darkness "wherein is born the fire as the eternal torment"; and the world

of light, wherein resides happiness and the Spirit of God. ("McCarthy and the Sacred" 223)

Arnold argues that "the three major interpolated narratives in *The Cross-ing*—those of the priest, the blind man, and the gypsy—told to Billy on his three journeys into Mexico, reflect Boehme's philosophy and serve as warn-ings to the boy against his own spiritual peril" (224). Such an analysis tends to support the notion that McCarthy views the world, and its individual inhabitants, as in grave peril from the secularizing impulse of modernity that seeks to abolish the spiritual at every turn.

Part of this peril, I would argue, is the tendency of individuals to act alone, to divorce themselves from communities of the like-minded—the need for modernity to produce the consuming "I" is extraordinarily power-ful. When Boyd becomes separated from Billy in *The Crossing*, John Grady Cole from Billy in *Cities of the Plain*, and again from Rawlins—and even the risible Blevins—in *All the Pretty Horses*, crises are not far distant. The message that secular modernity cannot be challenged by individuals acting alone is constantly reinforced in these novels. The Mexican woman, for example, and her pregnant daughter encountered by Billy Parham on his first journey across the border with the wolf fear the disparate and long for community: "She said that the young nowadays cared nothing for religion or priest or family or country or God" (87). Community ties are evaporat-ing, yet to live fully in the world, individuals must become part of that world; to defy community is to separate oneself catastrophically. The words of the "wild Indians," however, contain the essence of this message:

> [the leader of the Indians] said that the world could only be known as it existed in men's hearts. For while it seemed a place which contained men it was in reality a place contained within them and therefore to know it one must look there and come to know those hearts and to do this one must live with men and not simply pass among them. (134)

Only under these circumstances is it possible to achieve the profound union achieved by beings who do not possess the capacity for reason and technol-ogy: "Deer and hare and dove and groundvole all richly empanelled on the air for [the wolf's] delight, all nations of the possible world ordained by God of which she was one and not separate from" (127).

These are the lessons that allow spirituality to be recognized and the soul to develop. To join with others of like mind is a step along the road to a condition in which the world becomes a single entity, or consciousness. It is a move toward overcoming the separation and dualities of Western thought that sees even God as fundamentally removed from his creation. Such separations, of course, are precisely those that Silko's characters seek to bridge in their spiritual development. Indeed, this is characteristic of Native American perceptions of religion more broadly:

It is also important to note that the radical separation between God and the cosmos in Western thinking is also the origin of a series of other dualisms or separations which have profoundly influenced Roman Catholic and Protestant theology: cosmos-history, nature-grace, body-spirit, profane-sacred, world-church, individual-society, man-woman. (Peelman 54)

The notion of disunity that springs from dualism leads to the anchorite's doubts concerning God, and his obsession that without witness God could not continue to exist. [156] The Western mind seems incapable of viewing anything as undivided; seeking, always, to sunder that which should remain whole. There is:

> Nothing against which He terminated. Nothing by way of which his being could be announced to him. Nothing to stand apart from and to say I am this and that is the other. Where that is I am not. He could create everything save that which would say him no. (*The Crossing* 154)

Ultimately, however, despite the arguments of the anchorite, the priest perceives that without the participation of others and the presence of God, life is worthless:

> What the priest saw was that the lesson of a life can never be its own. Only the witness has the power to take its measure. It is lived for the other only. The priest therefore saw what the anchorite could not. That God needs no witness. Neither to Himself nor against. (156)

There are, indeed, warnings, as Edwin Arnold argues, and these warnings are against a failure to recognize that the spiritual is central to human existence. At a more fundamental, and precursory, level, however, they are warnings against solitude and disconnection from community. The priest's story of his relationship with the anchorite offers Billy stark examples of the danger of any attempt to fashion a self that is a hermetically sealed, unconsidered, unexamined "I." The lives of the anchorite and the priest are disfigured by the creation of this "I" until both, at last, come to accept that it cannot stand: "Ultimately every man's path is every other's. There are no separate journeys for there are no separate men to make them. All men are one and there is no other tale to tell" (157). The lesson of the *Seeleroman* is that nothing exists in isolation.

Although I am not entirely convinced by Arnold's projection of the philosophy of Boehme onto *The Crossing*, I *am* persuaded that the priest, the gypsy, and the blind revolutionary function as a triumvirate of spiritual advisors to Billy Parham. Such a feature is entirely consistent with the notion of a *Seeleroman*, and an essential part of this genre (as it is in the *Bildungsroman*) is that the protagonist should encounter "guides" who influence him as he journeys toward maturity. As I have suggested, however, it is not clear that Billy is swayed in significant ways by what he hears. At the conclusion of the priest's tale, for example, he returns to the US, but it is not obvious from his subsequent actions whether or not he has accepted that man cannot function as a single entity, separate from the world, if he is to challenge modernity. Similarly, after his encounter with the blind revolutionary, Billy "asks God about his brother" (295), but there is no reply; Billy falls asleep, and the experience is not mentioned again. Finally, after his meeting with the gypsies, who are returning the airplane to its original owner, Billy listens with great care to their leader and is willing to seek clarification of certain points (as he always is), but finally all he has to say to the gypsy's suggestion that they are both men of the road is that he is not, in fact, any such thing (413).

These encounters seem never to penetrate fully Billy's consciousness, just as the dialogue with the stranger appears to have little effect at the conclusion of *Cities of the Plain*. It appears that McCarthy is suggesting a means of resistance to modernity through the spiritual, but he does not allow his characters to take up these means of resistance in an instrumental fashion. As in *Ceremony*—and to a lesser extent Silko's *Almanac of the Dead*—McCarthy's characters are exposed to the wisdom of those who seek to reunite them with the world of the spiritual from which modernity has estranged them. The difference is that in Silko's narratives of spiritual formation Tayo and a number of the characters in *Almanac* absorb the lessons of their advisors and are redeemed; Billy Parham, a rough analogue of Tayo, does not, or cannot, heed these lessons and remains profoundly disconnected from redemptive spiritual experience. While the buds of transformative religious experience come to full flower in *Ceremony*, in McCarthy's version of the *Seeleroman* they wither on the stem.

Other than the priest, the blind man, and the gypsy—whose discourses deliver the major philosophical and spiritual import of the novel—there are a host of other characters to whom Billy also listens: the old Mexican wolf-trapper, the diva from the travelling opera, the singing girl hulling pecans, the Yaqui *gerente* of the *Babicora* who had earlier cut Billy and Boyd's horses out of the *Remuda*, even one of the kidnappers of Boyd's girl. Interestingly, what nearly all these characters from *The Crossing* have in common, and what Billy lacks, is a willingness to examine both the world in which they live, and themselves, in a questioning, philosophical fashion. There are no certainties and no conclusions, however: to repeat the words of the old Mexican concerning humanity in general at the beginning of the novel: "They see the acts of their own hands or they see that which they name and call out to one another but the world between is invisible to them" ( 47). The old Mexican implies that humanity has become estranged from itself, and lost its ability to connect with a richer, more spiritual world. And here I am reminded of Charles Taylor's remarks concerning the journey toward God:

> [Augustine's] concern was to show that God is to be found not just in the world but also and more importantly at the very foundations of

the person . . . And so at the end of its search for itself, if it goes to the very end, the soul finds God. The experience of being illumined from another source, of receiving the standards of our reason from beyond ourselves . . . is seen to be very much an experience of inwardness . . . But the way within leads above. When we get to God, the image of place becomes multiple and many-sided. In an important sense, the truth is *not* in me. I see the truth "in" God. Where the meeting takes place, there is a reversal. Going within . . . takes me beyond. (136–37)

"The way within leads above" and "going within takes me beyond" are key phrases for both novelists, and key phrases in the lexicon of the *Seeleroman*.

What Tayo, in Silko's *Ceremony*, finds is precisely this: that the process of self-examination unites him with land, community, and ultimately his broader spiritual heritage. McCarthy's narratives, however, can seem like a series of failed attempts to achieve what Taylor is advocating. None of these connections are made conclusively; the narrative of spiritual formation is never completed and the journey toward its God ends nowhere. The novels imply that this is, at least partly, a result of the character's reluctance to search inwardly; and I am drawn, once again, to Billy's early wanderings when he encounters the cave-dwelling "wild Indians" whose leader tells him that the reality of the world is within. Paradoxically, almost, given modernity's creation of the all-consuming "I," it is a focused scrutiny of the self that leads to its reconnection to something larger. Billy is informed—in a fairly straightforward fashion for a passage from McCarthy dealing with the spiritual—that the momentum for resistance must come from within, and until that occurs there can be no real union made with worlds that might exist beyond modernity. Without this union, the lessons of the spiritual journey cannot be learned.

If the evidence of McCarthy's fiction is to be believed then he feels, strongly, that a reconnection with the spiritual—a reenchantment of the world—is essential to counteract the pernicious and pervasive effects of modernity. He is, however, profoundly skeptical of Western humanity's ability to engage with the spiritual. These notions infuse his work with wistfulness, a profound feeling of loss, and a sense of permanent decline. Characters like Billy Parham are condemned to wander the Southwest in search of a kind of redemption that is always tantalizingly out of reach. The dialectic of modernity has almost run its course, McCarthy seems to imply; the end of history is nigh, and resistance is altogether futile. The explanation for this, I feel, is in part derived from McCarthy's embedded position within modernity. He is less well equipped to offer resistance than Silko as his work has been fashioned in an artistic tradition in which religion and the spiritual have been increasingly marginalized. Indeed—more broadly—it is at least arguable that the genre of the novel has become the standard-bearer of the secular Western tradition in art. Balancing this, of course, is McCarthy's obvious interest in, and wide knowledge of, spiritual matters, and his, equally obvious, recognition of the rifts, separations, and dualities inflicted on the world by modernity. The fact remains, however, that his Euroamerican background makes it less easy for him to have faith in the broadly spiritual as an antidote to modernity than someone like Silko, who is culturally immersed in the religious and sees no obvious and necessary separation of natural and supernatural. Salman Rushdie has suggested that

> [i]f one is to attempt honestly to describe reality as it is experienced by religious people, for whom God is no symbol but an everyday fact, then the conventions of realism are quite inadequate. The rationalism of that form comes to seem like a judgement upon, an invalidation of, the religious faith of the characters being described. A form must be created which allows the miraculous and mundane to co-exist at the same level—as the same order of event. (376)

Leslie Silko's *Ceremony* reflects Rushdie's remarks in its very mechanics, in the technical detail of its construction.

Not only does Silko treat the "natural" and "supernatural" as concurrent, the novel, while remaining descriptive and narrative in the Western novelistic tradition, from its opening word to its closing word, actually *performs* the religious ceremony of the title. Indeed, *Ceremony* might be regarded as exemplary of the stage I have suggested exists beyond the "romantic" response to modernity described by Jameson in the *Political Unconscious*. *Ceremony* is so infused with the antirational that natural and supernatural become one: the hunter and his female companion who Tayo encounters in his pursuit of the spotted cattle, and with whom he has a sexual relationship, are exemplary of this phenomenon. Neither Tayo, nor the reader, are certain of their status vis-à-vis "reality." Tayo's relationship with the woman Ts'eh is certainly naturalistic in its physical dimensions, and she offers specific details of the places her family live and how they earn a living, but when he relates his encounter to the tribal elders he receives a response that reads Ts'eh as a supernatural figure:

> A'Moo'ooh you say you have seen her
> Last winter
> up north
> with Mountain Lion
> the hunter
>
> All summer
> she was south
> near Acu
>
> They started crying
> the old men started crying

> "A'moo'ooh! A'Moo'ooh!"
> You have seen her
> We will be blessed
> again. (257)

Clearly, Silko wishes her readers to believe that Ts'eh exists both in the realm of the spiritual and the realm of the physical.

Stage by stage Tayo is transformed from a shell-shocked, alcoholic war veteran to a spiritually mature being able, once more, to live in harmony with his fellows and his environment. Indeed, the process is almost precisely analogous to the Christian narrative of spiritual formation summarized by William James over a hundred years ago:

> To be converted, to be regenerated, to receive grace, to experience religion, to gain an assurance, are so many of the phrases which denote the process, gradual or sudden, by which a self hitherto divided, and consciously wrong inferior and unhappy, becomes unified and consciously right superior and happy, in consequence of its firmer hold upon religious realities. (157)

What is so interesting here is that one of the most difficult aspects of *Ceremony* for the Western reader is the question of which parts of the novel are to be read literally, and which to be read figuratively. It is my contention that this is a redundant question, and that the novel is intended to be read wholly literally. Tayo's "supernatural" experiences are, in fact, "religious realities" of the kind described by James and elucidated in the work of Robert Bellah:

> "American Indians lack a word to denote what we call religion," writes Ake Hultkrantz in *The Religions of the American Indians* ... Of course, nothing else is to be expected in environments where religious attitudes and values permeate cultural life in its entirety and are not isolated from other cultural manifestations. (139)

Naturally, the "religious realities" James mentions are difficult for the increasingly secularized Western cast of mind to accommodate, and a corollary of this is that a novel taking the form of a *Seeleroman* tends to pass unnoticed as such, yet this does not lessen the boldness of its claim to a different kind of "reality."

McCarthy's fiction *does*, I think, approach the condition Rushdie describes in its engagement with romance and in its adoption of the genre of the *Seeleroman* but, finally, hope and salvation are mirages. As Rick Wallach reminds us, McCarthy's fiction is a graveyard of failed potentials from destroyed bodies, to wrecked buildings (especially churches), to mangled and useless vehicles, to abandoned careers (foreword to

Holloway xii–xiii). I believe the spiritual, more broadly, could be added to this list. The miraculous and the magical are certainly scrutinized by McCarthy, and worked into the texture of the fiction: beyond the narratives of spiritual formation to which Billy is exposed there are, of course, John Grady Cole's almost supernatural relationship with horses, and Billy's with the wolf. These relationships, though, are illusory or mistaken glimpses of resistance or salvation. The failure of the spiritual as the antidote to modernity is vividly illustrated toward the end of *Cities of the Plain* as Billy mistakes radar domes for the cupolas of Spanish missions, and rags of plastic for robed figures. "I aint nothing" says Billy a few words from the end of the novel, in spite of the exhortation following his encounter with his final spiritual guide of the Border Trilogy, to "honor the path [the man who is all men] has taken" (288) and "listen to his tale" (289).

Repeatedly, in the Border Trilogy, McCarthy's characters are offered glimpses of a scenario in which man is no longer sundered from man and is reunited with the world. But the message continually eludes them. As Edwin Arnold suggests: "There is always the possibility of grace and redemption even in the darkest of [McCarthy's] tales, although that redemption may require more of his characters than they are ultimately willing to give" ("Naming, Knowing and Nothingness" 46). This is insufficient: not only are McCarthy's characters unwilling, they are *unable* to give what is required for redemption; and so, to extrapolate, is modern humanity in its entirety. McCarthy's most recent novel, *The Road*—another version of the *Seeleroman*—offers strong support for this view. In the novel modernity has destroyed itself—and everything else—in some apocalyptic disaster that has left a handful of individuals to scavenge what they can from the ruined land. God seems to have departed for good:

> The road crossed a dried slough where pipes of ice stood out of the frozen mud like formations in a cave. The remains of an old fire by the side of the road. Beyond that a long concrete causeway. A dead swamp. Dead trees standing out of the gray water trailing gray and relic hag-moss. The silky spills of ash against the curbing. He stood leaning on the gritty concrete rail. Perhaps in the world's destruction it would be possible at last to see how it was made. Oceans, mountains. The ponderous counterspectacle of things ceasing to be. The sweeping waste, hydroptic and coldly secular. The silence. (231)

God never was, perhaps; or there is no God without belief, and faith is impossible after such a calamity; or all those going to Paradise have departed and God has abandoned the remainder; or utter ruination is what the secular has brought us to. There could be many explanations for the absence of the spiritual, but the argument that, unable to reach out and grasp grace and redemption, humanity has all but perished, is persuasive.

*The Road* offers the reader a dead world in which the spirit of the earth has been extinguished—and if there is any hope at all it is extraordinarily weak depending, as it does, on either an evolution into civilization from cannibalism, the success of the "good guys" against overwhelming odds, or the intervention of a god who seems absent. Religiosity, however, is never "weakened" to this extent in *Ceremony*, in spite of the ravages of humankind. Modernity may threaten to extinguish humanity, but Silko has Tayo understand that hope resides in the mysterious agency she imputes to natural phenomena. Tayo begins to understand that these phenomena have the power to withhold what is necessary for human survival and happiness, and it is only by embracing this, and realizing his place in a complex and entirely interdependent system, that Tayo is healed and returned to his culture. Exemplary of this is the benefit in the wider community from the rains that have been absent for so long as a result of the dysfunction affecting both Tayo and the Laguna Pueblo. Beyond a simple plea for harmony, Silko offers a complex, yet coherent, worldview that refutes great swathes of the thinking that drives the globally dominant strain of Eurocentric modernity—the economic apparatus of which many would argue now threatens the planet. To the Western ear—Christian or secular—schooled in separations and alienated from both the natural and spiritual worlds, the kind of power with which Silko invests the environment seems implausible, yet it is a system that offers no catastrophic threat to the earth; indeed what lies at its heart is sustainability for both human beings and the environment. The point at which Tayo becomes fully conscious of this is the culmination of the *Seeleroman*; the story has been told, the healing ceremonies completed, and balance restored. Tayo has been an audience for, witness to, and a participant in a pattern of storytelling and listening that has resulted in his redemption. Equally, Silko, in writing *Ceremony*, has been an active contributor to a process that holds out the possibility of a real engagement between storyteller and audience, and may even possess the potential to redetermine and restructure the world.

In McCarthy, redemption remains a faint hope. It is significant, perhaps, that the very last words of *Cities of the Plain*, and the Border Trilogy as a whole, are, "The story's told / Turn the page." What follows, of course, are a number of blank pages. Nothing, in other words—although this may simply be McCarthy penetrating our suspension of disbelief as readers and informing us that there really is nothing beyond the story, and the story ends with Billy. Similarly, however, at the end of *The Sunset Limited*, what remains is a "mysterious silence"—the dramatic equivalent, perhaps, of the blank pages at the end of *Cities of the Plain*. What both works suggest is that there is virtually nothing remaining in this world that has not been synthesized by modernity—even the spiritual. Only the faintest, most easily overlooked traces of previous worlds are detectable. As we learn of the domain of the wolves in *The Crossing*, it is:

A world construed out of blood and blood's alkahest and blood in its core and in its integument because it was that nothing save blood had the power to resonate against that void which threatened hourly to devour it. When those eyes and the nation to which they stood witness were gone at last with their dignity back into their origins there would perhaps be other fires and other witnesses and other worlds otherwise beheld. But they would not be this one. (73–74)

The atavistic and bloody hunting instincts of the wolf are uncontaminated by modernity and stand, therefore, in opposition to it, yet the wolf is on the verge of extinction.

Indeed, in *The Road*, humanity itself stands upon this very threshold: "He walked out into the gray light and stood and he saw for a brief moment the absolute truth of the world. The cold relentless circling of the intestate earth. Darkness implacable. The blind dogs of the sun in their running. The crushing black vacuum of the universe" (110). McCarthy has moved beyond hinting at the nothingness that must exist beyond unchecked modernity to an explicit description of the character of nullity. An "ultra-weakened" religiosity can be read into the death of the man and the passing of the boy into the hands of others who might sustain him, but with what will they sustain him and for how long? For the protagonists of McCarthy's *Seeleromane*, unlike those of Silko, the spiritual enlightenment the genre offers, remains heavily hedged and attenuated. As Theodor Adorno said of the work of that other great and profound nihilist of the twentieth century, Samuel Beckett, "hope skulks out of the world . . . and back to where it came from, death" ("Trying to Understand *Endgame*" 81). In McCarthy's Border Trilogy, in a moment simultaneously prolonged and evanescent, hope for spiritual redemption lingers in the magnificence of yet another blood-red desert sunset. In *The Road* hope exists merely in exploded fragments, ever-dispersing into a spiritual and empirical monochrome.

## NOTES

1. Anniken Telnes Iversen has a list of ninety-one features that characterize a novel in the genre, and a great deal of other useful material for those who wish to look at the history of attempts to define it. Marianne Hirsch's identification, however, of the *Bildungsroman* as "the novel of formation" is the one perhaps best suited to my purposes in this essay.
2. A detailed analysis of the variety of responses to modernity in McCarthy's fiction can be found in my essay, "'An Impulse to Action, an Undefined Want': Modernity, Flight and Crisis in the Border Trilogy and Blood Meridian." These responses tend to be focused on modernity's transformative power; its seeming irresistibility; its function as the cultural analogue of capitalism; its dependence on science, technology, and instrumental reason; its facility to "disenchant" the world; its Eurocentric nature; its pragmatic violence; its devotion to utility and calculability; its homogenizing effect; its relentlessly exploitative nature; its promotion of a hermetic "I"; and the challenge

to it from art. Added to this list should be the radical separation of mind and body that has been so thoroughly incorporated in Western thinking to the extent that when, for example, notions such as "holistic" medicine are mentioned, or hypnosis is used as a form of anaesthesia, such ideas and phenomena appear exotic or radical. Whether the weakening of the grip of the US and Europe on the global economy will allow other forms of modernity to come to the fore remains to be seen, of course.

3. I am grateful to Professor McClure for these formulations, which I first heard in a graduate seminar at Rutgers University in 2001. For McClure much contemporary fiction is postsecular, "because the stories it tells trace the turn of secular-minded characters back towards the religious; because its ontological signature is a religiously inflected disruption of secular constructions of the real; and because its ideological signature is the rearticulation of a dramatically 'weakened' religiosity" (3).

4. It should be noted that Jameson has elsewhere claimed that "spirituality virtually by definition no longer exists: the definition in question is in fact that of postmodernism itself" (*Postmodernism* 55). My view is that the difference between "spiritual" and "postmodern," in this case, is semantic rather than philosophical.

5. McCarthy's view of this disconnect is borne out in his remarks to Garry Wallace:

> [McCarthy] said that the religious experience is always described through the symbols of a particular culture and thus is somewhat misrepresented by them. He indicated that even the religious person is often uncomfortable with such experiences and accounts of them, and that those who have not had a religious experience cannot comprehend it through second-hand accounts, even good ones like James's "Varieties of Religious Experience." He went on to say that he thinks the mystical experience is a direct apprehension of reality, unmediated by symbol, and he ended with the thought that our inability to see spiritual truth is the greater mystery. (138)

> There is a fascinating counterpoint to this in Deloria's *God is Red* in which he argues that: "The question the so-called world religions have not satisfactorily resolved is whether or not religious experience can be distilled from its original cultural context and become an abstract principle that is applicable to all peoples in all places and at different times" (65). McCarthy seems to think such a process is certainly possible.

6. The anchorite, here, is the old man, of whom the priest speaks, who lives in the shadow of the teetering church at Caborca.

## WORKS CITED

Adorno, Theodor. "Trying to Understand Endgame". 1961. *Samuel Beckett: Modern Critical Views.* Ed. Harold Bloom. New York: Chelsea House, 1985. 51–81.

Arnold, Edwin T. "McCarthy and the Sacred: A Reading of *The Crossing.*" James D. Lilley, ed. *Cormac McCarthy: New Directions.* Albuquerque: U of New Mexico P, 2002. 215–38.

———. "Naming, Knowing and Nothingness: McCarthy's Moral Parables." Arnold, Edwin. T. ed. *Perspectives on Cormac McCarthy.* Jackson: University Press of Mississippi, 1999. 45–69.

Bellah, Robert. *The Broken Covenant: American Civil Religion in Time of Trial.* 2nd ed. Chicago, IL: University of Chicago Press, 1992.

Deloria, Jr., Vine. *God is Red: A Native View of Religion.* 3rd ed. Golden, CO: Fulcrum Publishing, 2003.

Frye, Steven. "Cormac McCarthy's 'world in its making': Romantic Naturalism in *The Crossing.*" *Studies in American Naturalism.* International Theodore Dreiser Society,2007: 46–65.

Hall, Wade, and Rick Wallach, eds. *Sacred Violence: A Reader's Companion to Cormac McCarthy.* Volume 2: *Cormac McCarthy's Western Novels.* El Paso: Texas Western Press, 2002.

Hirsch, Marianne. "The Novel of Formation as Genre: Between Great Expectations and Lost Illusions." *Genre* 12 (1979): 293–311.

Holloway, David. *The Late Modernism of Cormac McCarthy.* Foreword, Rick Wallach. Westport, CT: Greenwood Press, 2002.

Iversen, Anniken Telnes. "Towards a Polythetic Definition of the *Bildungsroman*: The Example of Paul Auster's *Moon Palace.*" *Literatûra* 49.5 (2007): 68–75.

James, William. *The Varieties of Religious Experience.* 1902. Cambridge: Harvard UP, 1985.

Jameson, Frederic. *The Political Unconscious: Narrative as a Socially Symbolic Act.* London: Methuen, 1981.

———. *Postmodernism: The Cultural Logic of Late Capitalism.* London: Verso, 1992.

Luce, Dianne C. "The Vanishing World of Cormac McCarthy's Border Trilogy." *A Cormac McCarthy Companion: The Border Trilogy.* Edwin Arnold and Dianne C. Luce, eds. Jackson: UP of Mississippi, 2001. 161–97.

———. "First Thoughts on McCarthy's New Play, *The Sunset Limited.*" Cormac McCarthy: Novels of the Border Panel. Cormac McCarthy Society. ALA Convention. Hyatt Regency Hotel, San Francisco. 27 May 2006.

McCarthy, Cormac. *All the Pretty Horses.* New York: Vintage, 1993.

———. *Blood Meridian.* New York: Random House, 1985.

———. *Cities of the Plain.* New York: Knopf, 1998.

———. *The Crossing.* New York: Knopf, 1994.

———. *No Country for Old Men.* 2005. London: Picador-Pan Macmillan, 2006.

———. *Outer Dark.* 1968. London: Picador, 1994.

———. *The Road.* New York: Knopf, 2006.

———. *Suttree.* 1979. London: Vintage, 1992.

McClure, John A. *Partial Faiths: Postsecular Fiction in the Age of Pynchon and Morrison.* Athens: Georgia UP, 2007.

Monk, Nick. "'An Impulse to Action, an Undefined Want': Modernity, Flight and Crisis in the Border Trilogy and *Blood Meridian.*" Hall and Wallach 83–103.

Peelman, Achiel. *Christ is a Native American.* Maryknoll: Orbis, 1995.

Rushdie, Salman. *Imaginary Homelands.* London: Granta-Penguin, 1991.

Silko, Leslie Marmon. *Almanac of the Dead.* New York: Simon & Schuster, 1991.

———. *Ceremony.* 1977. New York: Penguin, 1986.

Taylor, Charles. *Sources of the Self.* Cambridge: Cambridge UP, 1989.

Wallace, Garry. "Meeting McCarthy." *Southern Quarterly* 30 (1992): 134–39.

# Contributors

**Nicholas Monk** is Assistant Professor at the University of Warwick's Institute for Advanced Teaching and Learning. His research interests include literatures of the American Southwest, Native American literature, and literature and pedagogy.

**John Cant** teaches Film Studies part-time at Essex University. He gained his PhD there in 2002. He has published articles on McCarthy and the Coen Brothers; his book *Cormac McCarthy and the Myth of American Exceptionalism* came out in 2008.

**Tom Cornford** is a freelance theatre director and teaches acting and directing for institutions including The Guthrie Theater/University of Minnesota, Shakespeare's Globe and the Royal Scottish Academy of Music and Drama. He directed a performance-with-scripts of The Sunset Limited with actors Michael Gould and Wale Ojo while working as an artist-in-residence at the CAPITAL Centre at The University of Warwick.

**Ciarán Dowd** is a Galway Doctoral Research Fellow whose research explores the interplay of metaphysical and scientific concepts in the works of Cormac McCarthy. His work is supported by funding received from the *Galway Doctoral Research Fellowship Scheme* of the College of Arts, Social Sciences, & Celtic Studies, National University of Ireland, Galway.

**John Ferer** is a literary scholar living in South Florida. His research interests include Cormac McCarthy, dystopian novels and animal studies. He researches at the University of La Laguna in Tenerife, Spain.

**Euan Gallivan** was awarded a PhD in American Studies from the University of Nottingham in 2010, where his research focused on the connections between southern literature and the philosophy of Arthur Schopenhauer. He currently teaches English at The Priory Academy in Lincoln, UK.

**Peter Josyph** works concurrently as an author, painter, photographer, and in theatre and film as an actor-director. His books include *Adventures in Reading Cormac McCarthy*; his films include *Acting McCarthy: The Making of Billy Bob Thornton's All the Pretty Horses*; and his exhibition *Cormac McCarthy's House* has shown at the Centennial Museum in El Paso, Texas; the CAPITAL Centre in Coventry, England; the Kulturens Hus in Luleö, Sweden; and the Loyal Jones Appalachian Center in Berea, Kentucky.

**Dianne C. Luce** is the author of *Reading the World: Cormac McCarthy's Tennessee Period* (University of South Carolina Press, 2009). Currently she is writing a chronicle of McCarthy's literary career based on his letters and manuscripts.

**Michael Madsen** is assistant/external lecturer at Aarhus School of Business, Aarhus University, Denmark. He has published newspaper articles and essays on representations of the city and suburbia in American literature and popular culture, and the fiction of Cormac McCarthy.

**Megan Riley McGilchrist** is the author of *The Western Landscape in Cormac McCarthy and Wallace Stegner*. A native Californian, she has lived in England since 1983.

**Jan Nordby Gretlund** is Senior Lecturer in American Literature at the Center for American Studies, University of Southern Denmark. He has held ACLS or Fulbright fellowships at Vanderbilt, Southern Mississippi, and South Carolina universities and has taught several terms at the two latter universities. He is the author of *Eudora Welty's Aesthetics of Place, and Frames of Southern Mind: Reflections on the Stoic, Bi-Racial & Existential South.*

**David Williams** is Associate Professor of philosophy at Azusa Pacific University in Los Angeles, CA. He specializes in the history of Ancient Greek philosophy.

# Index